On Psychoanalysis

On Psychoanalysis

Writings and Lectures, Volume 1

Paul Ricoeur

Translated by David Pellauer

polity

This collection first published in French as *Écrits et conférences 1 – Autour de la Psychanalyse* © Éditions du Seuil, 2008

This English edition © Polity Press, 2012

Polity Press
65 Bridge Street
Cambridge CB2 1UR, UK

Polity Press
350 Main Street
Malden, MA 02148, USA

ISBN-13: 978-0-7456-6123-0
ISBN-13: 978-0-7456-6124-7(pb)

A catalogue record for this book is available from the British Library.

Typeset in 11 on 13 pt Sabon
by Toppan Best-set Premedia Limited
Printed and bound in Great Britain by the MPG Books Group

The publisher has used its best endeavours to ensure that the URLs for external websites referred to in this book are correct and active at the time of going to press. However, the publisher has no responsibility for the websites and can make no guarantee that a site will remain live or that the content is or will remain appropriate.

Every effort has been made to trace all copyright holders, but if any have been inadvertently overlooked the publisher will be pleased to include any necessary credits in any subsequent reprint or edition.

For further information on Polity, visit our website: www.politybooks.com

Table of Contents

Acknowledgments

The publishers gratefully acknowledge the following publications for permission to reproduce translations of some of the chapters:

"The Question of Proof in Freud's Psychoanalytic Writings", *Journal of the American Psychoanalytic Association*, vol. 25 (Sage Publications, 1977), pp. 835–72.

"Image and Language in Psychoanalysis", *Psychiatry and the Humanities*, 3 (Yale University Press, 1978), pp. 293–324.

"The Self in Psychoanalysis and in Phenomenological Philosophy", *Psychoanalytic Inquiry*, 6 (Taylor and Francis Group Ltd, 1986), pp. 437–58.

"Psychiatry and Moral Values", in *American Handbook of Psychiatry, vol. 1: The Foundations of Psychiatry* (Basic Books, 1974), pp. 976–90.

"Psychoanalysis and the Work of Art", *Psychiatry and the Humanities*, 1 (Yale University Press, 1976), pp. 3–33.

"Life: A Story in Search of a Narrator", in *Facts and Values: Philosophical Reflections from Western and Non-Western Perspectives* (Martinus Nijhoff Philosophy Library, 19, 1986).

Editor's Introduction

"Essays and Lectures"

This volume is the first in a series meant to bring together and publish Paul Ricoeur's essays and lectures. Preserved – often rediscovered – in the archives that are now held by the Ricoeur Foundation (the *Fonds Ricoeur*) in Paris, many of them are not well known, or have been forgotten, or were unknown in French, and a good number of them have become impossible to find or inaccessible.[1] They include both older and more recent articles, sometimes ones published in foreign journals and in foreign languages (even when a manuscript in French exists), transcripts of lectures (for which the *Fonds Ricoeur* has the original written text, sometimes with annotations, or with large or small editorial additions by the author), and a few articles still available in other languages but not in print in French. The origin and place of first publication for each article are given in the listing at the end of this volume (see pp. 232–3), along with any editorial decisions that were made when different versions of a text exist.

---

[1] Praise must be rendered here to Thérèse Duflot, who served as Ricoeur's typist over the years, and who during the 1980s and 1990s preserved the French originals of his articles published in foreign journals, and often prepared a fair text of his many public statements.

Like many people invited, even pestered, to write an article or give a lecture on the same or similar topics, in France and abroad, Ricoeur drew from presentations already given in other places and at other times. It is striking, however, to see how meticulous he was in this "cutting and pasting" if time was pressing. It rarely came down to simple cut and pasting. His manuscripts bear witness in almost every case to some reworking or partial rewriting, sometimes in important ways, of what already existed – a rewriting due sometimes to new reflections as a result of what he had been asked to address and the public involved, but also often due to the advance in his own thinking after having read something that struck him as significant or owing to the discussion that had followed an earlier presentation.[2] Those who knew him and "followed" him as he developed his work over his lifetime up to the end know how "reactive" he always was, never indifferent, but always capable of picking up on what was happening in regard to his own thought as well as what was happening in public affairs. And those who heard one of his lectures can verify how well prepared they were, how this non-orator was able to captivate large audiences, seduced by his rigor and finesse, and how humor was not absent even given a topic marked by austerity or that was difficult to understand.

Yet, to understand the spirit in which these essays and lectures have been edited, it is necessary to note that Ricoeur did not like the long-established practice, which continues to grow, of publishing oral presentations – course lectures, conference presentations, public interventions – even when they had been prepared beforehand or, *a fortiori*, were impromptu. Requests to him to do so were not lacking. He almost always obstinately refused them, to the despair of some editors. A few unscrupulous ones ignored his reticence – and even his refusals – and published his "unauthorized" texts without permission. In other cases, which sometimes were the result of his giving in to and sometimes owing to his feeling of gratitude toward and trust of those who had invited him, Ricoeur did allow the publication of his courses or of recorded

[2] The first two chapters can serve as an example of this. The second one, "Psychoanalysis and Hermeneutics" draws heavily on the first one, "The Question of Proof in Psychoanalytic Writings," as regards the problem of "criteria."

and transcribed lectures, although he never thought this was a good idea.

Some may find his scruples excessive. However, they did not stem from some jealous or narrow-minded idea of the *rights* of an author (he always welcomed being paid for such publication), but from an ethics regarding the philosophical text and the responsibility of a philosopher as author who ought not to accommodate himself to "something like" in how he expressed things or in what he said (even less so in an age where everything, including philosophy, is caught up in the mania for "communication"). The "endurance of thinking," to take up an old phrase which has a Heideggerian resonance, requires careful writing and demands the stamp of the living author's signature. One can well understand that Paul Ricoeur, a formidable and scrupulous reader of others' writings, would turn out to be as intransigent about his own. Whatever the case may be, before he died, he asked the Editorial Committee for which he had himself chosen the first members carefully, to oversee the publication of any future books, and to make a clear distinction between his written work that had become a book or a part of a book during his lifetime, hence something that was edited by him or published with his explicit approval, and all future publications of things written by him but brought together by others, those who had been given his full confidence about what they were doing.

It is in this spirit, and strictly respecting what he asked, that this book was put together, as will be any future volumes.

"On Psychoanalysis"

This first volume begins in a sense with the prickliest, or in any case the most controversial, case in the development of the philosophy of Paul Ricoeur, his reflections on psychoanalysis. The reason for this choice is the fact that these texts are among those most difficult to find, not some desire to reawaken old quarrels, very French ones to be sure (which were ignored in psychoanalysis and philosophy in most other countries). Bringing them together will allow French and other readers access to some texts not so well known as others because they were not part of this battle, but rather come from the earlier and the more intermediate part of Ricoeur's reflections. Several of these "papers" were published abroad, where they remain much in demand, and French philosophers, psychoanalysts, and the general public therefore can learn from them.

This volume brings together essays and lectures, published or unpublished, from four decades. This time span allows one in the end to verify the continuities and shifts in accent of a stream of thought. The continuity is one of an effort aimed at philosophical understanding, of a willingness to think through psychoanalysis by means of a "second-degree" approach, one that defines the reflective philosophy so dear to Ricoeur. He considered it the very heart of the whole philosophical enterprise beginning with its dawn in ancient Greece. In fact, these texts are first of all illuminating, in the sense of the Enlightenment tradition and of an important part of contemporary philosophy, about Freud and his work. What is more, even if it comes to being "on psychoanalysis," one could as well have titled this volume *Paul Ricoeur: Freud's Reader.* Freud, whom Ricoeur interprets with precision, empathy, and admiration, with that *Redlichkeit*, that intellectual probity, which is "the single ethical 'value' . . . that conforms to the ethical neutrality of the psychoanalytic relation." With as well an awareness of the troubling break that the man from Vienna represents for the rational tradition of philosophy. Freud, to be sure, is not alone in this respect for modern philosophy, but the step he took is particularly troubling, upsetting, threatening, owing to its "uncanniness," and he transports philosophy, whether or not it wants to be transported, "elsewhere," to a country of dissimilitude, where the rule and the criterion of reflexive reason gets shifted. The famous *Verstellung*, the "displacement" that Freud places at the heart of work of the unconscious and of transference, leaves no one untouched. As the history of psychoanalysis has demonstrated, this displacement is not risk free, the more so when it is prolonged or borne by a practice that aims at a unique type of proof test: the analytic experience.

Ricoeur does not look for the theoretical or practical flaw in Freud. He takes him up as he is, so to speak, with the philosopher's wonder, first of all by patiently reading the author of an oeuvre, of written texts, then by questioning them along different axes, which assuredly correspond to his own intellectual interests but are not limited to them.

In a collection drawn from scattered texts left to those who follow him, it would be arbitrary to look for a "plan," but one can, broadly speaking, find three directions of thought at work here.

Several of these texts have to do with the project and validity of psychoanalysis as a "science," its way of proceeding and its results, its interpretation of culture and its place in culture, its intentions, well or poorly formulated, or not spoken of at all. So what science is psychoanalysis? What truth is at issue, what proofs furnished, in what way? "How are its assertions justified, its interpretations authenticated, its theory verified?" These are the questions Ricoeur takes up. It is not epistemology, in the sense of a critique of scientific knowledge, that interests Ricoeur above all else, but rather the problem of the "truth" of psychoanalysis and the means it makes use of. If it is acknowledged that "what counts as a fact in psychoanalysis is of a different nature than what counts as a fact in the natural sciences and in general in those sciences based on observation," the question follows necessarily, as with every human science, of the "hermeneutical character of psychoanalysis." It is important to recognize, however, that even if "the notion of a fact in psychoanalysis presents a certain kinship with the notion of a text" and if "the theory stands in relation to the psychoanalytic fact in a relation analogous to that of the exegesis of texts in the hermeneutical sciences," Ricoeur gives a prudent, nuanced answer regarding the hermeneutical status of psychoanalysis, as a "mixed discipline," with an "ambiguous status."

As regards this central question, his hesitation is all the more justified in that the kinship between the notion of a psychoanalytic fact and that of a text does not exhaust the contents of the psychoanalytic "thing" or "object." In the text "Image and Language in Psychoanalysis," not previously published in French, which in earlier years would undoubtedly have given rise to lively arguments (and, in other circumstances, could have revived some acrimonious ones), Ricoeur insists on the necessity to add to the "field of speech and language" in psychoanalysis that of the image, which possesses a misunderstood "semiotic" dimension that cannot simply be brought without remainder to language. Beyond any critique of Lacan, it would be necessary to tie this insistence on Ricoeur's part regarding the "image family" to the importance of the imagination, to the "space of fantasy" or of *Phantasieren*

throughout his work.[3] In the end, the philosopher's most basic
reservation regarding psychoanalysis would perhaps be the absence
of that force of the future coming through the imagination, a force
present not only in utopias but in the creative capacity of human
beings to project themselves toward what is still to come.

With the presentation and discussion of Heinz Kohut and his
"self psychology," we totally change ground and language, but
not object. It is still a matter of questioning psychoanalysis about
what it is, what it wants to be, and maybe cannot be (Kohut's
telling but too little-known theoretical criticisms of the Freudian
tradition figure largely in this text). Some may surely object that
with Kohut one has left Freud, and that the connections that Paul
Ricoeur establishes with Hegel and Levinas, which are neither
"eclectic" nor "concordant," may even justify the reproach of a
return to better-known territory than that of Freud's "disturbing
uncanniness." Still the suggestive fruitfulness of this shift of
grounds in relation to Freudian orthodoxy remains and does contribute to staking out the difference that is Freud's from the interest of other "schools" than his.

A further series of texts is devoted more to the problem of
culture. What does psychoanalysis make of the existing culture?
Of culture from the point of view of values, religion, the perception of art? This more "classic," better-known register, that of
comprehending a thematic approach qualified by Ricoeur himself
in a now well-known expression as the "philosophy of suspicion,"
may be an illuming rediscovery for a generation of analysts and
analysands confronted today with the quarrel over therapies, the
success of the neurosciences, and the attacks of behavioral-
oriented psychologies, whose analytic horizon needs to be broad-
ened and contextualized in relation to the philosophical tradition
and, more broadly speaking, both ancient and present culture.
Here we are confronted not with psychoanalysis as an object but
with the object in psychoanalysis, an object that is not "desire"
but "human desire caught up in a more or less conflictual relationship with a world of culture" encompassing art, ethics, and religion. It is not difficult to understand what connections and

[3] Allow me to recall that *Phantasie* in German means "imagination."
For more on this subject, see the Introduction by Michaël Foessel to
Paul Ricoeur, *Anthologie* (Paris: Seuil, 2007).

personal interests tie these themes to his philosophical concerns and even Ricoeur's own existence. Would it be out of place to risk a hypothesis here or would it mean forcing our interpretation were we to believe that we can see in Ricoeur's fine reflections on "Psychoanalysis and Art" a rare autobiographical element: a proximity, an empathy with Leonardo da Vinci, who like Ricoeur was born a precocious orphan, or who shared the pain of such an origin? With the *Mona Lisa*, "Leonardo's brush does not re-create the memory of his mother, but creates it as a work of art, by creating *the* smile as seen by Leonardo." "The true smile, which will be sought in vain, is not behind it in some actual event that could be relived, it is in front of us, on the painted canvas." A philosophical work is not a work of art, but it is a work. Did not Paul Ricoeur construct his from the hurt of a life that from early infancy had been torn from the peacefulness of the mother's smile?

Two more texts, finally, are the fruits and representative of Ricoeur's own work on narrative and narrativity. The first one, "Life: A Story in Search of a Narrator," by its very title recalls the meaning and importance of biographical narrative for the narrator's own identity. In the second one, "Narrative: Its Place in Psychoanalysis," Ricoeur spells out how his reflection comes from "my increasing dissatisfaction regarding Freudianism" and its "metapsychological doctrine" insofar as this represents a discordant theory in relation to a certain practice: "there is more in the Freudian discovery than in the theoretical discourse Freud offers regarding it." Risking reinterpreting "psychoanalysis by taking as [his] starting point, not the theory but what happens in analytic experience itself," that is, in the relation between the analyst and the analysand, Ricoeur acknowledges that it is "imprudent" to venture into a territory that stems from a practice he himself never experienced. Hence it is up to analysts and practitioners to say whether this approach to psychoanalysis through the theory of "narrative" is well founded or if it has any contribution to make, and whether, moreover, psychoanalysis is not one of those regions of life and culture where the "narration of a life" finds a place.

Even if the references to the history of philosophy are muted, the impression might arise that there is too much effort to integrate or reintegrate psychoanalysis into the continuity of Western thought and culture, to neutralizing its rupturing power, in short to manifesting a more "Hegelian" accent than Ricoeur himself might have wished, thereby removing the sting of psychoanalytic "science," that "disturbing uncanniness" which, to cite Freud's own expression, best characterized it and which, moreover, Ricoeur himself so readily assumed in order to indicate what was original about Freud. Readers will have to make their own judgment on the basis of the texts gathered here. Those who wish to discredit this effort or project, to consider them as "out of date," even to indicate to the layman that he is forbidden to undertake to do so (a prohibition that radically contradicts Freud's own opinion and practice) are free to do so. But good reasons have to be given. Those that were produced at the time when Lacan rejected Ricoeur's work were often not really honorable; others, which came later, do not shine because of their philosophical brilliance. It is an irony of history that those who today might stand accused in a "black book of psychoanalysis," who yesterday were Ricoeur's own accusers, should find in him one of their best defenders.

But that doesn't really matter. The past is past. Beyond the momentary conflicts that they may have provoked or led to, the texts brought together here belong, as such, to the history of the relations between philosophy and psychoanalysis in the twentieth century. In this regard, beyond the contingencies that marked their own original publication, they deserve to be drawn from their dissemination and reclusion in difficult-to-locate sites and proposed, in a different context, to new readers.

Jean-Louis Schlegel

Note about this Edition

The "essays and lectures" in this book were brought together and prepared by Catherine Goldenstein and Jean-Louis Schlegel, with the attentive help of Mireille Delbraccio. The preparation consisted in "getting hold" of some of the texts, translating parts of them, integrating missing passages (indicated or referred to clearly by Paul Ricoeur), verifying the notes and citing French versions, completing them where necessary, and in adding a good number of others in order to give the interested reader necessary or useful information. No change was made to the chosen text, which generally could be found in manuscript form in the archive and which was the most complete version. Changes in form had to do with punctuation, spelling, and the translation of a few words, as well as the use of references to more recent translations for a few quotations. All the important changes are indicated in the notes and indicated as having been introduced by the editors.

C.G. and J.-L.S.

Translator's Note

As the Editor's Introduction to this volume states, the French edition of this book was meant to make available important essays by Paul Ricoeur on psychoanalysis that had not previously been published in French. These include some texts that had previously appeared in languages other than French and a few texts that had not previously been published in any language, but whose manuscript in French is now contained in the Ricoeur Archive in Paris. A number of these essays were previously published in translation in English, some of them in my translations from the time when I worked as Ricoeur's assistant at the University of Chicago. For this volume, I have taken the French book as now published as definitive and corrected my existing English versions of individual chapters where necessary, incorporating any changes or additions Ricoeur may have made subsequent to their original publication in English. In the case of earlier English translations by other hands, I have translated them anew on the basis of the French text as now published in order to ensure consistency of style and voice across these pages. Where an earlier English version does not exist, the translation given here appears for the first time.

Citations of Freud's works are taken from the 24-volume Standard Edition, edited by James Strachey (London: Hogarth Press and The Institute for Psychoanalysis, 1953–74), which is the English version used by Ricoeur. They are given as S.E. volume number: page number(s).

David Pellauer

The Question of Proof in Freud's Psychoanalytic Writings

The question of proof in psychoanalysis is as old as psychoanalysis itself.[1] Even before being a demand addressed to psychoanalysis by epistemologists, it is an internal exigency of psychoanalysis itself. The 1895 "Project" aims at being a project of scientific psychology. The interpretation of dreams claims to be a science and not a fantastic construction, a "fine fairy tale," to use Krafft-Ebing's remark, hurled at Freud at the close of one public presentation. Each of Freud's didactic works – *The Introductory Lectures*, *The New Introductory Lectures*, and the *Outline* – represents a new effort to communicate to the non-specialist the conviction that psychoanalysis is genuinely related to what is intelligible, what claims to be true. And yet, psychoanalysis has never fully succeeded in stating how its assertions are justified, how its interpretations are authenticated, how its theory is verified.[2] This relative failure

---

[1] My presentation is limited in two ways. First, I am restricting myself to Freud's work and I will refrain from making any judgment concerning developments in the problematic of psychoanalysis or its epistemology after Freud. Second, I am limiting myself to Freud's written work, not having had access to his oral teaching, his working notes, or any information apart from his published works.

[2] Cf., for example, the discussion that followed Heinz Hartmann's paper "Psychoanalysis as a Scientific Theory," at the New York University Symposium in 1958, in *Psychoanalysis, Scientific Method and Philosophy*, ed. Sydney Hook (New York: New York University Press,

of psychoanalysis to be recognized as a science results, I think, from a failure to ask certain preliminary questions which I propose to elaborate in the first two parts of my paper, before attempting in the third part to reply directly to the original question.

The first question has to do with what counts as a fact in psychoanalysis. The second deals with the type of relations existing between analytic theory and experience, in its double sense of being both a method of investigation and a therapeutic treatment.

The Criteria for "Facts" in Psychoanalysis

As regards the first question, we can begin by noting that traditional discussions about the epistemological status of analytic theory take it for granted that theories consist of propositions whose role is to systematize, explain, and predict phenomena comparable to those that verify or falsify theories in the natural sciences or in the human sciences, which, like experimental psychology, themselves adopt the epistemology of the natural sciences. Even when we are not dealing with a narrow empiricism that requires a theory to be directly validated by observable facts, we nevertheless continue to ask the same questions we would put to a science based on observations. In this way, we ask by what specific procedures psychoanalysis connects this or that theoretical notion to definite and unambiguous facts. However indirect the verification process may be, definitions must become opera-

1959), 3–37. I also refer to the mordant commentary of Ernest Nagel published under the title "Methodological Issues in Psychoanalytic Theory," in the same volume. [In the French version of this text published as "La psychanalyse confrontée à l'épistémologie," *Psychologie française* (1986): 211–22, which makes use of part of this chapter, Ricoeur adds a reference to "the recent book" by Adolf Grünbaum, *Foundations of Psychoanalysis* (Berkeley: University of California Press, 1984), which "confirms the misunderstanding that reigns between psychoanalysts and epistemologists formed by the Vienna School, prolonged by logical positivism." – Eds.]

tional; that is, they must be shown to generate procedures for verification and falsification.

But this is precisely what is in question: what in psychoanalysis merits being considered as a verifiable fact?

My thesis is that psychoanalytic theory – in a certain sense that will be described in the second part of this essay – is the codification of what takes place in the analytic situation, or more precisely in the analytic relationship. It is there that something is produced that merits being called the analytic experience. In other words, the equivalent of what the epistemology of logical empiricism calls "observable" facts is to be sought first in the analytic situation, in the analytic relationship. Our first task, therefore, will be to show in what way the analytic relationship brings about a selection among the facts that are likely to be taken into account by the theory. I propose retaining four criteria of this process of selection as useful for further discussion.

First criterion: there enters into the field of investigation and treatment only that part of experience which is capable of being said. There is no need to insist here on the talk-cure character of psychoanalysis. This restriction to language is first of all an inherent restriction on the analytic technique. It is the particular context of noninvolvement with reality, belonging to the analytic situation, that forces desire to speak, to pass through the defile of words, excluding every substitute satisfaction as well as any regression toward "acting out." This screening through discourse in the analytic situation also functions as a criterion for what will be held to be the object of this science; not instinct as a physiological phenomenon, not even desire as energy, but desire as a meaning capable of being deciphered, translated, and interpreted. Hence the theory necessarily has to account for what from here on we can call the semantic dimension of desire.

We can already see the misunderstanding that prevails in the usual epistemological discussions: facts in psychoanalysis are in no way facts of observable behavior. They are "reports." We know dreams only as told upon awakening; and even symptoms, although they are partially observable, enter into the field of analysis only in relation to other factors verbalized in the "report."

It is this selective restriction that forces us to situate the facts of psychoanalysis inside a sphere of motivation and of meaning.[3]

Second criterion: The analytic situation singles out not only what is sayable, but what is said to another person. Here again, the epistemological criterion is guided by something absolutely central to the analytic technique. The transference stage, in this regard, is highly significant, for we might be tempted to confine the discussion of transference to the sphere of psychoanalytic technique and thereby overlook its epistemological implications in our search for relevant criteria.[4] To demonstrate this, let us consider a text crucial for analytic technique, the 1914 essay titled "Remembering, Repeating, and Working Through." In this essay Freud begins with the precise moment in the cure when the memory of traumatic events is replaced by the compulsion to repeat, which blocks remembering. Focusing on the relation

---

[3] Despite efforts as remarkable as those of David Rapaport in *The Structure of Psychoanalytic Theory* (New York: International Universities Press, 1960), psychoanalysts have not managed to convince epistemologists that psychoanalysis is capable of satisfying the requirements of operational analysis as it is defined, for example, by P.W. Bridgman. We need only recall here B.F. Skinner's strident criticism in the discussion of psychoanalysis in Herbert Feigel and Michael Scriven, eds., *The Foundations of Science and the Concepts of Psychology and Psychoanalysis* (Minneapolis: University of Minnesota Press, 1956). For Skinner, Freud's mental entities are the same sort of thing as phlogiston or aether are in physical theory; the forces alleged by psychoanalysis cannot be quantified, so they cannot be integrated into an empirical science worthy of the name. Moreover, it is doubtful whether reformulations of psychoanalysis to a modified or revised form of operationalism would meet the requirements of operational analysis any better than did Freud's own presentation in the *Outline of Psychoanalysis*. In order to assimilate psychoanalytic entities to operationalism's "intervening variables" and "dispositional concepts," they would have to refer to facts that were themselves observables in the sense that this term is used in logical empiricism.

[4] I will leave for later discussion whether in saying this, motive is to be opposed to cause, meaning to energy, and understanding to explanation. This may be too hasty a conclusion, one that does not take into account as yet unexamined facts and that, at first glance, are not in agreement with the semantic – signifying and sayable – characteristic singled out by the analytic situation and relationship.

between this compulsion to repeat, resistance, and transference, he writes, "The greater the resistance, the more extensively will acting out (repetition) replace remembering." And he adds, "the patient repeats instead of remembering and repeats under the conditions of resistance."[5] Then he introduces transference, which he describes as "the main instrument . . . for curbing the patient's compulsion to repeat and for turning it into a motive for remembering."[6] Why does transference have this effect? The answer to this question leads to epistemological considerations directly grafted onto what appears at first to be strictly a matter of technique. If the resistance can be cleared away and remembering made free to occur, it is because the transference constitutes something like "a playground in which [the patient's compulsion to repeat] is allowed to expand in almost complete freedom."[7] Extending this analogy of the playground, Freud makes things more specific by adding: "The transference thus creates an intermediate region between illness and real life through which the transition from one to the other is made."[8]

It is this notion of transference as a "playground" or "intermediate region" that guides my remarks on the second criterion for what is psychoanalytically relevant as a fact. In this "playground," this "intermediate region," in effect, we can read the relationship with the other as constituting an erotic demand addressed to another person. It is in this regard that "transference" has its place, not only in a study of analytic technique, but also in an epistemological inquiry about criteria. It reveals this constitutive trait of human desire: not only is it able to be spoken, to be brought to language, but it is also addressed to another; more precisely, it is addressed to another desire which is capable of mistaking its request. What is thereby singled out from human experience is the immediately intersubjective dimension of desire.

We should therefore not overlook the fact that if we speak of objects, of "wish objects" – and we cannot fail to speak of them in such contexts as the object-choice, the lost object, and the substitute object, which we shall return to below – this object is

[5] S.E. 12:151.
[6] Ibid., 154.
[7] Ibid.
[8] Ibid.

another desire. In other words, the relationship to the other is not something added onto desire. In this respect Freud's discovery of the Oedipus complex in the course of his self-analysis is to be included within the very structure of desire, seen as a triangular structure bringing into play two sexes and three persons.

[It follows from this that what the theory will articulate as symbolic castration is not an additional, extrinsic factor, but something that attests to the initial relation of desire to an agency of prohibition that imposes the standards lived out in fantasies by the child as a paternal threat directed against its sexual activities.][9] This is why, from the outset, all that might be considered a solipsism of desire is eliminated, as would be the case for a definition of desire simply in terms of energy, tension, and release. The mediation of the other is constitutive of human desire as addressed to. . . . This other can be someone who responds or who refuses to respond, someone who gratifies or someone who threatens. He may be, above all, real or a fantasy, present or lost, a source of anxiety, or the object of a successful mourning. Through transference, psychoanalysis controls and examines these alterative possibilities by transposing the drama that generated the neurotic situation onto a sort of miniature artificial stage. Thus it is the analytic experience itself that forces the theory to include intersubjectivity within the very constitution of libido and to conceive of it less as a need than as an other-directed wish.

Third criterion: The third criterion introduced by the analytic situation has to do with the coherence and the resistance of certain manifestations of the unconscious, which led Freud to speak of "psychical reality" in contrast to material reality. It is the distinctive features of this psychical reality that are psychoanalytically relevant. And this criterion is paradoxical to the extent that what common sense sets in opposition to reality is what constitutes this psychical reality.

In his *Introductory Lectures*, for example, Freud writes, "phantasies possess *psychical* as contrasted with *material* reality . . . *in the world of the neuroses it is psychical reality which is the decisive kind.*"[10] Symptoms and fantasies "abstract from the object

[9] The brackets here are to be found in the French manuscript in the Ricoeur Archive.
[10] S.E. 16:368.

and thus renounce every relation with external reality." He then goes on to refer to infantile scenes which themselves "are not always true." This is an especially important admission if we recall how difficult it was for Freud to give up his initial hypothesis of the father's real seduction of the child. Fifteen years after the publication of *The Interpretation of Dreams*, he remarks how disturbing this discovery remained for him.[11] What is so disturbing is precisely that it was not clinically relevant whether the infantile scenes are true or false. This is what is expressed by the phrase "psychical reality."

But resistance to the notion of a psychical reality does not come only from common sense. It apparently also contradicts the basic opposition in psychoanalysis between the pleasure principle, from which comes the fantasy, and the reality principle. This is why this concept meets resistance not only from common sense and the attitude formed by the observational sciences, but also from psychoanalytic theory itself and its tenacious dichotomy between the imaginary and the real.

The epistemological consequences of this paradox from analytic experience are considerable: whereas experimental psychology does not encounter a similar paradox in that its theoretical entities are all said to refer to observable facts and ultimately to real movements in space and time, psychoanalysis deals only with psychical reality and not with material reality. So the criterion for this reality is no longer that it is observable, but that it presents a coherence and a resistance comparable to that of material reality.

The range of phenomena satisfying this criterion is wide. Fantasies deriving from infantile scenes (observing the parents' sexual relations, seduction, and above all castration) constitute the paradigmatic case to the extent that, in spite of their fragile

---

[11] Confronted with a patient who takes no account of the difference that exists between reality and imagination, "We are tempted to feel offended at the patient's having taken up our time with invented stories. Reality seems to us something worlds apart from invention, and we set a very different value on it. Moreover the patient, too, looks at things in this light in his normal thinking" (ibid.). Here, then, is the paradox: in what follows, Freud says that the administration of the cure forbids us either to rid the patient of his illusions or to take him at his word, that is, to consider the difference between the imaginary and the real as relevant.

basis in the real history of the subject, they present a highly structured organization and are inscribed in scenarios that are both typical and limited in number.

But the idea of psychical reality is not exhausted by that of the fantasy, in the sense of archaic scenes. The imaginary, in the broad sense, covers all the sorts of mediations implied in the unfolding of desire. Close to the infantile scene, for example, we may put the whole domain of abandoned objects which continued to be represented as fantasies. Freud introduces this notion in connection with the problem of symptom formation. Objects abandoned by the libido provide the missing link between the libido and its points of fixation in the symptom.[12]

And from the notion of abandoned objects, the transition to that of the substituted object, which places us at the very heart of the analytic experience, is easy. The *Three Essays on Sexuality* starts from the variability of the object in contrast to the stability of the aim or goal of the libido and derives from this gap the substitutability of love objects. And in "Instincts and their Vicissitudes," Freud goes on to construct in a systematic fashion on this basis the typical configurations arising from the combinations of substitutions – through inversion, reversal, etc., the ego is capable of putting itself in place of the object, as in the case of narcissism.

Substitutability, in turn, is the key to another set of phenomena central to the analytic experience. At the time of *The Interpretation of Dreams*, Freud had noted the remarkable feature of dreams that they could be substituted for a myth, a folktale theme, or for a symptom, a hallucination, or an illusion. In effect, the entire reality of these psychic formations consists in the thematic unity that serves as a basis for the interplay of their substitutions. Their reality is their meaning, and their meaning is their capability of mutually replacing one another. It is in this sense that the notions of the lost object and the substitute object – cardinal notions for analytic experience – deserve to occupy a key position in the

---

[12] "They or their derivatives are still retained with a certain intensity in phantasies. Thus the libido need only withdraw on to phantasies in order to find the path open to every repressed fixation. . . . The libido's retreat to phantasy is an intermediate stage on the path to the formation of symptoms" (ibid., 373).

epistemological discussion as well. Put quite simply, they forbid our speaking of a "fact" in psychoanalysis in the same way as in the observational sciences.

I do not want to leave this criterion of psychical reality without adding a final link to the chain of examples that has led us from fantasy to the lost object, then to the substitute object. This final link will assure us that the entire chain stems fully from the analytic experience. This example is the work of mourning. Mourning, as such, is a remarkable case of reacting to the loss of an object.[13] It is, to be sure, reality that imposes the work of mourning, but a reality that includes the loss of the object, therefore a reality signified as the verdict of some absence.[14] Consequently, mourning consists in "the compromise by which the command of reality is carried out piecemeal."[15] But this realization consists precisely in the internalization of the lost object, concerning which Freud says, "the existence of the lost object is psychically prolonged."[16]

If I conclude this examination of the criterion of psychical reality with the work of mourning, it is not only to emphasize the wide range of phenomena arising out of the abandonment of the object, but to show at what point the phenomenon of mourning is close to the very core of psychoanalysis. Psychoanalysis begins by acknowledging the fantasy as the paradigm of what represents psychical reality, but it continues by means of a labor that may itself be understood as a work of mourning, that is, as an internalization of the lost objects of desire. Far from restricting itself to vanquishing the fantasy to the benefit of reality, the cure also recovers it as a fantasy to situate it, without confusing it with what is real, on the level of the imaginary. This kinship between the cure and the work of mourning confirms, if any further confirmation is required, that it is the analytic experience that requires that

---

[13] Freud defines it specifically in the following terms: "Mourning is regularly the reaction to the loss of a loved person, or to the loss of some abstraction which has taken the place of one, such as one's country, liberty, an ideal and so on" (*Mourning and Melancholia*, S.E. 14:243).
[14] "Reality-testing has shown that the loved object no longer exists and it proceeds to demand that all libido shall be withdrawn from its attachments to that object. This demand arouses understandable opposition" (ibid., 244).
[15] Ibid., 245.
[16] Ibid.

we add the reference to fantasies to the two preceding criteria; for what has been said (the first criterion) and what is asked of the other person (the second criterion) bear the mark of the particular imaginary formations that Freud brings together under the term *das Phantasieren*. It follows that what is relevant for the analyst are not observable facts or observable reactions to environmental variables, but the meaning that the same events which the behavioral psychologist considers as an observer assume for a subject. I will venture to say, in summation, that what is psychoanalytically relevant is what a subject makes of his fantasies.

Fourth criterion: The analytic situation selects from a subject's experience what is capable of entering into a story or narrative. In this sense, "case histories" as histories constitute the primary texts of psychoanalysis.[17] This "narrative" character of the psychoanalytic experience is never directly discussed by Freud, at least to my knowledge. But he does refer to it indirectly in his considerations about memory. We recall the famous declaration from the *Studies on Hysteria* that "hysterics suffer mainly from reminiscences."[18] Of course many memories will appear to be merely screen-memories and fantasies rather than real memories when Freud seeks the real origin of neurotic suffering. But such

[17] There are other senses in which psychoanalysis presents historical features. If, for example, we emphasize the expression "case history," we can characterize the analytical situation in the sense that what unfolds there only happens once. Even if a typology may serve as a guide to the diversity of individual situations, types remain the intellectual instruments of an understanding governed by singular instances. The type is not a law for which the individual would be only an example. On the contrary, it is in the service of the "case" that the type offers the mediation of its intelligibility. In this sense the word "case" does not have the same sense in psychoanalysis as in the observational sciences due to this inverse relation of the type to the case. Later we shall see what difficulties this specific relation causes for the question of proof in psychoanalysis. The analytic experience also has many other historical features. It will suffice here to recall the archaism of the unconscious, the stages of the libido, the genesis of the object-choice, the history of the substitute objects, the relations between primary and secondary processes, and so on. All these features contribute in one way or the other to the narrative structure of the analytic experience.

[18] S.E. 2:7.

fantasies in turn will always be considered in their relation to forgetting and remembering due to their relation to resistance and to the connection between resistance and repetition. Remembering, then, is what has to replace repetition. The struggle against resistance – what Freud calls "working through" (*Durcharbeiten*) – has no other aim than to reopen the path of memory.

But what is it to remember? It is not just to recall certain isolated events, but to become capable of forming meaningful sequences and ordered connections. In short, it is to be able to constitute one's own existence in the form of a history where a memory as such is only a fragment of the narrative. It is the narrative structure of such life histories that makes a case a case history.

That such an ordering of one's life episodes in the form of a history constitutes a kind of work – as the phrase "working through" suggests – is attested by the role of one fundamental phenomenon of fantasy life, namely, the after-the-event phenomenon (*Nachträglichkeit*) that Jacques Lacan has brought out so well. It is the fact that "experiences, impressions, and memory-traces may be revised at a later date to fit with fresh expressions or with the attainment of a new stage of development. They may in that event be endowed not only with a new meaning but also with psychical effectiveness."[19] Before raising a theoretical problem, this phenomenon is implied in the work of psychoanalysis itself. It is in the process of working through just mentioned that Freud discovers that the subject's history does not conform to a linear determinism that would place the present in the firm grasp of the past in a univocal fashion. On the contrary, recovering traumatic events through the work of analysis reveals that, at the time they were experienced, they could not be fully integrated in a meaningful context. It is only the arrival of new events and new situations that precipitates the subsequent reworking of these earlier events. Thus in the Wolf Man, it is a second sexually significant scene that after the event confers upon the first scene its effectiveness. Generally speaking, numerous repressed memories only become traumas after the event. It is a question of more than

[19] Jean Laplanche and Jean-Baptiste Pontalis, *The Language of Psychoanalysis*, trans. Donald Nicholson-Smith (New York: W.W. Norton and Company, 1967), 111.

just a delay or a deferred action. Here we see that we are far removed from the notion of a memory that would simply reproduce real events in a sort of perception of the past; this is instead a work that goes over and over extremely complex structuralizations. It is this work of memory that is implied, among other things, by the notion of the history or narrative structure of existence.

For the fourth time, then, a vicissitude of the analytic experience reveals a pertinent feature of what, psychoanalytically, counts as a "fact."

Investigatory Procedure, Method of Treatment, and Theoretical Terms

The second preliminary question concerning proof in psychoanalysis is that of the nature of the relation that can be found between the theory and what counts as a fact in psychoanalysis. From the perspective of operational analysis, the theoretical terms of an observational science must be capable of being connected to observables by way of rules of interpretation or translation that assure the indirect verification of these terms. The question here is to know whether the operative procedures that allow the transition between the level of theoretical entities and that of facts have the same structure and the same meaning in psychoanalysis as in the observational sciences.

To reply to this question, I would like to return to one of Freud's statements that deals precisely with the epistemological status of theory in psychoanalysis. In *Two Encyclopedia Articles: "Psychoanalysis" and "Libido Theory,"* we read that "psychoanalysis is the name (1) of a procedure (*Verfahren*) for the investigation of mental processes which are almost inaccessible in any other way, (2) of a method (based upon that investigation) for the treatment of neurotic disorders, and (3) of a collection of psychological information obtained along those lines, which is gradually being accumulated into a new scientific discipline."[20]

It is this triangular relation between a procedure of investigation, a method of treatment, and a theory that will hold our attention because it takes the place of the theory-fact relation in

[20] S.E. 18:235.

the observational sciences. Not only does psychoanalysis deal with "facts" of a special nature, as has just been established, but what takes the place of the operative procedures at work in the natural sciences is a unique type of relation between the investigatory procedure and the method of treatment. It is this relation that mediates between the theory and the facts.

Now, before anything can be said about the role of the third term, theory, in relation to the other two terms, the relation between the investigatory procedure and the method of treatment is itself not easy to grasp. If this relation may appear to be non-problematical for a practice that is little concerned with theoretical speculation, it does raise considerable difficulties for epistemological reflection. Broadly speaking, we may say that the investigatory procedure tends to give preference to relations of *meaning* between mental productions, while the method of treatment tends to give preference to relations of *force* between systems. The function of the theory will be precisely to integrate these two aspects of psychical reality.

The investigatory procedure has, in effect, a strong affinity with the disciplines of textual interpretation. We read this, for example in the *Interpretation of Dreams*, whose very title (*Traumdeutung*) is revealing: "The aim which I have set before myself is to show that dreams are capable of being interpreted (*einer Deutungfähig sein*). . . . My presumption that dreams can be interpreted at once puts me in opposition to the ruling theory of dreams . . . for 'interpreting' a dream implies assigning a 'meaning' (*Sinn*) to it – that is, replacing (*ersetzen*) it by something which fits (*sich einfügt*) into the chain of our mental acts as a link having a validity and importance equal to the rest."[21] In the same context, interpretation is often compared to the translation from one language into another, to deciphering a hieroglyph, or to the solution of a rebus.[22] Freud never doubted that, however inaccessible the unconscious might

---

[21] S.E. 4:96.
[22] "A dream is a picture-puzzle of this sort and our predecessors in the field of dream-interpretation have made the mistake of treating the rebus as a pictorial composition: and as such it has seemed to them nonsensical and worthless" (ibid., 277). In his essay "The Unconscious," Freud will again say: "It is of course only as something conscious that we know it, after it has undergone transformation (*Umsetzung*) or translation (*Übersetzung*)" (S.E. 14:166). In the same sense, "it may be pointed out that the interpretations of psychoanalysis are first and foremost

be, it still participates in the same psychic structures as does consciousness. It is this common structure that allows us "to interpolate" unconscious acts into the text of conscious acts. This feature belonging to the method of investigation coheres with the criteria for "facts" in psychoanalysis, in particular with the criteria of sayability and substitutability. If the investigatory procedure may be applied to both neurotic symptoms and dreams, it is because dream-formation (*Traumbildung*) and symptom-formation (*Symptombildung*) are homogeneous and substitutable.[23] This deep kinship among all the compromise formations allows us to speak of the psyche as a text to be deciphered.

This broadly inclusive notion of a text encompasses the profound unity not only of dreams and symptoms, but of these two taken together with phenomena such as daydreams, myths, folktales, sayings, proverbs, puns, and jokes. The gradual extension of this method of investigation is assured by the special kinship that is shown to exist between, on the one hand, the group of fantasies referred to earlier as infantile scenes (classed in the *Interpretation of Dreams* along with typical dreams: dreams of nudity, of death of someone dear, etc.), and, on the other hand, the most highly organized and most permanent mythical structures of humanity. From the same investigatory procedure comes most notably the "textual" structure common to the Oedipus complex discovered by Freud in his self-analysis and the Greek tragedy *Oedipus Rex* transmitted to us as one of the masterpieces of literature. There is thus a correspondence between the extension of the investigatory procedure and what could be termed the

translations from an alien method of expression into one which is familiar to us" (*The Claims of Psychoanalysis to the Interest of the Non-Psychological Sciences*, S.E. 13:176). Elsewhere Freud compares censorship to press censorship. "If the analogy is not perused too strictly, we may say that repression has the same relation to other methods of defence as omission has to distortion of the text, and we may discover in the different forms of this falsification parallels to the variety of ways in which the ego is altered" (*Analysis Terminable and Interminable*, S.E. 23:236–7).

[23] See S.E. 4:605–6. This was recognized as early as 1893, where the "Preliminary Communication" already treats the relation between the determining cause and the hysterical symptom as a "symbolic tie," akin to the dream process.

space of fantasy in general, in which psychic productions as diverse as daydreams, children's games, psychological novels, and other poetic creations find a place. In the same way, the psychic conflicts inscribed in stone by Michelangelo's *Moses* lend themselves to interpretation by virtue of the figurable and substitutable nature of all the sign systems that are included within the same investigatory procedure.

But if we were only to follow the suggestion of the concepts of the text and interpretation, we would arrive at an entirely erroneous notion of psychoanalysis. Psychoanalysis could be purely and simply subsumed under the aegis of the historical-hermeneutical sciences, alongside philology and exegesis. We would then overlook the very features of interpretation that are grasped only when the investigatory procedure is joined to a method of treatment. Why are the meaning of the symptom and of the dream so difficult to decipher, if not because of the distortion mechanisms (*Entstellung*) interposed between the manifest and the hidden meaning – the mechanisms Freud listed under the term dreamwork in the *Interpretation of Dreams*? (The forms are well known: condensation, displacement, and so forth; we are not dealing with the theory of dreams here, but with the relation between interpretation and the method of treatment.)

This "distortion" is indeed a strange sort of phenomenon, and Freud employs all sorts of quasi-physical metaphors to render this transformation, which he says, "does not think, calculate, or judge in any way at all."[24] We have already mentioned condensation and displacement which are quasi-physical metaphors for the dreamwork. But it is the central metaphor of *repression* that orders all the others to the point of becoming a theoretical concept whose metaphorical origin is forgotten (as, moreover, is that of the concept of distortion itself, which literally signifies a violent

[24] Freud speaks of it cautiously in the following terms: "Two separate functions may be distinguished in mental activity during the construction of a dream: the production of the dream-thoughts, and their transformation into the content of the dream." This activity "is completely different (from waking thought) qualitatively and for that reason not immediately comparable to it. It does not think, calculate or judge in any way at all; it restricts itself to giving things a new form" (S.E. 5:506–7).

displacement as well as a deformation). The semi-metaphor of regression belongs to the same cycle.[25]

Another quasi-physical metaphor of equal importance is that of *cathexis*, concerning which Freud does not conceal the kinship with the operation of a capitalist entrepreneur (the daydreamer) who "invests" his money: "the capitalist who provides the psychical outlay for the dream is invariably and indisputably, whatever may be the thoughts of the previous day, a wish from the unconscious."[26] This metaphor allows regression to acquire not only a topographic signification, but also a dynamic one, to the extent that regression to an image proceeds from "changes in the cathexes of energy attaching to the different systems, changes which increase or diminish the facility with which those systems can be passed through by the excitatory process."[27] This play of metaphors becomes extremely complex when Freud goes on to interweave textual metaphors (translation, substitution, overdetermination, etc.) and energy metaphors (condensation, displacement, repression), producing mixed metaphors such as disguise, censorship, and so on.

Why does Freud get himself into such difficult straits with concepts that remain semi-metaphors and, in particular, with inconsistent metaphors polarized between, on the one hand, the textual concept of translation and, on the other hand, the mechanical concept of compromise, itself understood in the sense of the outcome of various interacting forces? I suggest that it is the conjunction of the investigatory procedure with the method of treatment that compels the theory to operate in this way, using semi-metaphorical concepts which moreover lack coherence.

I would like to pause here to consider the word "treatment" (*Behandlung*), which we earlier distinguished from the method of investigation. The notion of a "method of treatment" must be

---

[25] Evidence of this can be found in chapter 7 of the *Interpretation of Dreams*, which gives a graphic representation of this by means of the famous schema of the psychical apparatus that Freud calls an "auxiliary representation." Thanks to this topographic representation, regression acquires its properly topographic meaning in conjunction with the forces that compel this backward movement.

[26] S.E. 5:561.

[27] Ibid., 543–44.

understood in a sense that extends far beyond the strictly medical sense of "cure," to designate the whole analytic procedure insofar as analysis itself is a sort of work. This work is both the inverse of what we just described as the dream-work and the correlative of what earlier was termed the work of mourning. To the question of how analysis is a work, Freud gives a constant reply: Psychoanalysis is essentially a struggle against resistances.[28] It is this notion of resistance that prevents us from identifying the investigatory procedure with a simple interpretation, with a purely intellectual understanding of the meaning of symptoms. Interpretation, understood as translation or deciphering, in short as the substitution of an intelligible meaning for an absurd one, is only the intellectual segment of the analytic procedure. Even transference (which appeared above as an intersubjective criterion of desire) must be treated as one aspect of the handling of

---

[28] As is well known, it is the acknowledgement of the strategic role of resistances and of the struggle against resistances that made Freud decide to abandon Breuer's cathartic method insofar as it was aimed at reaching an anamnesis without work. Speaking in 1910 of "The Future Prospects of Psychoanalytic Therapy" (S.E. 11:141–51), Freud described his technical innovations in these terms: "As you know, our technique has undergone a fundamental transformation. At the time of the cathartic treatment what we aimed at was the elucidation of the symptoms; we then turned away from the symptoms and devoted ourselves instead to uncovering the 'complexes,' to use a word which Jung has made indispensable; now, however, our work is aimed directly at finding out and overcoming the 'resistances,' and we can justifiably rely on the complexes coming to light without difficulty as soon as the resistances have been recognized and removed" (144). This very struggle against resistances invites us to be forewarned against overestimating interpretation in its analytic form. It is completely ineffective for revealing to the patient the meaning of his symptoms so long as the entirely intellectual understanding of their meaning has not been incorporated into the work of analysis. Moreover, as Freud wrote in 1910 in " 'Wild' Psychoanalysis," "informing the patient of his unconscious regularly results in an intensification of the conflict in him and an exacerbation of his troubles" (S.E. 11:225). Freud even goes so far as to warn beginners in analytic treatment against trying to make an exhaustive interpretation of dreams for this can be used by the resistances to delay the healing process (see "The Handling of Dream-Interpretation in Psychoanalysis," S.E. 12:91–6).

resistances (as is apparent in "Remembering, Repeating, and Working Through"). This is why the three themes – compulsion to repeat, transference, and resistance – are found to be connected at the level of analytic praxis.

What does this signify for our epistemological inquiry? Essentially the following: the pair formed by the investigatory procedure and the method of treatment takes exactly the same place as the operative procedures in the observational sciences that connect the level of theoretical entities to that of observable data. This pair constitutes the specific mediation between theory and "facts" in psychoanalysis. And this mediation operates in the following manner: by coordinating interpretation and the handling of resistances, analytic praxis calls for a theory in which the psyche will be represented both as a text to be interpreted *and* as a system of forces to be manipulated. In other words, it is the complex character of actual practice that requires the theory to overcome the apparent contradiction between the metaphor of the text to be interpreted and that of the forces to be regulated; in short, practice forces us to think meaning and force together in a comprehensive theory. It is through the practical coordination of interpretation and the handling of resistances that the theory is given the task of forming a model capable of articulating the facts acknowledged as relevant in the analytic experience. It is in this way that the relation between the investigatory procedure and the method of treatment constitutes the necessary mediation between theory and "facts."

Now, does psychoanalysis possess a theory that satisfies these requirements? It seems to me that it is in light of these questions that Freud's theoretical work – essentially, his "metapsychology" – should be examined today. If Freud's metapsychology has been turned into a fetish by some and scorned by others, it is because they treat it as an independent construction. Too many epistemological works examine the great theoretical texts – from the "Project" of 1895 and chapter 7 of the *Interpretation of Dreams* to *The Ego and the Id* – outside of the total context of experience and practice. Isolated in this way, the body of doctrine can only lead to premature and truncated evaluations. The theory must therefore be relativized, placed back into the complex network of relations that encompass it.

For my part, I should like to submit two theses, apparently opposed to each other, but which taken together in their unstable equilibrium attempt to consider Freud's theoretical work as the imperfect yet indispensable starting point for any reformulation of this theory.

On the one hand, I am prepared to acknowledge that Freud's theoretical model is not adequate to analytic experience and practice as these are formulated in his other writings (among them the "case histories," the writings on psychoanalytic technique, and on applied psychoanalysis). More specifically, Freud's metapsychology does not succeed in codifying and integrating into a coherent model meaning and force, textual interpretation and the handling of resistances.

In the first place, Freud always tends to reverse the relations between theory, on the one hand, and experience and practice, on the other, and to reconstruct the work of interpretation on the basis of theoretical models that have become autonomous. He thereby loses sight of the fact that the language of the theory is narrower than that in which the technique is described. What is more, he tends to construct his theoretical models in the positivist, naturalistic, and materialist spirit of the sciences of his day. Many texts assert the exclusive kinship of psychoanalysis with the natural sciences and even with physics, or announce that in the future psychoanalysis will be replaced by a more refined pharmacology.

In this respect, in the extended discussion he devotes to psychoanalysis in *Knowledge and Human Interests*, Jürgen Habermas is correct in speaking of the "self-misunderstanding of psychoanalysis as a natural science."[29] According to Habermas, technique and experience call for a structural model that is betrayed by the preferred model of energy distribution. This latter model is superimposed upon analytic experience, and in many ways precedes it, as we see in the 1895 "Project," which imposes on experience its system of reference (quantifiable energy, stimulation, tension, discharge, inhibition, displacement, etc.). Even when the psychical apparatus only includes "psychical localities" that are not anatomically localizable (as is the case in chapter 7 of the *Interpretation of Dreams*), the spatial arrangement and the temporal sequence of the systems continues to support the

[29] Jürgen Habermas, *Knowledge and Human Interests*, trans. Jeremy J. Shapiro (Boston: Beacon Press, 1971), 247.

energy-distribution model. The great article on "The Unconscious" placed at the center of the essays on metapsychology is the principal witness to the sovereignty of this model.

What is lost from sight in a model like this, however, is the very specificity of the "psychoanalytic" fact, with its fourfold property of being able to be said, to be addressed to another person, to be fantasized, figured, or symbolized, and to be recounted in a life history. This set of criteria requires that elements which are capable of accounting for what occurs in the analytic relation be introduced at the theoretical level in a suitable manner. This is why I can adopt, up to a certain point, the suggestions Habermas offers in light of the work of Lorenzer.[30] These two authors assume as their frame of reference the symbolizing process at work in human communication and in human interaction generally. The disturbances that give rise to psychoanalytic intervention are then considered as the pathology of our linguistic competence and are placed on the same level as the distortions uncovered, on another level, by the Marxist and post-Marxist critique of ideologies. Psychoanalysis and the critique of ideologies, in effect, share a common obligation, namely, to explain and interpret these distortions, which are not accidental, but systematic in the sense that they are systematically organized in the text of interhuman communication. These distortions are the occasion for a subject's self-misunderstanding. This is why, in order to account for this, we need a theory that is not limited to restoring the integral, unmutilated, and unfalsified text, but one that takes as its object the very mechanisms responsible for distorting the text. And this explains why, in turn, the interpretive decoding of symptoms and dreams goes beyond a simply philological hermeneutic, insofar as it is the very structure of the distorting mechanisms that requires explanation. This is also why the economic metaphors (resistance, repression, compromise, etc.) cannot be replaced by the philological metaphors (text, meaning, interpretation, etc.).

But the opposite thesis is no less true: neither can the economic metaphors replace the exegetical metaphors. Nor can they lose their metaphorical character and set themselves up as an energetic

---

[30] Alfred Lorenzer, *Über den Gegenstand der Psychoanalyse: Sprache und Interaktion* (Frankfurt: Suhrkamp, 1973). I note my hesitation regarding parts of this work below.

theory to be taken literally. It is essentially against this reduction to the literal nature of the energy-distribution model that our authors formulate their own theories in terms of communication and symbolic interaction. According to these alternative models, the mechanisms of the unconscious are no longer held to be things: they are "split-off symbols," "delinguisticized" or "degrammaticized motives." Like banishment or political ostracism, repression banishes a part of language from the public sphere of communication and condemns it to the exile of a "privatized" language. This is how mental functioning simulates a natural process, but only to the extent that it first has been objectified and reified. If, as a result, we forget that this reification results from a process of "desymbolization," hence from "a specific form of self-alienation," we end up constructing a model wherein the unconscious is literally a thing. But at the same time, we are then unable to understand how "resymbolization" is possible, that is, how analytic experience itself is possible. We can understand this only if we interpret the phenomena revealed by this experience in terms of communication disturbances, and analytic experience as a reappropriation that inverts the process of splitting off symbols.[31]

---

[31] Our authors concede that Freud's second topography – the ego, id, and superego – preserves more of the features of this twofold process of desymbolization and resymbolization than does the first topography (which alone, moreover, deserves to be called a topography). The three agencies, in effect, designate positions in relation to this twofold process: the neuter id designates the derivation of that part of ourselves that was banished from public communication; the "über" (super, over) of the superego designates the agency of interdiction, itself objectified and reified, which bars the way of the subject's becoming an ego. But it is in relation to the capacity to become an ego that there is an id and a superego, in accordance with Freud's own celebrated adage: *wo es war, soll ich werden* ("Where id was, shall ego be"). It is therefore necessary to give up the idea of an a-symbolic unconscious, that is, one foreign to the very fate of desymbolization. If Freud nevertheless clung to this idea as, for example, in *The Ego and the Id*, it was doubtless for a lack of a suitable linguistic model, as Marshall Edelson has convincingly demonstrated in *Language and Interpretation in Psychoanalysis* (New Haven: Yale University Press, 1975). But it was also, and especially because of, an obstinate will to pattern psychoanalysis on the natural sciences and to maintain its discovery within the aura of the *Aufklärung* that presided over its birth.

To the extent we take seriously this critique of the energetic model of Freudian metapsychology, we accept classifying psychoanalysis among the critical social sciences, which are guided by the interest in emancipation and motivated in the final analysis by the wish to recover the force of *Selbstreflexion*.

Yet, in return, I would not want this comparison to the critical social sciences nor this ultimate reference to self-reflection to go beyond the goal of placing the theory back into the complex network of psychoanalytic experience and practice. This is why I want to defend with equal vigor the complementary thesis, which holds that we must always start from the Freudian system in spite of its faults, even – I would venture to say – because of its deficiencies. As Habermas himself has remarked, the self-misunderstanding of psychoanalysis is not entirely unfounded. The economic model, in particular, even in its most literal energetic reading, preserves something essential, which a theorizing introduced from outside the system is always in danger of losing sight of, namely, that man's alienation from himself is such that mental functioning does actually resemble the functioning of a thing. This simulation keeps psychoanalysis from constituting itself as a province of the exegetical disciplines applied to texts – as hermeneutics in Gadamer's sense – and requires that the epistemology of psychoanalysis incorporate into the exegetical procedures applicable to the process of self-understanding explanatory segments akin to those at work in the natural sciences.

This requirement may be illustrated through a brief critique of those efforts at reformulating the theory that exclude in principle this simulation of a thing. I am thinking here especially of those reformulations that borrow from phenomenology, from ordinary-language analysis, or from linguistics. All these reformulations omit the task of integrating an explanatory stage into the process of desymbolization and resymbolization.[32]

I will limit myself here to those efforts that arise from consideration of the semantics of action in the school of linguistic analysis. I discussed the phenomenological interpretation at length in

[32] See my "Image and Language in Psychoanalysis," included in this volume.

my *Freud and Philosophy.*[33] I will also confine myself to what are linguistic reformulations, properly speaking. Under the name of the "philosophy of action," an autonomous discipline has been constituted, one influenced by Austin, Wittgenstein, and the philosophy of ordinary language, which assigns itself the task of describing the logic implicit in our discourse on action when it uses terms designating actions, intentions, motives, individual or collective agents, etc. Some of the analysts who practice this discipline – although less numerous today, it is true, and subjected to increasingly rigorous criticism by other semantic theorists – have maintained that discourse on action brings into play criteria of intelligibility distinct from and different than the criteria for physical movement or observable behavior. One of the implications of this dichotomy between two "language games" for action and movement bears directly on the point at issue in our discussion: According to these language analysts, our motives for acting can in no way be assimilated to the causes by which we explain natural events. Motives are reasons for action, while causes are the constant antecedents of other events from which they are logically independent.

Can psychoanalytic theory be reformulated on the basis of this distinction? Some authors have thought so and have interpreted psychoanalysis as an extension of the vocabulary of action (intention, motives, etc.) beyond the sphere where we are conscious of what we do. Psychoanalysis, according to this interpretation, adds nothing to ordinary conceptuality except the use of the same concepts of ordinary language in a new domain characterized as "unconscious." In this way, for example, it is said of the Rat Man analyzed by Freud that he experienced a feeling of hostility toward his father without being conscious of it. Understanding this assertion rests on the ordinary meaning we give to this sort of hostility in situations where the agent is able to recognize such a feeling as his own. The only novelty here is the use of clauses such as "without being conscious," "unknowingly," "unconsciously," etc.

[33] Paul Ricoeur, *Freud and Philosophy: An Essay on Interpretation,* trans. Denis Savage (New Haven: Yale University Press, 1970), 344–418.

In one sense, this is true. Freud himself declares that in the unconscious we do find representations and affects to which we can give the same name as their conscious counterparts and which lack only the property of being conscious. But what is completely omitted in this reformulation is the very paradox of psychoanalytic theory, namely, that it is the becoming unconscious as such that requires a specific explanation, so that the kinship of meaning between conscious and unconscious contents may be recognized. The explanatory schema capable of accounting for the mechanisms of exclusions, banishment, reification, etc., radically challenges the separation of the domains of action and movement, along with the dichotomy between motive and cause. In this regard, Michael Sherwood's demonstration in the critical part of his *The Logic of Explanation* is entirely convincing.[34] What characterizes psychoanalytic explanation is that it brings into view motives that are causes and that require an explanation of their autonomous functioning. What is more, Freud could not oppose motive to cause by giving motives the sense of "reason for," inasmuch as rationalization (a term he borrowed from Ernest Jones) is itself a process that calls for an explanation and, by this very fact, does not permit us to accept an alleged reason as the true cause.

As a result, Freud is correct in completely ignoring the distinction between motive and cause and even in making its theoretical formulation impossible. In many ways his explanation refers to "causally relevant" factors, whether this is in terms of the initial phenomenon (the *origin* of a neurosis), intermediary phenomena (the *genesis* of a symptom, of a libidinal structure, etc.), its *function* (compromise formation, etc.), or, finally, its *meaning* (substitution or symbolic value, etc.). These are the four modes of explanation retained by Sherwood, not only in Freud, but in general as well. Freud's use of the idea of cause and of causal explanation is perhaps both complex and flexible – Sherwood quotes a text from Freud which also distinguishes between preconditions, specific causes, and concurrent causes[35] – but he leaves no room for an opposition between cause and motive. All that is

[34] Michael Sherwood, *The Logic of Explanation in Psychoanalysis* (New York: Academic Press, 1969).
[35] See ibid., 172.

important to him is to explain through one or another of the explanatory modes just mentioned, or through an "overdetermined" use of several of them, what in behavior is "the incongruity" in relation to the expected course of human action.

It is the attempt to reduce these incongruities that forbids distinguishing between motives and causes because it calls for an *explanation* by means of causes in order to reach an *understanding* in terms of motives. This is what I try to express by saying that the facts in psychoanalysis arise both from the category of the text, and hence of meaning, and from the categories of energy and resistance, and hence of force. To say, for example, that a feeling is unconscious is not just to say that it resembles conscious motives occurring in other circumstances; rather it is to say that it has to be inserted as a causally relevant factor in order to explain the incongruities of an act of behavior, and that this explanation is itself a causally relevant factor in the work – the working through – of analysis.

From this brief discussion it follows that psychoanalytic theory cannot be reformulated from the outside on the basis of an alien conceptuality, if we wish to avoid mistaking the initial situation in psychoanalysis, namely, that the human psyche under certain conditions of self-alienation is unable to understand itself by simply expanding its immediate interpretive capacities, but requires instead that the hermeneutics of self-understanding take the detour of causal explanation.

If Freud's economic model can therefore legitimately be accused of generating misunderstanding concerning the relation between theory and the analytic situation, it must also be said with equal force and in the opposite direction, that a model of understanding – be it phenomenological, linguistic, or symbolic – that does not integrate some explanatory segment, some economic phase, misunderstands the very facts that are brought to light by analytic experience. This is why today we can neither be satisfied with the Freudian metapsychology nor find another starting point to rectify and enrich the theoretical model, and that it is true to say that "the misunderstanding of psychoanalysis as a natural science is not without basis."[36]

---

[36] I therefore find myself in agreement with some of Habermas's remarks concerning the incorporation of causal explanation into *Selbstreflexion*.

Truth and Verification

I am now going to attempt to deal directly with the specific question of proof in Freud's psychoanalytic writings.

As I said in my introduction, we cannot pose this question in a useful way so long as two preliminary questions have not been resolved, that of the criteria or what counts as a fact in psychoanalysis and that of the relation to be established between the theory and analytic experience through the double mediation of procedures of investigation and method of treatment.

To inquire about proof in psychoanalysis is to ask two separate questions: (1) What truth claim is made by the statements of psychoanalysis? And (2) what sort of verification or falsification are these statements capable of?

What truth claim is made by psychoanalytic statements? This question is not only one of degree, but also has to do with the nature of truth; it is not just a question of quantity, but also of the quality of truth. Or, to put it another way, the degree of exactitude that can be expected of psychoanalytic statements depends on the sort of truth that can be expected in this domain.[37] For lack of an exact conception of the qualitative diversity of the types of truth in relation to the types of facts, verificational criteria appropriate to the sciences, in which facts are empirically given to one or more external observers, have been repeatedly applied to psychoanalysis. The conclusion has then been either that psychoanalysis does not in any way satisfy these criteria or that it satisfies them only if they are weakened. But the question is not,

But is this mixture of self-understanding and causal explanation clarified by a return to the Hegelian theme from the Jena period of the "causality of destiny"? And is the process of resymbolization, to the extent that it intends to overcome causal connections in order to recover the current of personal motivations and public symbolization, capable of being assimilated to the Hegelian *Begreifen* which is precisely the counterpart of the causality of destiny? Already in *Freud and Philosophy*, I noted this "fated" side of causality in Freudian explanation.

[37] Aristotle already noted at the beginning of his *Nichomachean Ethics* that we cannot call for the same *acribie* in human things as in the natural sciences, and that it is always the nature of the things characteristic of an area of investigation that determines the type of adequation appropriate to that discipline.

I think, how to use more or less strict criteria loosely and so place psychoanalysis higher or lower on a single scale of verifiability (and undoubtedly quite low on the scale), but how to specify the truth claim as a function of the kind of "facts" in the psychoanalytic domain.

Let us return to our enumeration of the criteria for facts in psychoanalysis and ask ourselves what sort of adequation of statements is appropriate to them.

First, if analytic experience is based on desire coming to discourse, the sort of truth that best answers to it is that of a "saying-true" rather than a "being-true." This saying-true is negatively designated through the characterization of the mechanisms of distortion as disguise, falsification, illusion, and in general as misunderstanding. The truth here is closer to that of Greek tragedy than to that of modern physics. *Pathei mathos*, learn through suffering, says the chorus in Aeschylus's *Agamemnon*. And what, indeed, is truth for Oedipus, if not the recognition of himself as one who has already . . . already killed his father and married his mother?

This movement from misunderstanding to recognition is also the typical itinerary of analytic experience; it designates what might be called the veracity threshold in psychoanalysis.[38] At the price of certain reservations, which will be introduced below, we may say along with Habermas, that this sort of truth involves above all the subject's capacity for *Selbstreflexion*. The truth claim of psychoanalysis is primarily its claim to increase this capacity by helping the subject to overcome the distortions that are the source of self-misunderstanding.

Second, if the analytic situation filters – principally by means of the act of transference – what is said to the other, the truth claim of psychoanalysis can legitimately be placed within the field of intersubjective communication.[39] Everything that affects self-understanding also affects misunderstanding the other. All Freud's

[38] This is the *Redlichkeit* – the intellectual probity – dear to Nietzsche. In my study on "Psychiatry and Moral Values" (also included in this volume), I suggest that *Redlichkeit* is the only ethical "value" that remains within the ethical neutrality of the analytic relationship.

[39] I stated earlier in what way the incongruities of behavior giving rise to psychoanalysis may be considered as disturbances in communication, as modes of excommunication, due to the privatization of disconnected symbols.

analyses concerning object choice, the lost object, substitutions for the lost object, mourning and melancholia suggest that the place of misunderstanding is first of all another person. If this is the case, the truth claim, for which the misunderstanding of oneself and others constitutes the negative side, can be defined as a function of the positive task of pursuing self-recognition through the recognition of others and by means of extending the symbolic process in the public sphere of communication. In this sense, psychoanalysis pursues in its own way the project of recognition that Hegel placed at the summit of ethical life in his Jena philosophy. This thesis will seem less banal if we see its critical point in relation to the danger of manipulation, which seems to me implicit in any reduction of the historical sphere of communication to the empirical sphere of observable facts. If it is true, as Habermas says, that the sphere of empirically verifiable statements coincides with the one governing our interest for control and domination, then reducing the historical to the empirical would entail the danger of placing the order of symbolic communication under the same system for control and domination as that of our instrumental action.[40] This warning is not empty if we consider a certain tendency of psychoanalysis to take the process of self-recognition and of recognizing the other as an "adjustment" to the objective conditions of a society that is itself diseased.

With the third criterion for psychoanalytic facts, we come to the major difficulty facing the truth claim of psychoanalysis. I concluded from the study of the third criterion that what is psychoanalytically relevant is what a subject makes of his fantasies. What becomes of the truth claim of psychoanalysis when it is set within the framework of a more positive acknowledgement of fantasy than Freud himself allowed?[41] By losing its reference to

[40] It is therefore of fundamental importance to distinguish clearly the criteria for extending self-consciousness and for liberating our capacities for interaction and symbolic communication from the criteria for instrumental action.

[41] Freud was not overly troubled by his own discovery of the range and ramifications of the imaginary domain because he remained faithful to the threefold idea that fantasy in the broad sense of *Phantasieren* was set in opposition to the real, that in the final analysis it derives from an

present reality and by giving wider rein to the liberation of fanta-
sizing, to emotional development, and to enjoyment that Freud
wanted to do, are we not breaking the final connection between
veracity and truth? It seems so, at least as a first approximation.
Nevertheless, the claim to truth is not lost in a positive approach
to fantasies. In saying this, I base myself on certain texts of Freud
himself, such as "The Dissolution of the Oedipus Complex" and
"Analysis Terminable and Interminable."[42] These texts invite us
to understand the analytic cure as a work of mourning that, far
from eliminating the fantasy, recovers it as a fantasy, in order to
situate it clearly in relation to the real on the plane of the imaginary, in the strong sense of *Einbildungskraft* used by Kant and
the great post-Kantians.[43] The truth claim then would have to do

actual experience either in the individual's childhood or in the archaic
experience of humanity, that finally it is something to be cleared away
in favor of the reality principle (see the short paper from 1911,
"Formulations on the Two Principles of Mental Functioning," S.E.
12:218–26). In this way he was able to tie his truth principle in psychoanalysis to that of reality inasmuch as the real is the opposite of the
fantasy, the origin of the fantasy, and the ultimate horizon beyond the
death of the fantasy. And so, entering that foreign inner country he
called "psychical reality," Freud never relinquished the stubborn conviction that the fantasy stood out against the background of a primordial
contact with a nondeceptive reality. This nondeceptive reality therefore
continued to be at once the measure of the fantasy's reality, the real
origin of the fantasy, and the principle that was to prevail over the
pleasure principle under which the fantasy was classed and dismissed.
We may say that it was on the basis of this concept of reality that Freud
felt he was able to maintain the continuity between psychoanalysis and
the physical and biological sciences.

[42] S.E. 19:171–80, and S.E. 23:216–53.

[43] It is this hypothesis that the cure is itself a liberation of fantasies as
much as a struggle against resistances that made me take the recognition
of fantasy as a criterion for deciding what counts as a fact in psychoanalysis. It is because psychoanalysis is concerned with the fate of the
fantasy that its domain cannot be reduced to that of physiology or
psycho-physiology. It is in the same sense that I suggested in *Freud and
Philosophy* (472–7) that analytic experience aims at articulating several
prime signifiers of existence (phallus, father, mother, death, etc.) in order
to make their structuring function appear.

with the passage from the fantasy, as alienating, to it as symbolic, as founding individual and collective identity.[44]

The fourth criterion for psychoanalytic facts – the criterion of narrativity – will perhaps rid us of some of the difficulties raised by the preceding criterion. Someone might raise the objection to the preceding analysis that by introducing something like a "rational mythology" to the recognition process – for self-recognition as well as for the recognition of others – we also introduce fiction into the circumscription of truth. How, to borrow Goethe's title, can *Dichtung und Wahrheit* be reconciled? If we remember that fiction is pretending and that pretending is doing or making, are we not substituting making-true, i.e., make-believe, for saying true? Perhaps. But are not saying-true and making-true reconciled in the idea of constructing or reconstructing a coherent history from the scattered debris of our experience? Let us follow this pathway opened by the narrative character of psychoanalytic facts. Here the truth claim is tied to what Sherwood calls the "narrative commitment of psychoanalytic explanation." It seems to me that this author has shown quite correctly that ultimately what is at issue in psychoanalysis is giving "a single extended explanation of an individual patient's entire case history."[45] Hence, to explain here is to reorganize the facts into a meaningful whole which constitutes a single and continuous history (even if it does not cover an entire life span).

I think it is wise to approach things in this way. The narrative interest or involvement at issue here has no parallel in an observational science where we speak of "cases" but not of "case histories." The psychoanalytic explanation of a case is a narrative

---

[44] I have proposed such an analysis in my essay "Fatherhood: From Phantasm to Symbol," in *The Conflict of Interpretations* (Evanston: Northwestern University Press, 1974), 468–97.

[45] Sherwood, *The Logic of Explanation in Psychoanalysis*, 4. It is in a history of this kind that the incongruities appear, that is, behaviors, experiences, and feelings which do not "fit together." This is why Sherwood chooses to pose the question of the logic of analytic explanation at the level of the case history. For different reasons which he states, he chooses Freud's Rat Man as his primary example and in this regard asks: what is "the psychoanalytic explanation of an individual act of behavior?" In asking this question at this level, the narrative structure of psychoanalytic explanation is immediately evident.

explanation in the sense that the generalizations or law-like statements that are implied by the explanatory segments referred to in
the second part of our study contribute to the *intelligible narrative*
toward which each individual case study leads. If I could state
earlier that causal connections are explanatory segments in a
process of understanding, even of *Selbstreflexion* in Habermas's
sense, this is because the understanding in question is narrative
and because the partial explanatory segments of this or that fragment of behavior are integrated in a narrative structure.[46] So the
validation of analytic statements draws its specific nature from
this ultimate reference to a "narrative commitment" in the name
of which we try to integrate isolated or alien phenomena in "a
single unified process or sequence of events."[47]

We are thus invited to reflect upon the concept of narrative
intelligibility that psychoanalysis has in common with the historical sciences. It is not easy to define this concept inasmuch as the
criteria of adequacy are difficult to handle on this level. To be

[46] Sherwood speaks of "a fairly unified narrative within which a great
deal of previously unexplained material takes on comprehensible forms"
(ibid., 169). From this point of view, the narrative property of statements
in case histories encompasses their explanatory capacity. The explanation involves episodes – fragments initially isolated, then reorganized
into a comprehensive whole – but the ultimate context is narrative. In
the same sense, Habermas, basing himself on Arthur Danto's logic of
narrative statements, in *Analytic Philosophy of History* (New York:
Cambridge University Press, 1965), also develops a narrative theory of
interpretation and of the "the process of self-formation" (see *Knowledge
and Human Interests*, 258–60). Can we conclude from this narrative
structure of psychoanalytic statements that "the logic of psychoanalytic
explanation then resolves itself into the logic of psychoanalytic narratives" (Sherwood, *The Logic of Explanation in Psychoanalysis*, 191)? I
will state some reservations at this point for reasons which have to do
with the very place of "case histories" in the constellation of psychoanalytic statements. Although I am prepared to say that its truth claim is
related to the narrative character of the facts in psychoanalysis, I question the assertion that the logic of explanation simply resolves itself into
that of narration. It will be the object of the second part of my discussion to consider the role of theory in the validation process. However,
it is perfectly legitimate to isolate the truth claim that is tied to the narrative aspect of psychoanalytic facts.
[47] Sherwood, *The Logic of Explanation in Psychoanalysis*, 169.

sure, it is precisely in psychoanalysis that reduction of the "incongruities" raises the question of knowing what is meant by an intelligible account. A history that would remain inconsistent, incoherent, incomplete would clearly resemble what we know of the course of life in ordinary experience, namely, that a human life as a whole remains strange, disconnected, incomplete, and fragmented.

We might be tempted therefore to give up any attempt to tie a truth claim to the idea of the intelligible narrative of an existence. But I do not think it would be correct to give in to this epistemological defeatism, for we would thereby turn psychoanalytic statements into the rhetoric of persuasion on the pretext that it is the account's acceptability to the patient that is therapeutically effective. Beside the renewed suspicion of suggestion by the analyst – which Freud never ceased fighting against – a more serious suspicion is then insinuated, namely, that the criterion of therapeutic success is exclusively the patient's ability to adapt to a given social milieu. And this suspicion leads in turn to the suspicion that the psychoanalyst finally represents, with regard to the patient, only the point of view of society, and that he imposes this on his patient by subtly involving him in a strategy of capitulation to which he alone holds the key. This is why we must not give up our effort to link a truth claim to the narrativity criterion, even if this claim is validated on a basis other than that of narrativity itself.[48] In other words, we must maintain the critical dimension of narrativity, which is just that of self-recognition, of recognition of others, and of recognition of the fantasy. We may even say, then, that the patient is both the actor and the critic of a history that he is at first unable to recount. The problem of self-recognition is the problem of recovering the ability to recount one's own history, to endlessly continue to give the form of a

[48] Sherwood himself grants this when he concedes that "adequacy" goes along with "accuracy" (ibid., 244–57), which poses the problem of validation in terms other than those of acceptability to the patient, therapeutic effectiveness, or finally adjustment to the surroundings. Habermas expresses this conjunction of narrative accuracy and reflection in the following terms: "Only the patient's recollection decides the accuracy of the construction. If it applies, then it must also 'restore' to the patient a portion of lost life-history: then it must be able to elicit a self-reflection" (*Knowledge and Human Interests*, 230).

history to reflections about oneself. Working through is nothing other than this continuous narration.

We can now turn to the second half of our question: What sort of verification are the statements of psychoanalysis capable of? To ask about procedures of verification and falsification is to ask which *means of proof* are appropriate to the truth claims of psychoanalysis. My thesis here is as follows: if the ultimate truth claim resides in the case histories, the means of proof reside in the articulation of the entire network: theory, hermeneutics, therapeutics, and narration.

The preceding discussion on narrativity is a good introduction to this final stage of our investigation. We have assumed that all truth claims of psychoanalysis are ultimately summed up in the narrative structure of psychoanalytic facts. But it does not follow that the means of proof are contained in the narrative structure of psychoanalytic facts. Nor does it follow that the means of proof lie in the narrative structure as such and the question remains whether the means of truth appropriate to narrative explanation are not provided by the non-narrative statements of psychoanalysis.[49] To prove this point it will suffice if we consider what makes a narration an explanation, in the psychoanalytic sense of the term. It is the possibility of inserting several stages of causal explanation into the process of self-understanding formulated in narrative terms. It is this explanatory detour that justifies the recourse to non-narrative means of proof.

These are spread over three levels: (1) the level of generalizations resulting from comparison with the rest of the clinical explanation; (2) the level of law-like propositions applied to typical segments of behavior (symptoms, for example), which are, as Sherwood has shown, themselves divided into explanations in terms of origin, explanations in terms of genesis, in terms of function, and in terms of meaning; finally (3) the level of very general

---

[49] If we consider the body of Freud's work – and this is all we are considering at this time – the "case histories" make up only a small part of it. And as Sherwood has shown, among Freud's works only the Rat Man satisfies the criteria for a good analytic explanation. Beside the analogical applications of analytic explanation to works of art, and to cultural facts like morality and religion, the greater part of Freud's written work concerns the theory, the investigatory procedure, and the analytic technique itself.

hypotheses concerning the functioning of the psychic apparatus, which may be taken as axiomatic. This last level is divided into the topography, the theory of agencies, and the successive theories of instinctual drives, including the death instinct. Generalizations, laws, and axioms, therefore, constitute the non-narrative structure of psychoanalytic explanation.

At its first level, that of generalizations, this non-narrative structure of explanation is already present in the ordinary explanations of individual behavior: alleged motives – for example, jealousy – are not single phenomena but classes of inclinations under which we place a particular action in order to make it intelligible. To say that someone acted out of jealousy is to invoke in the case of his particular action a feature that is grasped from the outset as repeatable and common to a variety of individuals. Such a motive draws its explanatory value from its power to place a particular action in a meaningful context characterized from the start by a certain universality of meaning. So to explain is to characterize a given action by ascribing to it as its cause a motive that exemplifies a class. This is all the more true when we are not dealing with classes of motives, identifiable as the general features of human experience, but with fantasies that present organized, stable, and eminently typical scenes, or with stages – oral, anal, genital, etc. – which themselves are also typical organizations of libidinal development. In this way, we are ready to understand the kind of excommunication on the basis of which an unconscious set of representations is autonomously structured to produce the stereotyped incongruities that are the real object of analytic explanation.

The transition from generalities to law-like statements broadly corresponds to an explanation not only in terms of unconscious motives but in terms of the mechanisms of distortion that render the motivational process unrecognizable.

Above these law-like statements we have the propositions concerning the theoretical entities posited by psychoanalysis: These statements constitute the metapsychology as such, which can be considered from the point of view of the structure of these statements as the metalanguage of psychoanalysis – all that can be said regarding instinct or drives, the representatives of drives, the destiny of instincts, etc., comes down to this level. And at this level, every narrative feature, by which I mean the reference to a case history, is abrogated, at least at the manifest level of its statements.[50]

This style of explanation has as its consequence that in Freud what Sherwood calls "narrative commitment" and "explanatory commitment" continually split apart, only to merge again in the case histories. Here we should note that even in the case histories, including the Rat Man, Freud juxtaposes the case study as such and theoretical considerations. In his other writings, which are far more numerous, they diverge again. We could even say that in these writings the relation between "narrative commitment" and "explanatory commitment" is reversed. Thus, case histories constitute just one pole of a very wide range of writings for which the essays on metapsychology constitute the opposite pole, which is basically non-narrative.[51] It is in this sense that it can be said that in psychoanalysis the means of proof reside in the articulation of the entire network constituted by the theory, the interpretive procedures, the therapeutic treatment, and the narrative structure of the analytic experience.

I am not unaware that this assertion leads to the most formidable objection of all against psychoanalysis; namely, that its

---

[50] We may, of course, agree with Sherwood – to whom we are indebted for having challenged the dichotomy between cause and motive and to whom we owe the schema of fourfold explanation in Freud – that in a case history the explanatory segments are incorporated into the narrative structure that forms their enveloping structure and reference. But must we not then say that the means of proof are carried by these explanatory segments themselves? Psychoanalysis is an analysis precisely because the meaning of the whole always proceeds from decomposition into fragments and from an explanation in terms of details.

[51] We could, to be sure, give preference to the case histories among all of Freud's writings and so emphasize the narrative commitment by subordinating the explanatory commitment to it. But then the great mass of Freudian writings would be arbitrarily directed against their dominant theoretical orientation. This strategy is not without certain advantages inasmuch as it cautions us against the hypostatization of the theoretical perspective, but, in return, its disadvantage is that it tends to misconstrue the epistemological problem posed by the entire constellation of Freud's writings, divided as they are among the theory, the investigatory procedure, the method of treatment, and the case histories.

statements are irrefutable and therefore unverifiable if the theory, method, treatment, and interpretation of a particular case all confirm themselves at one time as a single block. If this entire investigation of mine does nothing more than formulate this objection correctly and assemble the means to reply to it, it will have attained its goal.

I will leave aside the crude form of this objection, namely, that the analyst suggests to his patient that he accept the interpretation that verifies the theory. I am taking for granted the replies that Freud opposes to this accusation of suggestibility. They are worth what the measures taken at the level of the professional code and the analytic technique itself against the suspicion of suggestion are worth. I grant that these measures define a good analyst – and that there are good analysts.

It is more interesting to take Freud at his word and to contend with a subtler form of the accusation of self-confirmation; that is, that validation in psychoanalysis is condemned to remain circular since everything is verified at once. It is all the more important to consider this argument since the notion of a circle is not foreign to all the historical-interpretive disciplines, in which a "case" is not only an example to be placed under a law, but something that possesses its own dramatic structure which makes it a "case history." The problem, Heidegger says with reference to the hermeneutic circle, is not avoiding the circle but entering into it correctly. This means: taking measures so that the circle is not a vicious circle. A circle is vicious if the verification in each of the areas considered is the condition for verification in all the other areas. The circle of verification will not be vicious, however, if validation proceeds in a cumulative fashion through the mutual reinforcement of criteria which taken in isolation would not be decisive, but whose convergence makes them plausible and, in the best cases, probable and even convincing.

I will say, therefore, that the validation most likely to confirm the truth claim belonging to the domain of psychoanalytic facts is an extremely complex process that is based on the convergence of partial and heterogeneous criteria. If we take as our guideline the idea of a constellation formed by the theory, the investigatory procedure, the treatment technique, and the reconstruction of a case history, we can then say the following:

(1) A good psychoanalytic explanation must be coherent with the theory, or, if one prefers, it must conform to Freud's psychoanalytic system, or to the system by which this or that school claiming his name is identified – recall, however, that I have limited my consideration in this essay to Freud's writings.

This first criterion is not peculiar to psychoanalysis. In every field of inquiry explanation establishes a connection of this kind between a theoretical apparatus of concepts and an array of facts relevant to this theoretical style. In this sense, all explanations are limited by their conceptual framework. Their validity extends as far as the correlation between theory and facts works. For the same reason, any theory can be questioned. A new theory is required, as Kuhn has argued, as soon as new facts are recognized that can no longer be "covered" by the ruling paradigm.[52] Something like this is happening today in psychoanalysis, perhaps. The theoretical model of energy distribution appears more and more inadequate, but no alternative model seems to be powerful enough to "cover" all the accepted facts relevant to psychoanalysis or to account for their paradoxical nature.

(2) A good psychoanalytic explanation must satisfy the universalizable rules set up by the procedures of interpretation for the sake of decoding the text of the unconscious. This second criterion is relatively independent of the preceding one to the extent that it relies on the internal consistency of the new text substituted by means of translation for the unreadable text of symptoms and dreams. In this respect, the model of the rebus is quite appropriate. It shows that the character of intelligibility of the substituted text resides in its capacity to take into account as many scattered elements as possible from those provided by the analytic process itself, especially as a result of the technique of free association.

A corollary of this second criterion deserves attention. It has to do with the expansion of the procedures of interpretation beyond the native domain of psychoanalysis, i.e., symptoms and dreams, along the analogical lines that connect tales, puns, jokes, etc., to the first analogon of this series, the dream. A new kind of coherence appears here which concerns not only the internal intelligibil-

[52] Thomas S. Kuhn, *The Structure of Scientific Revolutions* (Chicago: University of Chicago Press, 1962).

ity of the translated text, but also the structural analogy that obtains between all the members of the series of psychic productions. This second criterion of validation may be formulated accordingly in two complementary ways: as a criterion of intratextual consistency and a criterion of intertextual consistency. The second formulation may even be the more decisive one insofar as the universalization of the decoding rules relies on the soundness of the analogical extrapolation from symptoms and dreams to other cultural expressions. At the same time, the merely analogical character of this extrapolation reminds us of the problematic value of this means of proof.

But even this limitation, resulting from the analogical structure of this criterion of validation, proceeds from structural reasons distinct from those that impose a limitation on the first criterion. The second criterion is not just relatively independent of the first one, it may correct and even shatter it, inasmuch as it is under the guidance of these procedures of investigation that new facts are brought to light that may make difficulties for the claim of the theoretical framework to "cover" them. This is what happens, for example, to the energy distribution model when it is confronted with the facts yielded by the procedures of interpretation in conjunction with the methods of treatment.

(3) A good psychoanalytic explanation must furthermore be satisfactory in economic terms; in other words, it must be able to be incorporated into the work of the analysand, into his "working through," and so become a therapeutic factor of amelioration. This third criterion, too, is relatively independent of the first one since it implies something that *happens to* the analysand under the condition of his own "work" (hence the substitution of the term analysand for that of patient, and even of client). What is more, this third criterion is relatively independent of the second one, to the extent that an interpretation that is only understood, i.e., intellectually grasped, remains ineffective and may even be harmful so long as a new pattern of energies has not emerged from the "handling" of resistances. The therapeutic success resulting from this new energetic configuration constitutes in this way an autonomous criterion of validation.

(4) Finally, a good psychoanalytic explanation must raise a particular case history to the sort of narrative intelligibility we ordinarily expect from a story. This fourth criterion should not

be overemphasized as would be the case in a purely "narrative" account of psychoanalytic theory. But the relative autonomy of this criterion must not be overlooked either, because narrative intelligibility implies something more than the subjective acceptability of one's own life story. This criterion comes down to the general acceptability that we apply when we read any story, be it true or fictional. In the terms of W.B. Gallie, a story has to be "followable," and in this sense, "self-explanatory."[53] We interpolate explanation when the narrative process is blocked and in order to "follow-further." This explanation is acceptable to the extent that it may be grafted onto the archetypes of storytelling, which have been culturally developed and which govern our current competence to follow new stories. Here psychoanalysis is not an exception. Psychoanalytic narratives are kinds of biographies and autobiographies whose literary history is a part of the long tradition emerging from the epic tradition of the Hebrews, the Greeks, the Celts, and the Germans. It is this whole tradition of storytelling that provides a relative autonomy to the criterion of narrative intelligibility as regards not only the consistency of the interpretive procedures, but also the efficacy of the change introduced in the balance of libidinal energies.

When these criteria of validation do not derive from one another, but mutually reinforce one another, they constitute the proof apparatus in psychoanalysis. It may be granted that this apparatus is extremely complex, very difficult to handle, and highly problematical. But it can at least be granted that this cumulative character of the validation criteria is the only one suited to both the criteria for psychoanalytic facts that specify the truth claim of psychoanalysis and the complex relations between the theory, the investigatory procedure, and the method of treatment that govern the means of proof in psychoanalysis.

[53] W.B. Gallie, *Philosophy and the Historical Understanding* (New York: Schocken Books, 1968).

Psychoanalysis and Hermeneutics

What questions do we have to pose when we ask ourselves about the relations between psychoanalysis and hermeneutics? Let us begin with hermeneutics. By hermeneutics I mean a discipline close to exegesis, that is, to the interpretation of texts. But whereas exegesis is a first-order discipline that deals with the rule for interpretation of a specific category of texts, hermeneutics is a second-order discipline that undertakes to disengage the conditions of possibility for the interpretation of texts in general. Historically, exegesis was applied to three broad categories of texts: religious texts (principally the Bible in the Western, Jewish, and Christian tradition), literary texts (principally those of Greek and Roman antiquity, from the Renaissance to the Enlightenment), and finally juridical texts (insofar as no law applies directly to singular cases without some recourse to precedents whose coherent sequence is the object of jurisprudence). Hermeneutics gets constituted as an autonomous discipline when the general problem of the relationship between a text and its interpretation is superimposed on the problem of the particular rules to be applied to some category of texts.

As for psychoanalysis, I borrow its definition from Freud himself in his essay titled "Psychoanalysis and Libido Theory": "Psychoanalysis is the name (1) of a procedure (*Verfahren*) for the investigation of mental processes which are almost inaccessible in any other way, (2) of a method (based upon that investigation) for the treatment (*Behandlungsmethode*) of neurotic disorders, and (3) of a collection of psychological information (*Einsichten*) obtained along those lines, which is gradually being accumulated into a new scientific discipline."[1] This triangular relation between a procedure of investigation, a method or treatment, and a theory is to me most important. It is this quite specific relation between the theory, on the one hand, and the pair constituted by the procedure of investigation and method of treatment, on the other, that introduces the question we are considering here regarding the relation between psychoanalysis and hermeneutics.

The question does not arise – and in fact, was not posed – so long as one could take psychoanalysis, without discussion, as a science based on observation; that is, a science with the same epistemological status as the natural sciences. In these sciences, theoretical statements serve to systematize, explain, and predict phenomena that, directly or indirectly, fall under empirical investigation. Even if we do not require – as in the period of strict empiricism – that a theory should be directly validated by observable data, and even if we allow the introduction of theoretical entities that are not directly observable but only bound indirectly to experience through "correspondence rules," even if, moreover, we substitute (with Karl Popper) a criterion of falsifiability for the old criterion of verification, it is still through observable facts that a theory must finally be falsified at the end of a sequence of intermediary procedures, however large we might want to make their number. In the end, it is the relationship between theory and empirical fact that determines the status of being an empirical science, which to today only the natural sciences have fully satisfied. But it is this relationship between theory and fact that is finally called into question in psychoanalysis. And the question of the hermeneutic status of psychoanalysis is born from the failures of every attempt to deal with psychoanalysis as another science based on observation among others, that is, finally as a natural science.

Freud himself, in his theoretical writings, never seriously doubted that psychoanalysis belonged to the natural sciences. We can read his unequivocal assertions, from the "Project" of 1895, then in chapter 7 of *The Interpretation of Dreams*, the *Introductory*

[1] S.E. 18:235.

Lectures on Psychoanalysis, the writings on metapsychology, up to *An Outline of Psychoanalysis*, about the kinship between psychoanalysis and the other natural sciences, in particular, with biology. Beyond these declared intentions, the theoretical entities constructed in Freudian theory in the writings on metapsychology – libido, repression, compromise formations, unconscious, conscious, preconscious, ego, id, superego, etc. – are said to be inscribed within an economic type of model; that is, a model that only brings into play energies and their distribution in systems themselves assimilated to places (unconscious, conscious, preconscious). In turn, the representation of these places stems from a topological model, associated with this economic model. If we add the laws of development of systems, libidinal stages, etc., a genetic dimension comes to complete the topological-economic model. In this way, we obtain a complex model, but a perfectly homogeneous one, for the distribution and transformation of energies. It is this model in Freud's eyes that assures that psychoanalysis belongs to the group of natural sciences as well as its being submitted to the same epistemological model.

Doubt concerning the empirical, observational, naturalist – or however one may want to put it – character of psychoanalysis did not first come from psychoanalysis itself, but from logicians and epistemologists, mostly in the English-speaking world. In general, they argued that psychoanalysis did not satisfy the minimal criteria for an empirical science. Its theoretical entities were denounced as being no more verifiable or falsifiable than were the entities of medieval science prior to Galileo. As for its procedures of validation, they were too dependent on the analytic session, which, not being open to public inspection, did not allow for criticism of its results by a community of independent researchers. I will not hesitate to say that so long as one tries to situate psychoanalysis among the sciences based on empirical observation, the epistemological attack against it will find no answer.

Two ways are thus open to us: either to reject psychoanalysis as a whole, as not being scientific, or to reopen the question of its epistemological status. It is the second way that I shall attempt to follow here. If I take this risk, it is because the last word about psychoanalysis is not in what Freud said about it, but in what he did. With this formula, I do not mean to deprive psychoanalysis of any theoretical status by reducing it to a practice not based on principles. By what psychoanalysis "does," I mean instead the overall ensemble constituted by the procedure of investigation, the method of treatment, and the theoretical apparatus, following Freud's own statement given at the beginning of this essay. The thesis I want to develop about this is threefold.

(1) What counts as a fact in psychoanalysis is of another nature than what counts as a fact in the natural sciences and in general in those science based on empirical observation, owing to the specific character of the procedure of investigation and the method of investigation that leads to picking out these facts.

(2) The theory itself has to be reformulated on the basis of other models than that of the distribution of energy, owing to the specific relationship between the theory and the psychoanalytic facts stemming from the procedure of investigation and the method of treatment. With these first two theses we find the hermeneutic character of psychoanalysis. To anticipate what will follow, I will say that the notion of a fact in psychoanalysis presents a kind of kinship with the notion of a text, and that the theory stands in relation to the psychoanalytic facts in a relation analogous to the one between exegesis and a text in the hermeneutical disciplines.

(3) A third thesis will temper these first two. It seems to me that the reformulation of psychoanalysis runs up against unsurpassable limits which make psychoanalysis a "mixed" discipline, whose ambiguous status accounts for the hesitations of epistemological critics regarding its place among the sciences.

What is a Fact in Psychoanalysis?

This prior question is generally not raised in those accounts of psychoanalysis that limit themselves to consideration of its theory separate from its procedures of investigation and method of treatment. Critics forget that psychoanalytic theory, in a way that I shall have more to say about in the next part, is the codification of what took place in the analytic situation and more precisely in the analytic relation. That is where something takes place that can be called the analytic experience. In other words, the equivalent of what the epistemology of logical empiricism calls something "observable" is first to be sought in the analytic situation, in the analytic relation. The first thing that needs to be done, therefore, is to show in what way the analytic relation brings about a selection among the facts that have to be taken into account by the theory. For this discussion, I shall propose four criteria that guide this process of selection.

First criterion: All that enters into the field of investigation and treatment is that portion of experience capable of being put into words. It is not necessary to stress here the "talk-cure" aspect of psychoanalysis. This restriction to language is above all else a restriction inherent to the analytic technique. It is the particular context of not making a commitment about what counts as reality, belonging to the analytic situation, that forces desire to speak, to pass through the defile of words, to the exclusion of any substitute satisfaction as well as any regression in the direction of "acting out." This screening by discourse in the analytic situation thus functions as one criterion of what will be taken to be the object of this discipline: not an instinct as a physiological phenomenon, not even desire as a kind of energy, but desire as a meaning capable of being deciphered, translated, interpreted. The theory must therefore take into account what I will call the semantic dimension of desire. We can already see the mistake that is made by the usual epistemological discussions of psychoanalysis. The facts in psychoanalysis are in no way facts of observable behavior. They are "reports." Any partially observable symptoms enter the field of analysis only in relation to the other verbalized factors of the report. It is this selective restriction that forces us to situate the facts in psychoanalysis in a sphere of motivation and meaning.

Second criterion: The analytic situation not only screens out what is sayable, but what is said to another. Here, too, the epistemological criterion is guided by something absolutely central to the analytic technique. The transference stage in this respect is very important. We might be tempted to confine discussion of transference to the sphere of psychoanalytic technique, in the strictest sense of the term, and thereby not recognize the epistemological implications having to do with the search for relevant criteria. In an important essay from 1914, "Remembering, Repeating, and Working Through," Freud describes transference as the principal "instrument . . . for curbing the patient's compulsion to repeat and for turning it into a motive for remembering."[2] If transference has this virtue, it is because it constitutes something like "a playground in which it is allowed to expand in almost complete freedom."[3] The transference, Freud adds, is "an intermediate region between illness and real life through which the transition from the one to the other is made."[4] It is this notion of transference as a "playground" or "intermediate region" that will guide my comments about the second criterion of what is psychoanalytically relevant as a fact. Indeed, we can read in the transference situation a kind of abbreviated form of the relation to the other constitutive of the erotic demand. It is in this way that transference finds a place not only in a study of analytic technique but also in an epistemological search for criteria. Transference reveals the following constitutive feature of human desire: not only its power to be spoken about, to be brought to language, but also to be addressed to another; more precisely, it addresses itself to another desire, one that may refuse to recognize it. What is thereby sifted out from human experience is the intersubjective dimension of desire. In other words, the relation to the other is not something added on to desire. In this regard, Freud's discovery of the Oedipus complex in the course of his self-analysis, in relation to all his later discoveries, has a premonitory value. There, desire is grasped straightaway in its triangular structure, bringing into play two sexes and three persons. The result is that what the theory will articulate as a symbolic castration is not an additional, extrinsic factor, but rather attests that the initial relation of desire includes an agency of prohibition, which imposes ideals, experienced by the child at the level of fantasy as a paternal threat directed against his sexual activities.

From the beginning, then, everything that might be considered as a solipsism of desire is eliminated, as might be the case for a purely energetic determination of desire as just tension and release. The mediation of the other is constitutive of human desire as addressed to. . . . This other person may respond or refuse to do so, gratify or threaten. What is more, he or she may be real or imaginary, present or lost, a source of anxiety or the object of a

[2] S.E. 12:154.
[3] Ibid.
[4] Ibid.

successful work of mourning. Through transference, psychoanalysis puts all these possibilities into play by transposing the drama that engendered the neurotic situation into a kind of artificial scene in miniature. So it is the analytic experience itself that constrains the theory to include intersubjectivity in the very constitution of the libido and to conceive of it as less as a need and more as a wish directed to another.

Third criterion: The third criterion introduced by the analytic situation has to do with the coherence and resistance of certain manifestations of the unconscious that led Freud to speak of a "psychical reality" in contrast to material reality. It is the features that differentiate this psychic reality from material reality that are psychoanalytically relevant. This criterion is paradoxical inasmuch it is what common sense opposes to reality that constitutes psychic reality.

In the *Introductory Lectures on Psychoanalysis*, Freud writes: "phantasies possess psychical as contrasted with material reality. . . . In the world of the neuroses it is psychical reality which is the decisive kind."[5] Symptoms and fantasies "disregard objects and in so doing abandon their relation to external reality."[6] Freud then refers to "scenes from infancy," which are "not always true."[7] This is a particularly important remark, if we recall the difficulty Freud had in abandoning his initial hypothesis of a real seduction of the child by the father. Fifteen years later, he again emphasizes how troubling this discovery had been for him. What was disconcerting was that it should turn out that it was not clinically relevant whether the infantile scene was true or not. This is precisely what is expressed with the notion of a "psychical reality."

But the resistances to the notion of a psychical reality do not come only from common sense. In a certain way this notion stands in contradiction to the fundamental opposition in psychoanalysis between the pleasure principle, the source of the fantasy, and the reality principle. Therefore for psychoanalysis itself, this concept is paradoxical.

The epistemological consequences of this paradox for the analytic experience are considerable. Whereas experimental psychol-

[5] S.E. 16:368.
[6] Ibid., 366.
[7] Ibid.

ogy does not encounter such a paradox, inasmuch as its theoretical entities are supposed to refer to observable facts and finally to real movements in space and time, psychoanalysis works only with psychical reality and not with material reality. So the criterion for this reality is no longer that it should be observable, but that it present a coherence and resistance comparable to those of material reality.

The range of phenomena satisfying this criterion is huge. The fantasies deriving from infantile scenes (observation of sexual relations between the parents, seduction, and, above all, castration) constitute the paradigmatic case insofar as, despite their fragile basis in the real history of a subject, these fantasies present a highly structured organization and are inscribed in scenarios that are both typical and limited in number.

But the notion of psychic reality is not exhausted by that of a fantasy in the sense of these archaic scenarios. The imaginary, in the broad sense, covers every kind of mediation implied in the development of desire.

Close to the infantile scene, we can place the whole domain of lost objects that continue to be represented as fantasies. Freud introduces this notion in connection with the problem of the formation of symptoms. The libido's abandoned objects provide the missing link between the libido and its points of fixation in the symptom.

From the notion of the lost object, the transition is easy to that of the substituted object, which places us at the heart of the analytic experience. The *Three Essays on Sexuality* find their starting point in the variability of the object in contrast to the stability of the libido's goal and derive the substitutability of love objects from this variability. On this basis, in the essay "Instincts and their Vicissitudes,"[8] Freud constructs the combinations of these substitutions, by inversion, reversal, and so forth, it being taken for granted that the ego itself can take the place of the object, as in the case of narcissism.

Substitutability, in turn, is the key to another series of phenomena fundamental to the analytic experience. From the time of the *Interpretation of Dreams*, Freud had noticed the remarkable feature of dreams that they could stand for a myth, a theme from

[8] S.E. 14:111–40.

folklore, a symptom, a hallucination, or an illusion. In sum, the whole reality of these psychic functions lies in the thematic unity that serves as the basis of the rule-governed play of their substitutions. Their reality is their meaning, and their meaning is their capacity to stand for one another. It is in this sense that the notions of a lost object or a substitute object – cardinal notions of the analytic experience – deserve to have an equally key position in the epistemological discussion. To put it simply, they forbid our speaking of "facts" in psychoanalysis as we do for the sciences based on observation.

If we next consider that the work of mourning gets linked in turn to the problematic of the lost and the substituted object, we catch sight of the scale of the phenomena that can graft themselves onto the abandoned object. But there is more. The phenomenon of mourning brings us to the very heart of psychoanalysis. Psychoanalysis begins, in fact, by recognizing the fantasy as the paradigm for what, for it, constitutes psychical reality. But it continues by means of a work that itself can be understood as a work of mourning; that is, as the internalization of the lost objects representing our most archaic desires. Far from limiting itself to eradicating the fantasy to the benefit of reality, the cure restores the fantasy as fantasy with a view toward situating it on the symbolic plane, without confusing it with what is real. This kinship between the cure and the work of mourning confirms, if there is still a need to do so, that it is the analytic experience that requires us to add the reference to the make-believe to the preceding two criteria. It is not an accident that in Freud's German the term *Phantasieren* has a broader scope than does the French *fantasme* or even the English "fantasy." It covers the whole field we have been considering. The result is that what is relevant for the analyst are not observable facts or reactions to variables in the environment, but rather the meaning that a subject attaches to these phenomena. I will risk trying to sum this up by saying that what is psychoanalytically relevant is what a subject makes of his or her fantasies (giving this word the full scope of the German *Phantasieren*).

Fourth criterion: The analytic experience selects from a subject's experience what is capable of entering into a history, in the sense of a narrative. In this sense, the "case histories" as histories constitute the primary texts for psychoanalysis. This "narrative" character of analytic experience was never the object of a direct discussion by Freud, at least not to my knowledge. Still, he does refer to it indirectly in what he has to say about memory. We recall the well-known declaration from the *Studies on Hysteria*: "Hysterics suffer principally from reminiscences."[9] It is true that these "reminiscences" subsequently reveal themselves to be screen-memories and fantasies, not real memories. But these fantasies, in turn, must always be considered in relation to the phenomena of forgetfulness and remembering, given their connection to resistance and the tie between resistance and repetition. Remembering is what has to take the place of repetition. The struggle against resistances – what Freud calls "working through" – has no other goal than to reopen the path to memory.

But what is it to remember? It is not just the power to recall certain isolated events, but to become capable of forming meaning sequences, orderly connections. In short, it is the power to give one's experience the form of a history for which an isolated memory is just one fragment. It is the narrative structure of these "life histories" that make a "case" into a "case history."

That the ordering of the episodes of one's life into the form of a history constitutes a kind of work – and even of working-through – is attested to by the role of one fundamental phenomenon of imagined psychic life, the phenomenon of "after the factness" (*Nachträglichkeit*), emphasized by Jacques Lacan. This is the fact that "experiences, impressions, and memory-traces may be revised at a later date to fit with fresh expressions or with the attainment of a new stage of development. They may in that event be endowed not only with a new meaning but also with psychical effectiveness."[10] Before constituting a theoretical problem, this phenomenon is implied in the very work of psychoanalysis as psychoanalysis. It was in the process of working through just referred to that Freud discovered that the history of a subject did not conform to a linear determinism, which would place the present under the control of a past in a univocal way. On the contrary, the work of analysis shows that traumatic events, "at

[9] S.E. 2:7.
[10] Jean Laplanche and Jean-Baptiste Pontalis, *The Language of Psychoanalysis*, trans. Donald Nicholson-Smith (New York: Norton, 1973), 111.

the moment they were experienced, were not able to be fully integrated into a meaningful context."[11] It was only the arrival of new
events and new situations that precipitates the subsequent reorga-
nization of these past events. Thus, in the Wolf Man, it was a
second sexually significant scene that, after the fact, conferred its
efficacity on the earlier scene.

Generally speaking, many repressed memories only become
traumatisms after the fact. The question is not just that of a delay
or a deferred action. We see how much the psychoanalytic notion
of memory takes its distance from the idea of a simple reproduc-
tion of real events through a kind of perception of the past. What
is at issue is rather a work that has to pass through ever more
complex structurations. It is this work of memory that is implied,
along with other things, by the notion of a history or narrative
structure of existence. For the fourth time, a vicissitude of the
analytic experience reveals a relevant feature of what in psychoanalysis counts as a "fact."

Psychoanalysis as Hermeneutic

We can now return to Freud's definition of psychoanalysis. This
definition, we recall, put the accent on the relation bringing
together the "procedure of investigation," the "method of treatment," and the "theory." Now it is this triangular relation that
will draw our attention. Not only does psychoanalysis work with
"facts" of a particular nature, as we have just established, but
what takes the place of the operative procedures in the natural
sciences is a unique type of relation between its procedure of
investigation and method of treatment. It is this relation that plays
the mediating role between fact and theory.

I want to show, in this second part of my presentation, that this
mediation by way of the procedure of investigation and the method
of treatment justifies to a certain point a hermeneutic reformulation of psychoanalytic theory. I shall hold in reserve, for part three
of my discussion, showing that this same mediation makes a uni-
lateral hermeneutic interpretation fail, and imposes what I called
in my introduction a mixed, half-hermeneutic, half-naturalist
epistemology.

[11] Ibid., 112.

Let us begin with a general comment about the mediation exercised conjointly by the procedure of investigation and the method of treatment. We can say that this mediation is not only poorly interpreted but quite simply misconceived in most discussions of psychoanalytic theory. If Freud's metapsychology has been set up as a fetish by some and scorned as marginal by others, this is because it has been dealt with as an independent construction. All too many epistemological works try to examine Freud's theoretical texts, from the "Project" of 1895, to chapter 7 of the *Interpretation of Dreams*, to *The Ego and the Id*, apart from the total context of experience and practice. When isolated in this way, the body of doctrine has to lead to premature and truncated evaluations. The theory, therefore, needs to be relativized, that is, set back within the complex network of relations that frame it. In this regard, we have to admit that Freud himself was largely responsible for this misunderstanding of the epistemological structure of psychoanalysis. In general, he tends to invert the relation between theory, on the one hand, and experience and practice, on the other, and to reconstruct the work of interpretation on the basis of theoretical models that themselves have become autonomous. In this way he loses sight of the fact that the language of his theory is narrower than that constituted through the analytic experience. What is more, he tends to construct his theoretical models in the positivistic, naturalistic, and materialistic spirit of the sciences of his day. Many texts refer to an exclusive kinship of psychoanalysis and the natural sciences, even physics, or announce the future replacement of psychoanalysis by a more developed pharmacology. What I am proposing here, in response to the encounter with every over-evaluation of the theory or every attempt to treat it as autonomous, is that its function is to codify the "facts" brought to light by the analytic experience in a metalanguage guided conjointly by the procedure of investigation and the method of treatment.

It is within this general framework, whereby the theory is both legitimated and relativized, that the problem is posed of a reformulation of the theory in terms closer to hermeneutics; that is, in terms of a theory of interpretation appropriate to the exegesis of texts.

We may say, in general terms, that this reformulation is suggested more by the procedure of investigation, at the price of a certain abstraction from the method of treatment. When so isolated, the procedure of investigation tends to give priority to the relations of meaning between mental productions. As I shall say below, the method of treatment tends instead to give priority to the relations of force between systems. It will be precisely the function of a mixed theory to integrate these two dimensions of psychical reality.

The kinship between the procedure of investigation and those disciplines dealing with textual interpretation shows itself in many ways. First of all, in the process of interpretation applied to dreams. It is not an accident that Freud's great work is titled *Traumdeutung*. Freud himself says, "The aim which I have set before myself is to show that dreams are capable of being interpreted (*Deutung*). . . . 'Interpreting' a dream implies assigning a 'meaning' (*Sinn*) to it – that is, replacing (*ersetzen*) it by something which fits (*sich einfügt*) into the chain of our mental acts as a link having a validity and importance equal to the rest."[12] In this respect, interpretation is often compared to translation of one language into another or to the solution of a rebus. Freud never doubted that, however inaccessible the unconscious might be, it always participates in the same psychic structures as does consciousness. It is this common structure that allowed him to "interpolate" the meaning of unconscious acts into the text of conscious ones.

This first feature from the method of investigation is perfectly coherent with the criteria for a "fact" in psychoanalysis discussed above, in particular with those of sayability and substitutability. If the procedure of investigation can be applied to both neurotic symptoms and dreams, it is because dream-formation (*Traumbildung*) and symptom-formation (*Symptombildung*) are homogeneous and substitutable. This feature is recognized in the *Studies on Hysteria* – the *Preliminary Communication* of 1892 had already dealt with the relation between the determining cause and the hysterical symptom as a "symbolic connection," akin to the dream process. It is this profound kinship among all the compromise formations that allows us to speak of the psyche as a text to be deciphered.

This broadly inclusive notion of a text encompasses not only the profound unity of dreams and symptoms, but of these two

[12] S.E. 4:96.

taken together with phenomena such as daydreams, myths, folk-tales, sayings, proverbs, puns, and jokes. The gradual extension of this method of investigation is assured by the special kinship that exists between, on the one hand, the group of fantasies referred to earlier as infantile scenes and, on the other hand, the most highly organized and most permanent mythical structures of humanity. From the same investigatory procedure comes most notably the "textual" structure common to the Oedipus complex discovered by Freud in his self-analysis and in the Greek tragedy *Oedipus Rex* transmitted to us as one of the masterpieces of literature. There is thus a correspondence between the extension of the investigatory procedure and what could be termed the space of fantasy in general, in which psychic productions as diverse as daydreams, children's games, psychological novels, and other poetic creations find a place. In the same way, the psychic conflicts given material form in stone by Michelangelo's *Moses* lend themselves to interpretation by virtue of the figurable and substitutable nature of all the sign systems that are included within the same investigatory procedure.

These are the features of the method of investigation that, when joined to the criteria for a fact in psychoanalysis, suggest a reformulation of psychoanalytic theory in terms of a hermeneutical one.

This reformulation is equivalent to the substitution of one metalanguage for another. The metalanguage of Freud's theoretical writings, we have seen, consists in the construction of a topological-economic model, completed by a genetic dimension. This model brings into play only phenomena of energy distribution among distinct sites appropriate to systems that themselves obey specific laws.

What metalanguage might be more appropriate to the nature of such "facts" and to the method of investigation in psychoanalysis?

Two series of suggestions have been offered, independently of each other.

In the English-speaking world, under the influence of Wittgenstein, Austin, and the philosophy of ordinary language, authors who have sought to reformulate the theory rather than simply rejecting it as a whole have taken as their frame of reference the type of linguistic analysis that predominates in what is called "action theory." According to this analysis, our discourse about action brings into play a "grammar" (that is, a morphology and a syntax) irreducible to the "grammar" that governs our usage of physical concepts, those of movement, force, energy, and the like in first place. To speak of action is to accept the rules of a wholly distinct "language game," which admits notions such as intention, motive, agent, and so on. One of the implications of this dichotomy between two "language games" for action and movement directly has to do with our discussion: According to these analysts, our motives for acting can in no way be assimilated to the causes by which we explain natural events. Motives are reasons for acting, whereas causes are the constant antecedents of other events from which they are logically distinct. It is on the basis of this distinction that a reformulation of psychoanalytic theory can be attempted. Some authors, for example, have interpreted psychoanalysis as an extending of the vocabulary of action (intention, motive, etc.) beyond the sphere where we are conscious of what we do. Psychoanalysis, according to this interpretation, adds nothing to ordinary conceptuality except the use of the same concepts from ordinary language in a new domain characterized as "unconscious." In this way, for example, one says of the Rat Man, analyzed by Freud, that he felt hostility toward his father "without being conscious of it." Understanding this assertion rests on the ordinary meaning we give to this kind of hostility in situations where the agent is capable of recognizing such a feeling as his or her own. The only thing new is the use of clauses like "without being conscious," "without knowing," "unconsciously," and so on.

This reformulation is acceptable to a certain point. Freud himself says that in the unconscious we find representations and affects to which we can give the same name as to their conscious counterpart and which only lack the property of being conscious. However, we can already observe that what is completely omitted by this reformulation is the very paradox of psychoanalytic theory, namely, that it is the becoming unconscious as such that requires a specific explanation. This comes down to asking whether this explanation does not completely call into question the separation into domains of action and movement and, as a result, the dichotomy between motive and cause. I shall return to this below in part three.

Another frame of reference has been proposed for the reformulation of the theory. It was suggested by the kinship, glimpsed by some German-speaking authors, between psychoanalysis and what those in the Frankfurt School and related movements call the theory of ideologies. The theme common to these approaches has to do with the process of symbolization at work in human communication. The troubles that give rise to psychoanalytic intervention can then be considered as stemming from some pathology affecting our linguistic competence. In this way, these distortions can be placed in parallel with those discovered at another level by the Marxist and post-Marxist critique of ideologies.

Psychoanalysis and the critique of ideologies are said to share the same obligation to explain and interpret distortions that are not accidental, but systematic, in the sense that they form organized sub-systems within the text of interhuman communication. These distortions are the occasion for a subject's misunderstanding himself. This is why, in order to account for these distortions, we need a theory that is not limited to restoring an integral, unmutilated and unfalsified text, but that takes as its object the very mechanisms that alter and falsify the text. These mechanisms, it is true, demand that the interpretive decoding of symptoms and dreams surpass a purely philological hermeneutics, inasmuch as it is the very meaning of these mechanisms that is the problem. As we shall see below, here is the reason why the economic metaphors (resistance, repression, compromise) cannot be fully replaced by philological ones (text, meaning, interpretation). But the contrary is no less true: The economic metaphors cannot be substituted for their philological counterparts. They cannot lose their metaphorical character and be raised to the rank of an energetic theory that could be taken in a strictly literal sense. It is fundamentally against this reduction to a literal reading of the energy distribution model that these authors formulate their theories in terms of communication and symbolic interaction.

According to these alternative models, the unconscious mechanisms cannot be taken to be things; they are "dissociated symbols," "delinguisticized" or "degrammaticized" motives. Like banishment or political ostracism, repression banishes a part of language from the public sphere of communication and condemns it to the exiled state of a "privatized" language. This is how mental functioning simulates a natural process, but only insofar as it has been reified. Therefore, if we forget that this reification results from a process of "desymbolization," hence from a "specific self-alienation," we end up constructing a model where the unconscious is literally a thing. But, at the same time, we are incapable of understanding how "resymbolization" is possible; that is, how the analytic experience itself is possible. We can understand this only if we interpret the phenomena revealed by this experience as disturbances in communication and the analytic experience as a reappropriation that reverses the process of symbolic dissociation. As a result of this attempt at reconstruction, psychoanalysis has to be classed among the critical social sciences, that is, according to Jürgen Habermas, among those sciences guided by an interest in emancipation and motivated in the final analysis by the wish to recover the force of self-reflection.

For my part, I accept the starting point of this critique of the energetic model of the Freudian metapsychology. What is missing is a more positive evaluation of the economic dimension of psychoanalysis. It is this point that I am going to consider next.

Limits of a Hermeneutic Reformulation of Psychoanalysis

Attempts to reformulate psychoanalytic theory in hermeneutic terms all suffer from the beginning from a misunderstanding that is the inverse of that committed by naturalistic formulations of this theory. To uncover this error, we need to return to the mediating role conjointly exercised by the procedure of investigation and method of treatment between the facts and the theory. We then see that the initial error was to isolate the procedures of investigation from the method of treatment. If we reestablish the close connection between them, it is no longer possible to separate what I have called above the relations of meaning from those of force.

But first a word about the expression "method of treatment" (*Behandlungsmethode*). This notion has to be understood in a sense that extends well beyond the strictly medical meaning of "cure" to designate the whole set of analytic maneuvers (which is what the German term *Behandlung* means), insofar as analysis itself is a kind of work. To the question in what way analysis is work, Freud offers a constant answer: Psychoanalysis is essentially a struggle against resistances. It is this notion of resistance that prevents us from identifying the procedure of investigation with a simple interpretation, that is, with the purely cognitive understanding of what the symptoms mean. Interpretation understood as translation or deciphering, that is, as the substitution of an intelligible meaning for an absurd one, is just the cognitive segment of the analytic process. Even transference (which appeared above as the intersubjective criterion of desire) has to be taken as an aspect of the "handling" of resistances (as is evident from the essay titled "Remembering, Repetition, and Working Through"). This shows that the three themes of a compulsion to repeat, transference, and resistance are all connected to the same level of analytic praxis.

This struggle against resistances is so little just one aspect that we can isolate and confine to analytic technique, in the strictest sense of the word, that it insinuates itself into the procedure of investigation itself. Why, in effect, are the meaning of a symptom or the meaning of a dream so difficult to decipher, if not because, between the manifest and the latent meanings are interposed distortion mechanisms (*Entstellung*), those very mechanisms that Freud placed under the general heading of the "dream-work" in the *Interpretation of Dreams*? The diverse forms of this "work" are well known: condensation, displacement, etc. But we are not interested here in the theory about dreams as such, but in the relation between interpretation and method of treatment.

This "distortion," in fact, is a very strange phenomenon. Freud makes recourse to all sorts of quasi-physical metaphors to account for this operation, about which he says that it "does not think, calculate, or judge in any way at all: it restricts itself to giving things a new form."[13] We have already referred to condensation and displacement as quasi-physical metaphors for the dream-work. But it is the central metaphor of repression that reorganizes all the others; to the point of becoming a theoretical concept whose metaphorical origin is lost (as also happens to the concept of distortion itself, which literally signifies a violent displacement

[13] S.E. 5:506–7.

as well as a deformation). The half-metaphor of inhibition belongs to the same cycle.

Another quasi-physical metaphor of equal importance is that of cathexis (*Besetzung*), for which Freud does not conceal the kinship with the operations of a capitalist entrepreneur who invests his money in some affair. Thanks to this metaphor, regression takes on a meaning that is not only topological but also dynamic, inasmuch as the regression to an image proceeds from "changes in the cathexes of energy attaching to the different systems."[14] This play of metaphors becomes extremely complex in that Freud combines textual metaphors (translation, substitution, overdetermination, etc.) and energy metaphors (condensation, displacement, repression), producing mixed metaphors such as disguise, censorship, etc.

Why does Freud get himself into such difficult straits with concepts that remain semi-metaphors and, moreover, with inconsistent metaphors submitted to the polarity of, on the one hand, the textual concept of translation and, on the other hand, the mechanical concept of compromise, itself understood in the sense of an outcome of various interacting forces?

There can be no doubt about the answer. It is the conjunction between procedure of investigation and method of treatment that constrains the theory in this way to use semi-metaphorical concepts which lack coherence. But we must then draw all the epistemological consequences. If it is true that the pair constituted by the procedure of investigation and the method of treatment occupies exactly the same place as do the operative procedures in the sciences based on observation in bringing together the level of theory and that of the observable facts, the theory itself has to account for this inseparable solidarity between the interpretation of meaning and the handling of resistances. The theory has to represent the psyche as at once a text to be interpreted and a system of forces to be manipulated.

If we accept this way of posing the problem, we must also admit that psychoanalysis does not possess a theory capable of satisfying all these demands, one that can account for the criteria of what counts as a fact in psychoanalysis and provide the articulation that is needed to preserve the connection between the theory and

---

[14] Ibid., 543.

the pair constituted by the procedure of investigation and the method of treatment.

This is why I shall limit myself to one suggestion. If, as I believe, the naturalistic model cannot be corrected in such a way that it can integrate the interpretive dimension of psychoanalysis, can the hermeneutical model integrate into the course of interpretation an explanatory phase borrowed from the topological and economic models?

The answer would seem to be negative if we stay with the first frame of reference proposed above for such a reformulation. If we hold on to the incompatibility of two language games – one of motives and one of causes – affirmed by one whole branch of linguistic analysis, we render ourselves incapable of understanding what is precisely the problem in psychoanalysis: that the mechanisms responsible for the distortions in dreams and, more generally, the whole bundle of facts grouped around the term "resistance" call in question the dichotomy invoked by linguistic analysis between motives and causes. What psychoanalysis does is to put us face to face with motives that are causes and that require an explanation of their autonomous functioning. What is more, Freud could not oppose motive to cause by giving the word "motive" the sense "reason for" inasmuch as "rationalization" (a term he borrows from Ernest Jones) is itself a process that calls for an explanation and which, in that very way, does not permit accepting a proposed reason as a real cause.

It is no accident therefore that Freud completely ignored the distinction between motive and cause. His whole experience made the theoretical formulation of this distinction impossible. What, on the contrary, is characteristic of psychoanalysis is that it makes recourse to an explanation in terms of "causes" in order to reach an understanding in terms of "motives." This is what I try to express in my own terms by saying that the facts in psychoanalysis stem both from the category of the text, and therefore of meaning, and the category of energy, therefore of force. To say, for example, that a feeling is unconscious is not to limit oneself to saying that it resembles conscious motives observed in other circumstances, it is rather to say that it is necessary to interpolate it as a casually relevant factor in view of explaining the incongruities of an act of behavior, and that this explanation is itself a causally relevant factor in the work of analysis.

The frame of reference coming from the comparison of psycho-analysis and the theory of ideologies seems to me more appropriate for attempting a synthesis between the hermeneutic point of view and the economic one. The critique of ideologies, we have seen, gives itself the task of accounting for the not accidental, but systematic distortions in communication. It is prepared therefore to integrate into an understanding of meaning, as it unfolds at the level of the conscious significations in discourse, an explanatory phase, which is applied expressly to the causes of the systematic distortion.

This is not an inconsistent project. In other domains than psychoanalysis and the theory of ideologies – linguistic and nonlinguistic ones – we have learned to bring together understanding and explanation. The decoding of texts such as narratives appeals to mechanisms that are productive of meaning that are not accessible to the consciousness of speakers and hearers. Similarly, in the theory of ideology which serves as a parallel comparison to psychoanalysis, it is necessary, in order to analyze the systematic distortions of discourse, to bring to light more radical structures than the discourse itself, bringing into play its complex relation to work, money, power. An explanatory step must thus be integrated into the understanding of the processes of desymbolization and resymbolization.

It is in these terms that the epistemological problem of psychoanalysis should be posed, I think. What makes for its specific, even enigmatic character is what has been called, in comparison with the ideological phenomenon, "self-alienation from oneself," or the "reification of dissociated symbols," is the very reality that psychoanalysis takes into account. This symbolic reification is such that the mental functioning really simulates the functioning of a thing. This real simulation prevents psychoanalysis from constituting itself as a province of the exegetical disciplines applied to a text. It requires psychoanalysis to include in its process of self-understanding operations initially reserved for the natural sciences. In this sense, the misunderstanding of itself by psychoanalysis, which gets expressed in its exclusive identification with naturalistic models of explanation, is not entirely groundless. The economic model itself, with its literal and naive energetics, preserves something essential that a theorization coming from the outside is always in danger of losing sight of, namely, what I have called the simulation of a "thing" by mental functioning.

In return, the rectification of the hermeneutic interpretation must not go so far as to return purely and simply to a literal energetics. In this respect, we must not lose sight of the semi-metaphorical character of the energetic vocabulary, the only one, though, capable of conveying the sense of the mind's real simulation of a thing in situations of symbolic reification.

This is why I appeal to the idea of a depth hermeneutics in order to express the task of integrating into one complex model of interpretation the moment of causal explanation and that of understanding a meaning. The model remains hermeneutic, in the sense that, as in the theory of ideologies, the starting point is in the understanding, even if it should be falsified, that an individual has of him- or herself, and the end point lies in a deeper, more lucid understanding, one where conscious awareness returns enriched by what it at first misunderstood, then explained, and finally understood.

Allow me to conclude by reversing the terms of our initial problem. We asked at the beginning what help psychoanalytic theory could expect from hermeneutics, understood as the science of the rules of interpretation applied to everything that is a text or like a text. We should also ask what hermeneutics can expect in return from psychoanalysis.

It now appears that everything we have said about the necessity to integrate an explanatory step into the process of understanding does not just apply to others, but also to oneself. Let me sum up this recoil of psychoanalysis on hermeneutics by proposing three things.

First, I will say that we do not understand ourselves except by means of a network of signs, discourses, and texts, which make up the symbolic mediation of reflection. In this sense, it is necessary to renounce the Cartesian *cogito*, at least in its form based on direct intuition. We do not know ourselves in that way, we continue to interpret ourselves.

Next, we have to admit that this indirect, mediated understanding begins from misunderstanding. This is a rule of every hermeneutics. There is interpretation, Schleiermacher said, where there is first misunderstanding. This is the basis for what I have elsewhere called the hermeneutics of suspicion, which has always to be incorporated into the hermeneutics aimed at the recollection of meaning.

The third implication, the most radical of all, is that self-understanding has to pass through a letting-go of oneself, an abdication of any claim to dominate meaning. Appropriation of one's own meaning is first of all a disappropriation of oneself.

The result is that the idea of an ultimate self-understanding remains a limit idea, the idea of an understanding that will have integrated all the different critical resources applied to the illusions of self-consciousness. Reflection has to be converted to such a depth hermeneutics under the prodding of psychoanalysis and the critique of ideologies. Only this depth hermeneutics answers the Socratic warning that "the unexamined life is not worth living."

The Self in Psychoanalysis and in Phenomenological Philosophy

My contribution to the study of the last – and alas posthumous – work of Heinz Kohut, *How Does Analysis Cure?* does not have the ambition of arbitrating the quarrel among psychoanalytical schools concerning the respective place of such concepts as "consciousness," "ego," and "self."[1] Instead, by accepting as a quite plausible working hypothesis the metapsychology of self psychology and the analytic technique corresponding to it, I would like to reflect upon their import for philosophical reflection concerned with the relationships between subjectivity and intersubjectivity. Hence I will assume the same attitude that I held when I was writing *Freud and Philosophy*, namely, to let myself be instructed by analytic experience in order to learn what it can teach us about what philosophical reflection cannot draw from its own grounds.[2]

In the first part of this essay I shall present a summary of the themes that will figure in the confrontation with philosophy that will take place in the second part.

---

[1] Heinz Kohut, *How Does Analysis Cure?* ed. Arnold Goldberg, with the collaboration of Paul Stepansky (Chicago: University of Chicago Press, 1984).

[2] Paul Ricoeur, *Freud and Philosophy: An Essay on Interpretation*, trans. Denis Savage (New Haven: Yale University Press, 1970).

The Major Themes of the Metapyschology of Self

1. It is first of all important to obtain an exact measurement of the gap between Heinz Kohut's metapsychology and what he calls "traditional analysis," namely, that of Freud, as prolonged by ego-analysis.

The principal point of dispute has to do with the place of the Oedipus conflict in the genesis of those troubles capable of being treated by psychoanalysis, especially as this takes place through transference. Kohut's thesis is that the conflict centered on sexual drives, seduction, and aggression, from which emerges the formation of love-objects, is not as basic as is the conflict that affects the primitive relations between the self and its "selfobjects." By the self, Kohut does not mean a psychical apparatus constituted by various instances bound together by mechanisms, but rather an indivisible psychical life, only accessible by empathy – that is, a sort of vicarious introspection – by which one self transports itself into another self. (Below, we shall return to this notion of empathy, in discussing the experience of transference in which the technical form of empathy proper to the analytical cure is articulated.) In order to situate this debate with Freud and ego-analysis (which I shall discuss in the next section), let us say that Kohut defines the self by means of three needs: for cohesion, for firmness, for harmony. The notion of a cohesive self is the one that occurs most often in his writing. This need for cohesion makes narcissism an irreducible, primary phenomenon, one that becomes pathological only when, in early childhood, the self has experienced the lack or the loss of a supportive, reassuring, or approving response on the part of those archaic objects (in the psychoanalytic sense of the term) that Kohut calls selfobjects rather than love-objects, owing to the close tie between the cohesion required by the self and the expected response of its selfobject, which this need makes felt one's whole life long, up to one's last breath. Corresponding to the normal correlation between a cohesive self and supportive selfobjects are the traumas of the relation between the archaic self and selfobjects, those traumas that Kohut calls self-selfobject disturbances.

2. A brief comparison and contrast of *How Does Analysis Cure?* with *The Analysis of Self* will allow us to understand better

how bit by bit Kohut became more and more aware of the conceptual distinction between self and ego, a distinction that was proposed by Heinz Hartmann. In 1971, narcissism was still defined, following Hartmann, as a cathexis of the self, symmetrical to the cathexis of love objects, even though the notion of a selfobject had been already constituted.[3]

A tie to the Freudian tradition is thus preserved through the notion of "libidinal forces," along with that of cathexis or investment, common to the analysis of classical neuroses as well as to the "troubles of narcissistic personalities." The same filiation and the same overlapping are also found on the level of the central experience in analysis, transference. Its function was already clearly identified. It was to reactivate the libidinal cathexes characteristic of narcissistic problems and to accompany the working through upon which the outcome of the cure depended. This reactivation and working through allow us to group such problems around two poles: the omnipotent object (an idealized parental image as yet poorly distinguished from the image brought about by the internalization of the superego), and the grandiose self (itself still considered in terms of a prolonged autoeroticism as explicated by Freud). However, the specificity of these "selfobject transferences" – whether it was a question, as in the former case, of an "idealizing transference"[4] or, as in the latter case, of a "mirror transference"[5] – was not yet clearly distinguished from the transference neuroses simply called "transference" in the classical terminology. Thus in 1971, Kohut apparently still accepted the thesis of an homonymy between two uses of the word transference – transference as an "amalgamation of a repressed infantile, object-libidinal urge with (pre)conscious strivings that are related to the present"[6] – and the transference that takes place between two people, the analysand and the analyst. At the base of each of

[3] These selfobjects, according to this text, are "objects which are either used in the service of the self and of the maintenance of its instinctual investments or objects which are themselves experienced as parts of the self." Heinz Kohut, *The Analysis of Self* (New York: International University Press, 1971), xiv.

[4] See ibid., 37–101.

[5] Ibid., 105–99.

[6] Ibid., 24.

them we supposedly find the same mechanism, clinical transference being conceived of as the "specific example of interpsychical transference," to the extent that "the analysand's preconscious attitudes toward the analyst become the carriers of repressed infantile, object-directed wishes."[7] In any case, the question was already posed whether the narcissistic structures themselves stemmed from situations where repression prevailed, as in transference neuroses, or whether the dynamics of clinical transference in narcissistic problems was really identical to the dynamism at work in the treatment of classical neuroses.

The clear separation between analysis of the self and ego analysis takes place in *How Does Analysis Cure?*

The first task for an inquiry concerned with epistemology is to bring together the criticisms addressed to Freud that occur here and there in this volume.

First, it is the very notion of a "psychical apparatus," along with the associated one of "mechanisms" operating between regions external to one another in this apparatus that self psychology challenges by opposing to them the holistic concept of the self.

The second criticism is just as telling. By putting the accent on the dichotomy between consciousness and unconsciousness, Freud assigned an essentially cognitive function to analysis. It came down to a matter of extending the sphere of awareness, of pushing back the bounds of ignorance and misunderstanding regarding oneself. Despite all appearances, the addition of the topology of the ego, the id, and the superego did not really change the basic direction of analysis, the ego being characterized in the final analysis by the mastery conferred by knowledge, in particular by verbalized self-knowledge.

From this follows a third, more subtle reproach: the underlying motivation of traditional analysis is moralistic, as is revealed by its interpretation of resistances. These essentially are held to consist of a kind of flight from the anxiety caused by awareness of the archaic configurations of the libido object, the sexual orientation of drives, and the aggressiveness linked to them. Through this will-to-knowledge, and through the ethics of veracity at any price that prolongs it, Freudian metapsychology belongs to the

[7] Ibid.

heritage of the Enlightenment, triumphant in fin-de-siècle Vienna. In this regard, Freud quite clearly defined himself by associating the wounds to narcissism brought about by psychoanalysis with those brought about earlier by Copernicus and Darwin. In each case, mankind is forced to give up an illusion of domination. Human beings learn that they are not the center of the world, not the apex of life, not the master of their own house. Yet, as Kohut notes, even this discovery of a lack of mastery is the result of a Promethean undertaking. It is a victory for knowledge, one which magnifies the scientist all the more in that it reduces ignorance, prejudice, and superstition. In this sense, Freud was a child of his time.

To these three criticisms, self psychology opposes the following three arguments. The self cannot be defined as a mechanically articulated psychical apparatus, insofar as the need that defines it is the need for cohesion and insofar as its specific pathology is precisely fragmentation. In this regard, the ill person of today is not the ill person of Freud's day who suffered from inhibition and repression, which themselves expressed the state of a society that was itself conflicted, and wherein the forces of progress were held in check by the reactionary tendencies of surveillance and punishment that were still the dominant rule. Today's sick person suffers most of all from dispersion, depression, a lack of harmony among the three poles for which cohesion defines mental healthiness; that is, the pole of ambitions, that of talents and skills, and that of ideals. To face up to this threat of disarticulation, of the "arc of personality," a kind of thinking grounded on an analysis into parts, similar to the approach Dilthey had criticized in the experimental psychology of his day, is not adequate. On the contrary, a holistic conception of the self is better suited to dealing with the need for cohesion that Kohut holds to be more primitive than sexualized libido and the aggression that accompanies it.

Next, to its criticism of Freud's overestimation of the cognitive function, self psychology opposes the need for empathy, which distinguishes the relation between the self and its selfobjects from the relation between the ego and its love objects. Before being the key weapon of the psychoanalytic cure, empathy is the basic structure of the relation between self and selfobject, and this structure corresponds point by point to the definition of the self by the need for coherence, firmness, and harmony. The primary function of the archaic selfobject is to support the need for cohesion, to approve movements of self-assertion, and to provide appropriate ideals to a harmonious personality. The need for empathy should not therefore be opposed in a simplistic manner to the need for knowledge, as though it could be reduced to a purely emotional attitude. Empathy encompasses all the modalities of help that one self can bring to another in the quest for integration, identification, and individuation. The term "responsive self" is the one that best defines the selfobject required by a cohesive self. The pathology of this self consists precisely of those traumas that affect the relation self-selfobject in early childhood, where the two major terms are defined respectively by the cohesive self and the responsive selfobject.

Finally, to the militant ethics of veracity, which entails an attitude of confrontation between the analyst and the analysand's resistances, self psychology opposes the ethics underlying empathy, which may be summed up by one word that comes frequently from Kohut's pen, attunement or consonance. In this regard, if Freud is the heir of the Enlightenment, where the accent was on the conflict between the power of knowledge and the resistance of darkness, I would see an unstated filiation between Kohut and those British moral philosophers who have seen the fundamental human bond in pity, compassion, and sympathy. For my own part, I was quite moved by Kohut's repeated affirmation that human beings need the support of selfobjects capable of helping them realize their project of an integrated creativity up to their last breath, that is, up to the point of becoming moribund. (I shall return to this point below.)

3. Before we can begin a dialogue between Kohut's metapsychology of his analysis of the self and phenomenological philosophy, we need to consider the reasons that led him to center his analysis on the experience of transference, the fundamental medium of the psychoanalytic cure. This role is taken to be so crucial that his 1971 work was constructed on the dichotomy between "the therapeutic activation of the omnipotent object" and "the therapeutic activation of the grandiose self." And, of course, his last work is titled *How Does Analysis Cure?* Therefore his interpretation of psychoanalytic "treatment" does not constitute an appendix to his metapsychology, as if it were only a question

of "applied psychoanalysis." Rather this interpretation is situated at the center of his whole enterprise, as was already apparent in my preceding comments on his relationship to Freud.

Transference contributes to the cure in two ways that do not necessarily constitute two successive phases: the reactivation of archaic traumas of the self-selfobject relation, and working through these traumas. It is the reactivation of traumas that allows us to affirm that the problems in the relation between self and selfobject are more primitive than those of the oedipal stage. In this regard, the new typology of self-transferences which Kohut presents is important for the discussion we are aiming at. Whereas *The Analysis of Self* had distinguished two kinds of self-transferences – mirroring transference, where the reactivation is that of a merger of the grandiose self with its selfobjects which reproduced it, and idealizing transferences, where the merger of a self that overestimates itself and an overly idealized selfobject is reactivated – *How Does Analysis Cure?* distinguishes three self-transferences by dissociating from mirroring transference a kind that earlier had been only a variation of mirroring transference. This is "twinship transference," in which the self is seeking a partner that would be not so much its replica as its equal. The model here is of an alter ego, in the proper sense of the term. By way of these three types of transferences we can catch sight of the differentiated structure underlying the relation of the self and its selfobjects. But this is only brought to light by means of the reactivated transference of archaic and pathological forms of this relation.

As for the process of working through, it is the key element of the cure. Much of Kohut's theory is based upon it, and in the first place the destiny of narcissism. Indeed, it looks as if such working through does not lead to substituting an ideal relation to a love-object for some narcissistic form. A crucial point here is the equivalence set up between working through and transmuting internalization. Narcissism is not an archaic structure that needs to be replaced. Instead it has to be transmuted into a mature form of narcissism. This point is crucial for Kohut's whole theory of the self. There is a fundamental equivalence for him between the two notions of cohesive self and mature narcissism. However, this equivalence is itself the fruit of the process of working through as a transmuting internalization. I know of no better way he could have underlined the centrality of the analysis of transference in his metapsychology, something we must not forget in any philosophical discussion of his work.

4. The decisive contribution of his analysis of transference to the metapsychology underlying his analysis of self at the same time poses a difficult problem for any discussion of the epistemology of psychoanalysis. This question is whether the whole undertaking does not rest upon a vicious circle. The relation between the study of the kinds of self-transferences and the central thesis of self psychology – namely, the complementarity between the cohesive self and the responsive selfobject – is so tight that we may well ask whether transference does not turn by turn play the roles of a clinical verification and a presupposition of the metapsychological theory as a whole. This question arises both on the level of the reactivation of archaic traumas, taken as problems between the self and the selfobject, and on the level of working through, which is said to transmute, not to replace, the underlying narcissism. To dramatize this difficulty, we might say that empathy is both the object under investigation (in the self-selfobject relation) and the means of investigation (in self-transferences).

There are two replies to this objection. First, we can note that every hermeneutical discipline is circular in this sense. This comment applies to exegesis, to philology, to literary criticism, and even to history and to sociology. Each partial verification is at the same time a justification of the whole system of interpretation. It is true that the difficulty is more apparent in psychoanalysis than elsewhere because psychoanalysis is always under the suspicion of suggesting, if not dictating to the analysand how to transform each allegedly successful analysis into a therapeutic proof of the truth of the whole system. This, by the way, is why the debates between psychoanalysis and other forms of psychotherapies, and even more so the conflict internal to the psychoanalytic movement, cannot be decided by some "crucial experiment" in Bacon's sense of this term. This type of circularity has to be accepted as an inevitable destiny for the analysis of the self even more so than in other disciplines because of the role assigned to empathy at both the metapsychological and therapeutic levels of such analysis. From this destiny, the psychoanalyst has to draw the lesson of modesty and the need for critical vigilance. In this regard, Kohut was correct to emphasize that what can most hinder psychoanalysis is not this unavoidable paradox, which is merely more open and more frankly admitted in psychoanalysis than in other hermeneutical disciplines, but rather the spirit of orthodoxy and mutual ostracism that perverts psychoanalysis into a quest for power.

However, the psychology of self is not quite as powerless as it might appear to be in the face of this objection of circularity. It can also appeal to a second reply, one that belongs to it alone: the empathy brought into play through self-transferences is not the exact repetition of the empathy at work in the archaic relations of self and selfobject. What Kohut has to say in this regard about the place of empathy in the cure is quite instructive. The empathy by which the analyst responds to the analysand's self-transference, if the analyst wishes to guard against yielding to counter-transferences, is the fruit of much technical training. It makes the analyst at one and the same time both a substitute selfobject and a qualified scientific observer. And by making the analyst take on this double role, self psychology can claim to have made an original contribution to two classical discussions, almost to the point of becoming fastidious. The first of these discussions concerns the conflict between subjectivity and objectivity in the human sciences; the second has to do with the conflict between understanding and explanation. In relation to the former, Kohut goes so far as to compare self psychology to microphysics, where the observer is a part of the field under observation, as opposed to traditional analysis which seeks only to attain the untainted objectivity of macrophysics, of Newtonian physics. This comparison may leave us perplexed. Nevertheless, it does bear witness to an acute awareness of the specificity of empathy in the process of the psychoanalytic cure, in particular in the process of working through grafted onto the reactivation of archaic problems. That the analyst is subjectively involved in this process and is also an objective observer mutually imply each other in a unique way. As regards this second discussion, Kohut tries to distinguish a phase of understanding, wherein the analyst gives himself over to the transference in a relationship of close proximity, and a phase of explanation, where, by way of his more and more frequent interpretations, the analyst contributes to the working through from a more distant attitude. And he maintains that the empathy unfolded in self-transference is not limited to the first phase, that of understanding, but that it also applies to that of the explanatory phase.

What follows from these two discussions is that the empathy that is the object of the cure and the empathy that is its means are not on the same level. The former is archaic, the second, sophisticated. In this sense, we may legitimately claim the relation between these two kinds of empathy – and more generally, the relation between the metapsychological theory and therapeutic practice – is not so much a circle as it is a spiral.

5. I should like to end this review of important themes in Kohut's last book with a comment that has to do with his theory of self, which I referred to briefly above. A healthy self, I said, is characterized by cohesion, firmness, and harmony. And it requires a responsive selfobject, one that gives approval and foments ideals. My remarks regarding the means at the analyst's disposal for helping to cure the analysand allow us to add one further and important comment, namely, the structuring role of what Kohut calls optimal frustration. This role is revealed only through the reactivation of the archaic relations between the self and its self-object when these relations are submitted to the process of working through. For a mature narcissism to emerge from an archaic one, the self has to discover, at the price of inevitable blows, that it is not the omnipotent self that is reactivated by mirroring-transference. It must also discover that the other, essentially the mother or the father, is not a perfect, omniscient, always respon-sive selfobject. Nor is this other that reassuring twin who prevents the self from having to confront a different other, an other truly other than oneself in every way.

This corrective has considerable philosophical importance. It allows Kohut to make more precise his thesis that autonomy – particularly the autonomy that comes through knowledge – is not the final word of wisdom. We have already seen that the self always needs the support of a selfobject that helps it to maintain its cohesion. In this sense we might even speak of an autonomy through heteronomy which is expressed by the notions of attun-ement or consonance. What needs to be added now is that a certain degree of disillusionment about oneself, of deception as regards others, needs to be integrated into the self's education. Narcissistic wounds, at least those that are optimal, are part of life. It is this vulnerability that goes along with the human condi-tion that, in the final analysis, makes mental illness possible. Such mental illness comes about when the threshold of acceptable frustration is crossed, when the self suffers the loss of the responses of an empathetic selfobject capable of preserving its cohesion. Yet if what is at stake in life is not autonomy, what is it? Goodness, perhaps?

Here is where the true dialogue between self psychology and phenomenological philosophy gets under way.

A Philosophy Lesson

The preceding pages have been a long introduction to the following reflections. As I said at the beginning, I am not capable of arbitrating among the conflicts of analytical schools. My problem is to draw out what instruction the analytic situation, analytic practice, and analytic theory are able to provide for philosophy. This instruction comes from the dialogue the analyst may undertake with philosophy. What the philosopher brings to this dialogue is not, as one might believe, some naive reflection concerning himself, as though the analyst took his stand on empathy, conceived of as vicarious introspection, while the philosopher practiced direct introspection. Both of them make recourse to empathy and to introspection, although in different ways, ways which break with ordinary, everyday, naive experience.

What the analyst brings to this dialogue is an experience formed by the practice of transference; more precisely, those diverse configurations Kohut puts under the title of self-transferences. In a sense, this is a rare, even exceptional experience, one which, as is well known, requires both training and practice. Yet neither does the philosopher turn directly to himself by observing his lived experience. Instead of using the route of transference, the philosopher makes use of conceptual paradigms meant to articulate as one whole the constitution of a self and the relationship to another person who will be authentically another person. These paradigms are suggested by ordinary experience, it is true, but they are selectively elaborated and raised to the level of concepts by way of what we might call a thought experiment, parallel to the analytic experience of transference; that is, by a kind of experimentation based on hypothetical models that have their place in a quite specific philosophical undertaking. The examples of this process I shall propose below will help us better to understand what I mean by these conceptual paradigms of subjectivity and intersubjectivity.

Let us consider the central thesis of self psychology, namely, that a coherent, healthy, and harmonious self requires approval, support, and the idealistic summons of appropriate selfobjects if it is to come into being. It is this correlation between a cohesive self and a responsive selfobject that constitutes the potential philosophical core of self psychology and the analytic practice that goes with it.

How might philosophy respond to this notion of the needs of a self and not those of a consciousness, not even of an ego?

It is worth noting that in order to articulate subjectivity and intersubjectivity, contemporary philosophy provides not only a number of models, but highly different ones. For didactic reasons that will be justified by the course of our discussion, I would align them between two poles. On the one side lies the Hegelian model of the master and the slave, as we find it in the *Phenomenology of Spirit*.[8] On the other side, there is the model proposed by Emmanuel Levinas in his *Totality and Infinity*, which puts the accent, not on a struggle, but on the epiphany of the face that appears to me, or rather over me, and that says to me, "do not kill me" – the face of the master who teaches justice and calls for peace.[9] Two models, therefore, where the other first appears as a master. However, the mastery of the first is that of domination and its other is a slave. The mastery of the second signifies teaching and has a disciple as its other. Between these two poles, as in a way the transition between them, I would place the notion that Husserl elaborated in his fifth *Cartesian Meditation* of an analogical grasping of the other, as another ego, an alter ego, similar to me in that he too says "I" just as I do.[10]

Let us take a closer look at this span between one pole of mastery, where the master's other is a slave, and another pole,

---

[8] G.W.F. Hegel, *Phenomenology of Spirit*, trans. A.V. Miller (Oxford: Clarendon Press, 1977).
[9] Emmanuel Levinas, *Totality and Infinity: An Essay on Exteriority*, trans. Alphonso Lingis (Pittsburgh: Duquesne University Press, 1969).
[10] Edmund Husserl, *Cartesian Meditations: An Introduction to Phenomenology*, trans. Dorian Cairns (The Hague: Martinus Nijhoff, 1964).

where the other is a disciple, passing through what I will call the zero degree of mastery, the analogy of the similar.

1. What may come from a confrontation between Hegel and self psychology? Their common core is important inasmuch as the Hegelian dialectic consists of passing from the stage of mere consciousness to that of self-consciousness by way of a redoubling of consciousness upon itself. At the stage of mere consciousness, mind or spirit is entirely outside of itself, turned toward a world whose consistency exhausts the meaning of the consciousness unaware of itself. At the stage of self-consciousness, spirit turns back on itself. It knows itself. But its return is conditioned by the otherness of a second consciousness to which it opposes itself in order to be able to reflect itself back to itself by means of this second consciousness. It is this tie between self-consciousness and the duplication of consciousness that finds an echo in the correlation brought to light by Kohut between a cohesive self and a responsive selfobject. However, the similarity does not end there. The Hegelian subject does not attain the recognition that occurs between two equal self-consciousnesses except by having traversed all the stages of inequality and struggle – the famous struggle of master and slave – that constitute the archaism of self-consciousness. What is more, this equality results from the fact that the slave discovers its own self in the master, while the master merely gets enjoyment by way of the slave's work which transforms things. This archaism of the struggle for recognition finds an echo in the archaism of the self-selfobject relation from which stems the pathology of narcissism. This pathology has two faces, as Kohut already made clear in *The Analysis of Self*: absorption in an omnipotent object or the inflation of a grandiose self. The dialectic of such an omnipotent object and the grandiose self is one species of the dialectic of master and slave, one that can only be surmounted through a realistic recognition of the limitations of a selfobject that loses its omnipotence and a self that renounces its claim to omniscience. The working through initiated by transference consists precisely in making use of those optimal frustrations and the transmuting internalization that bring about a kind of equality and a mutual recognition between the self and its selfobjects.

On the basis of this overall similarity, the analyst and the Hegelian philosopher can question each other. The analyst will say first of all, as might be expected, that it is in early childhood that everything happens, in particular with those specific selfobjects which are a father and a mother. The dialectic of master and slave will seem to occur too late to the analyst, from the genetic and developmental point of view. To this the Hegelian philosopher will reply that the parental relation does certainly have a major role to play from the psychological point of view, but the social relation also has its archaic figures, which cannot be derived from the archaic selfobjects through a process of simple substitution. The discussion could go on for a long time on this level, the psychoanalyst responding that any new selfobjects capable of upholding the self throughout its life are still the image of or at least resemble the first selfobjects. It is always something like the image of a father and a mother that we seek to accompany us to our last breath.

However, this first line of discussion is not the most interesting one. What self psychology will most forcefully contest in the Hegelian schema is the primacy of struggle. Kohut insists that aggression, like the sexual seduction stemming from the Oedipus complex, is not the cause but rather the effect of earlier deficiencies affecting the support the self receives from its responsive selfobjects in earliest infancy. The absolutely primitive character of this relation of support and permanent need that the self undergoes up to its last breath shows that war is not the source of everything, but rather that it is the result of an acquired pathology, however archaic it may be. This is why empathy – a work of peace – is also the *Grundstimmung* that governs the carrying out of the cure. It is only in an atmosphere of confidence that archaic traumas can be reactivated and transmuted.

It is this basic discordance in the kinship of the analytic model of self-transference and the Hegelian model of the struggle for recognition that calls for a similar dialogue between self psychology and the Husserlian phenomenology of intersubjectivity.

2. There is a kind of kinship at this second stage as well that will allow us to advance in our dialogue. Husserl takes up the problem of intersubjectivity by way of an abstractive operation of a purely transcendental nature. That is, he approaches this problem through this abstractive operation aimed at obtaining the level of the conditions of the possibility of intersubjective experience and not on the level of this experience per se. This abstractive opera-

tion (the *epoché*) consists of putting into parentheses or suspending everything in the constitution of objects of perception and of science – and even more so as regards institutions and cultural objects (books, monuments, ethical norms, rules of law, aesthetic objects, etc.) – which are due to the contribution of intentional consciousnesses other than that form that defines itself as *ego cogito*. In this way is laid bare what Husserl calls the sphere of ownness that defines what is mine. A methodological solipsism is thus raised to the rank of a hypothetical thought experiment ("let us assume that . . ."). The core of ownness isolated in this way includes the intending of the world from a unique perspective, along with the grasping of oneself as a living body, whose feelings and drives I am the only one to experience. It is starting from this experience of pure ownness of the self by itself that the constitution of others is undertaken. Even though I cannot live the experiences of another subject, I can at least transport myself into this subject's consciousness and grasp its experience as analogous to my own. This is possible thanks to a *Paarung*, a pairing, at the level of the lived body, a lived body that feels its affinity for the lived body of the other by a sort of consonance. This *Paarung*, which recalls the reduplication of consciousness for Hegel, is not just bodily and emotional, it is also mental. I perceive the other person as a subject who perceives me and thereby enters into an exchange of signs with me. Furthermore, imagination fills out this experienced *Paarung*. Through empathy, I can imagine what I would perceive if I was over there, what I would feel if I inhabited that body over there that is the "here" of the other person.

Thus a dialogue between Husserlian phenomenology and self analysis rests first of all on the abstractive reduction to the sphere of ownness, without which the other person would not be other than me, as well as on the analogizing projection by means of which the other is intended as both other than me and similar to me at the same time. The counterpart in self psychology of this methodological solipsism is narcissism, considered not as an avatar of autoeroticism but as the primary core of self-esteem. Someone capable of self-esteem is required if there is to be a healthy relation with another person. The analytic counterpart of the analogical grasping of the other is the self-selfobject relation, where the very word "self" is redoubled. In this sense the notion of empathy, defined by Kohut as vicarious introspection, is the common good of both phenomenology and self psychology. I see an even closer kinship between what Husserl calls *Paarung* and what Kohut calls attunement or consonance. (In this regard it would be interesting to know whether Kohut was at all influenced by Husserl, whether directly or indirectly, by way of Dilthey, Heidegger, or perhaps Alfred Schutz, in elaborating his concept of empathy.)

On this common basis, self psychology brings complementary details and corrections from which phenomenology may profit greatly. In the first place, within the perspective of a genetic phenomenology, the developmental aspect of self psychology adds valuable information regarding the archaic forms of the intersubjective relation, linked to the child-parent pairing. Next, the experience of transference provides the phenomenologist with resources to unfold a typology that can enrich the notion of *Paarung*. As we have seen, in his last work Kohut distinguishes twinship transference from mirroring and idealizing transference. This alone is what corresponds to the alter ego in Husserl, to the extent that the support given by a selfobject is neither that of fusion nor that of idealization, but rather a relation of resemblance that makes the other person similar to me. In turn, the Husserlian phenomenologist will no doubt resist this identification of his notion of an alter ego with Kohut's notion of a supportive selfobject. For phenomenology, the relation of likeness is not one empirical relation among others but the transcendental basis of every intersubjective relation. In this sense, for phenomenology it is the analogical grasping of the other as alter ego that makes empathy itself possible as vicarious introspection. What is more, the phenomenologist will ask the analyst whether his concept of mental health, which defines the self in terms of cohesion, firmness, and harmony, does not constitute an a priori assumption of his empirical inquiry, one that allows the analyst to speak of the illness of the self of our day as one of fragmentation, depression, and disharmony. What the analyst will reply is that it is precisely from the cure process that this concept of mental health emerges.

The irony of the situation is that both the analyst and the phenomenologist are challenged today by a mode of thought stemming from Nietzsche that denounces any reference, whether clinical or transcendental, to a unified self. Here arises a crisis much more serious than any eventual divorce between phenomenology and self psychology. This crisis affects the very model of personal identity by means of which the self has traditionally been defined since Locke and Descartes. Do we not see here the erosion of the very model of mental health defined by Kohut in terms of cohesion, firmness, and harmony? If not, what are we to make of his references to the work of Proust, Kafka, and Joyce where this model finds itself radically called into question? Are we to say that these artists, without meaning to do so, restitute its purely transcendental character to the self, by depicting its foundering, at least in terms of some recognized sociological paradigm, which is contradicted not only by individual pathology but by social pathology? The question that would then be posed by such literature, for which fragmentation, depression, and disharmony have become inverted paradigms, is what still justifies the criteria of a healthy self. Must we say that culture itself, as the source of helpful selfobjects, is completely sick? But who can make such a diagnosis?

3. Pressed on by such questions, let us turn to that mode of thought where the transcendental status of the otherness of the other person takes on a deliberately ethical coloration. If, indeed, the description has become ambiguous, is it not the prescription that may make sense again of the paradigm of a healthy self, upheld by a healthy selfobject? It is at this stage of our discussion that Levinas's paradigm of otherness comes into play.

Here too the discussion is made possible by a deep-lying kinship concerning the cohesion of the self as well as the support of the selfobject. We need to emphasize this first point. Levinas forcefully asserts that the self-assertion of the ego is the necessary condition for the other to be presented in his total exteriority. Without the interiority of the ego, there is no exteriority of the other person. To bring this interiority about, Levinas elaborates a thought experiment that recalls the Husserlian reduction to the sphere of ownness. According to this paradigm, which he calls "separation," the affirmation of the ego by itself is pushed to an extreme that escapes all empirical verification. This is why I call it a thought experiment. Let us imagine a self with no external support. How does it maintain its existence? Essentially, by defining itself as living, as enjoying itself, and as identifying itself with itself by means of this enjoyment. We need not go so far here as to identify what Levinas calls enjoyment with Freud's pleasure principle, and even less so with autoeroticism. Enjoyment seals self-identification in all its forms in something like the way for Aristotle pleasure is a surplus that is added to every successful activity, "like the flower of youth." This is why enjoyment, as pure interiority without exteriority, crowns all the empirical modalities of selfhood and sets up this self as the transcendental condition of interiority. The a priori character of such selfhood is underscored by Levinas's recourse to the super-category of the Same, opposed to the super-category of the Other ever since Plato. The Same has to affirm itself, he says, so that, beginning from itself, it can welcome the Other. Is this not a way of grounding narcissism just as fundamental as Hegel's positing of a consciousness that is not yet self-consciousness, and just as fundamental as Husserl's methodological solipsism? Let me again emphasize the hypothetical aspect of the paradigm of separation for Levinas. We might even look for its origin in the notion of the "contraction" of the Absolute in the Kabala.

Still, someone may say, are we not far, too far from self psychology? Only in appearance, in my opinion. For the speculation on separation, by which the ego posits itself as Same, can be projected on the psychological plane as the ultimate justification for the affirmation of the primary character of narcissism beyond any pathological aspect. In other words, the separation of the ego for Levinas can be posited as the ultimate meaning of narcissism for Kohut.

Having said this, the parallelism in question can be pursued further on the level of the otherness of the Other. As we indicated above, it is in terms of another paradigm of the master that the other reveals his absolute exteriority (absolute in the sense of non-relatedness, of being without any external relation). Only the face of this other, the face that teaches justice, unilaterally announcing the commandment "thou shall not kill," is radically alien to the ego in its separateness. I am not the slave of this master, but rather the disciple. I enter into the language that binds the Same to the Other, not by speaking, but by listening. In this way, I make myself, as Levinas puts it, hostage to the Other.

Confronted with this discourse, what would self analysis say? Its initial response would undoubtedly be to indicate a reticence regarding this paradigm of the master/teacher at least equal to that which it bears toward the Hegelian paradigm of the master and the slave. What we have, it would say, is the same asymmetry of the Same and the Other in another form. And even more than this asymmetry, the ethical aspect linked to the epiphany of the other's face is shocking. Does Kohut not reproach Freud for the moral accent of his ferocious quest for truth as well as for the opposition he sets up between the reality principle and the pleasure principle? Perhaps, the philosopher will reply, yet Levinas's ethics of justice differs profoundly from that ethics of truth from which Kohut dissociates himself. It is more directed against the crime of murder than any lack of knowledge on the part of consciousness as regards the unconscious, or any lack of mastery of the ego over the id and the superego. Also, the face that condemns murder announces peace, not war.

At this point where Levinas is most opposed to Hegel, self psychology can face the philosopher's ethics. What self psychology does affirm, from start to finish, is the primacy of help, support, responding to any confrontation. The "healthy" selfobject is fundamentally supportive in relation to a cohesive self. Of course, the discussion may continue on from here. Unlike Kohut, Levinas accentuates the "height" of the face that teaches more than the resemblance of two twin subjects. So we might be tempted to establish another correlation between the philosopher's paradigm and another of the modalities of self-transference – that of idealizing self-transference. And in this sense, the primacy philosophy gives to the figure of the master is not wholly lacking an echo in self psychology. We may even say that at the archaic level of the selfobjects of early childhood, it is the parents who first represent this dimension of height. It is they who present themselves, on the plane of language and education, as the first teachers, the bearers of those ideals that the self has to internalize. Taking up the discussion, the metaphysician, who is also a moral philosopher, opposing his normative perspective to the developmental one, will ask: in the name of what do parents teach? If the prohibition of murder is not based on force, to what ultimate foundation may we appeal, if not to the absolutes of justice and peace, manifested by the face?

So, if for the analyst idealizing transference is just one form among others, along with mirroring and twinship transference, for the moral philosopher, the height of the teaching face has a greater intensity than every relationship of resemblance. For this type of philosopher, the Other becomes similar to me only if the relation of similarity has been abstracted from the tendency of the self to fuse itself with its selfobject. Indeed, how could this transcendence of the relation of similarity in relation to fusion be established if not by starting from the height of the Other's face in which I cannot immerse myself, that is, by starting from the master's face? To put it another way, as soon as we move from a developmental perspective to one of legitimation, the question of how to pass from archaic selfobjects to those of adult maturity arises in the most pointed fusion. Either the internal teleology of development itself requires a priori the maturity that mere psychology cannot provide or such psychology does so by means of a tacit borrowing from a transcendental style of thinking.

It is true that this argument can be questioned, and self psychology will question any ethics that sets the figure of the master above that of the father, by asking how the master can help the disciple. Is it not insofar as the law does not confine itself to condemnation, and where the face that bears witness to it is one that responds in a supportive way to the self's self-esteem? If so, in supporting the self in its quest for cohesiveness, the master must make himself a kind of co-disciple. In other words, the dialectic of master and disciple has to take on a kind of equality, like that of the master and the slave as it progresses. In short, the height of the face must stem from the similarity of Similarity. The truth of what Levinas says therefore is perhaps that only the fundamental asymmetry of the Same and the Other can justify resemblance and preserve distance within reciprocity. But the truth of what Kohut says is that this transmutation of the superior Other into an equal Other presupposes that the master is not just a substitute for the archaic ideal selfobject, but rather its extension and its transmutation. In short, that the master has to be like a father and like a mother, or, to put it differently, that the master has to be a supportive help to that unuprootable form of narcissism called self-esteem.

By posing these questions we return in concluding to the question raised by self analysis; if the highest value in life is not autonomy, what is it if not goodness? And this is Emmanuel Levinas's message in *Totality and Infinity*, when he says, "The ground of expression is goodness."[11]

[11] Emmanuel Levinas, *Totality and Infinity: An Essay on Exteriority*, trans. Alphonso Lingis (Pittsburgh: Duquesne University Press, 1969), 183.

Let me end by saying therefore that we do not overextend the parallels between the analysis of self and our three philosophical types if we say that the three configurations of self-transference described by Heinz Kohut – mirroring, idealizing, and twin trans-ference – find some echo in the three paradigms of intersubjectiv-ity arising out of the most radical forms of thought experiments in modern philosophy. We should not set these correlations up as some sort of rigid system, however, inasmuch as Kohut's three forms of self-transcendence belong to the same analytic field while the three hypothetical philosophical forms belong to ways of doing philosophy that are not reducible to one another. This is why we must avoid any eclecticism or easy reconciliation, leaving open the interplay of affinities and incompatibilities between the analytic approach and the philosophical ones.

Image and Language
in Psychoanalysis

My goal in this essay is to appraise the attempts by some recent theoreticians of psychoanalysis to reformulate psychoanalytic theory in terms of linguistic models borrowed either from structural linguistics, from Saussure to Jacobson, or from the transformational and generative linguistics coming from Chomsky. My line of argumentation will be as follows. In the first part I will present the reasons favoring such a linguistic reinterpretation, principally by dwelling upon analytic practice and more generally speaking on the analytic experience. At the same time, I will try to explain why Freud's metapsychological theory lags behind his own practice as regards recognition of the semiotic dimension of psychoanalysis.

In the second part, beginning from the partial failure of such linguistic reformulations, I will attempt to demonstrate that the universe of discourse appropriate to the analytic experience is not that of language, but that of the image. As we shall see, this thesis is not purely and simply opposed to the linguistic one. Unfortunately, we do not yet possess an adequate theory of the image and of the imagination to account for this discovery; more precisely, we lack a theory that would account for the semiotic aspects of the image. This explains why, at a time when linguistics has made considerable advances beyond the other human sciences, we should not have any other resources than to assign everything that presents a semiotic character to language. But by so doing we misunderstand the real discovery of psychoanalysis in another fashion than do the purely economic interpretations of it, i.e., in terms of the make-believe level of semiotics. My second part, therefore, will not be a refutation of my first part to the extent that the case in favor of language is in fact a case in favor of the semiotic aspects of the analytic experience. Rather it will be a question of reorienting the same arguments to the benefit of what I shall suggest calling a semiotics of the image.

The case in favor of a linguistic reinterpretation of psychoanalytic theory proceeds first of all from reversing the relation between the metapsychology and what in a general sense we may call the analytic experience. Many presentations of psychoanalysis, my own included, proceed from a certain misunderstanding of the organic connection between three things: the procedure of investigation (that is, the interpretation of symptoms, dreams, miscarried actions, rationalizations, and symbolic constructions of every kind); the method of treatment (that is, the therapeutic technique, including the use of the golden rule, the handling of resistances, of transference, and so on); and finally the theoretical apparatus (that is, the setting out of such theoretical entities as libido, cathexis, and repression, and the establishing of explanatory models like the theory of drives, the first and second topology, and so on). It is the misunderstanding of the circular connection between the procedure of investigation, method of treatment, and theoretical system that has led to overestimation of the theoretical system and, at the same time, to not noting the possible discordances between what psychoanalysis *does* and what it *says* it does.

The linguistic reinterpretations proceed from a revision of the theory starting from analytic experience, to bring together under this term what I have just called, using Freud's own vocabulary, the procedure of investigation and the method of treatment.

I propose therefore to proceed by summarizing the arguments to be considered according to their decreasing degree of proximity to the analytic situation, the whole theory in a way constituting the metalanguage of psychoanalysis.

The Analytic Situation as a Speech Situation

Let us say first of all that the analytic situation itself may be characterized as a speech relation. The "treatment" – to stay with the same vocabulary – is a talk-cure. And psychoanalysis continues to distinguish itself from every other therapeutic method by this veritable asceticism. The analysand is placed in a situation where desire is forced to speak, to pass through the defile of words, while excluding substitute satisfactions as well as every tendency to slip into acting out.

This simple starting point in analytic practice is heavy with theoretical consequences. What at first seems to be just a constraint inherent to the analytic technique conceals a theoretical requirement, namely, to include in the nomenclature of theoretical entities only those psychical realities having an affinity for language. If the theory speaks of instincts or drives, this will never be in terms of physiological phenomena, but only in terms of a *meaning* susceptible of being deciphered, translated, interpreted. Psychoanalysis knows desire only as what can be said. Let us be clear on this point. It is in no way a question here of an amputation of human experience reduced to discourse, but on the contrary, it is a question of an extending of the semiotic sphere as far as the obscure confines of mute desire antecedent to language. For only in this way will psychoanalysis claim to rejoin such preverbal experience through the subsequent symbolic constructions that assure its enduring efficacy. We can even say that psychoanalysis extends language beyond the logical plane of rational discourse to the alogical regions of life, and that in so doing it makes that part of us speak which is not so much dumb as it has been constrained to silence.

It does so by first making desire speak to another. The analytic situation offers desire what Freud, in one of his technical texts, calls "a playground in which it [the patient's compulsion to repeat] is allowed to expand in almost complete freedom."[1] Now why does the analytic situation have this virtue of reorienting repetition toward remembrance? Because it offers desire an imaginary face-to-face relation in the process of transference. Not only does desire speak, it speaks to someone else, to the other person. This second starting point in analytic practice, too, does not lack theoretical implications. It reveals that from its beginning human desire is, to use Hegel's expression, the desire of another's desire and finally for recognition. This reference to something other than

[1] S.E. 12:154.

itself is constitutive of desire as an erotic demand. The discovery of the Oedipus complex in Freud's self-analysis has no other signification: desire is structured as human desire when it enters into that triangular relation bringing into play two sexes and three persons, a prohibition, a death wish, a lost object, and so on. We can see how psychoanalytic theory is inadequate to the discovery made in psychoanalytic practice when it proposes a purely energetic definition of desire in terms of tension and discharge and when it does not take intersubjectivity into account in its definition of human desire. The same model ignores language as well as the other. For to speak is to address oneself to another.

To conclude this discussion of the analytic situation, let us add that the analysand becomes capable of speaking about himself in talking to the other person. Therefore to speak of oneself in psychoanalysis is to move from an unintelligible to an intelligible narrative. The analysand, after all, enters analysis not simply because he is suffering, but because he is troubled by symptoms, behaviors, and thoughts that do not make sense to him, which he cannot coordinate within a continuous and acceptable narrative. The whole of analysis will be only a reconstruction of contexts within which these symptoms take on meaning. By giving them, by means of the labor of talking about them, a reference framework wherein they can be appropriated, they are integrated into a history that can be recounted. So we can describe the analytic process, with Marshall Edelson, as the "rejection of immediate occasions or contexts . . . as sufficient grounds for understanding such acts" and the substitution of "more remote or distant occasions and extended contexts as these have been and are now symbolically reconstructed (according to other norms) by the actor."[2] This labor of decontextualization and recontextualization, principally with the help of "symbolizations he constructed as a child" (ibid.), implies that the analysand considers his experience in terms of texts and contexts; in short, that he enters into a semiotic reading of his experience and that he raises his experience to the rank of an acceptable and intelligible narrative. This narrative structure of personal experience has not received the recognition it deserves in psychoanalytic theory. Yet a good

[2] Marshall Edelson, *Language and Interpretation in Psychoanalysis* (New Haven: Yale University Press, 1975), 55.

portion of analytic knowledge is lodged within the case histories. This is so true that an epistemologist such as Michael Sherwood can claim that the epistemology of psychoanalysis must begin with the case histories and the conditions of intelligibility of their narrative structure and then proceed to the theory, which only furnishes explanatory segments which are to be interpolated into an essentially narrative intelligibility.[3] I shall not pursue this epistemological aspect of the problem here. I will retain from the concept of a case history only what it implies concerning the relations of language and the analytic experience. If Freud can write case histories, it is because every analytic experience takes place within a mode of discourse that we can call narrative discourse. The analysand recounts his dreams and the episodes of his past. He recounts what he does not understand, until he understands what he recounts. In this way, the whole of analytic experience is traversed by that discursive modality that requires us to say that analysis is a narrative analysis or an analytic narration.

Let us now take a little distance with regard to the analytic situation and turn toward what Freud's writings call the investigatory procedure. By so doing, we take our distance from the most formal aspects of the analytic relation and enter into the actual thickness of the analytic experience. What is more, we separate ourselves from the contemporary contexts of the pathological episodes in order to make the symbolic constellations, at first unknown to the analysand, emerge that allow us to confer intelligibility on the troubles which he suffers.

Within this phase of interpretation and explanation, what counts in favor of a linguistic reformulation of the theory taken as a whole? Essentially this: that analysis consists not just in listening to someone speak, but in listening to the analysand speak in another manner, in interpreting his symptoms as another discourse, even as the discourse of another. This idea that the unconscious is structured like a language, to the degree that it may be understood as another kind of discourse – an idea that finds its most pithy expression in the work of Jacques Lacan – constitutes the central thesis of what we are calling the linguistic reformulation of psychoanalysis.

[3] See Michael Sherwood, *The Logic of Explanation in Psychoanalysis* (New York: Academic Press, 1969).

Let us see to what extent Freud's written works may support such a reinterpretation.

Even before *The Interpretation of Dreams*, which will be the key document for our discussion, the *Studies on Hysteria* suggest for the first time a conception we may call a semiotics of symptoms. In the "Preliminary Communication" of 1892, Freud establishes a symbolic connection between the determining cause and the hysterical symptom. Already at this date, the parallelism is established between this symbolic connection and the dream process. As the apparent content of the dream the symbol counts as . . ., and its indicative value lies in its indirect function as a kind of remembering. Freud even speaks of "mnemic symbols" to indicate in an abbreviated fashion that the symptom, insofar as it is a symbol, is the mnemonic substitute for a traumatic scene whose memory has been repressed.[4] Mnemonic symbols are the means by which the traumatism continues to exist in the distorted form of the symptoms. The semiotic nature of these mnemonic symptoms is confirmed by the analysis itself to the extent that the symptom may be replaced by a discourse – a pain in the leg, for example, is equivalent to a linguistic expression of the relation between the patient's desire and the paternal figure. The transition from the symptom to the linguistic expression is even often assured by the metaphorical values of words, where the symbolization of a psychical state by a corporeal expression is in a way brought to language after having been buried in the body through hysteric conversion. Do we not say when we feel insulted that it was like a kick in the face? And when we are hopeless that we cannot take another step?

This possibility of translating a hysteric symptom into a metaphor – which Freud caught sight of very early on – announces a universal feature of the semiotic universe that Freud traversed in every direction, namely, the indefinite substitutability of one class of signs by another. The dream will be the first link in these semiotic chains, which we are going to consider next, and along which it may be exchanged for a symptom, a legendary theme, a myth, a proverb, or a perversion.

[4] S.E. 2:90–3. It is true that Freud will not continue to use the term symbol in this sense, which will be reserved for the cultural stereotypes revealed by "typical dreams."

That a dream should be a sort of text to interpret as another discourse, or as the discourse of another, is attested to in multiple fashions in *The Interpretation of Dreams*. This presupposition is what first confers meaning on the very task which Freud sets himself in placing his undertaking under the title of interpretation (*Deutung*) rather than explanation (*Erklärung*): "The aim which I have set before myself is to show that dreams are capable of being interpreted (*einer Deutungfähig sein*). . . . Interpreting a dream implies assigning a 'meaning' (*Sinn*) to it, that is replacing (*ersetzen*) it by something which fits into (*sich einfügt*) the chain of our mental acts as a link having a validity and importance equal to the rest."[5]

This kinship between the task of interpreting a dream and that of interpreting a text is confirmed by the fact that analysis takes place between the narrative of the dream and another narrative which is to the first what a readable text is to an unreadable rebus, or what a text in our maternal language is to a text in a foreign one.

The semiotic character of the dream is attested to a second time in the way that Freud designates the dream-matter. He does not hesitate, to our astonishment, to speak of dream-thoughts. Immediately after having said that the dream is "the fulfillment of a wish," he asks the question: "What alteration have the dream thoughts undergone before being changed into the manifest dream which we remember when we wake up?"[6] It is easy to see why the latent content is called a thought: When the dream has been interpreted as a wish-fulfillment it becomes intelligible, because to seek to attain a goal or satisfy a desire is what we fully understand in virtue of the veritable axiom that governs our whole comprehension of human action.[7] Consequently, to say which desire the dream is the disguised accomplishment of is to restore the context within which it becomes intelligible. Therefore in that it renders

[5] S.E. 4:96.

[6] S.E. 4:122.

[7] Edelson quotes Freud as saying, "It is self-evident that dreams must be wish-fulfillments, since nothing but a wish can set our mental apparatus at work" (S.E. 5:567), and comments that "this assumption in Freud's works, if we strain a bit, can be viewed as an axiomatic postulate of a general theory of human action" (*Language and Interpretation in Psychoanalysis*, 46).

the dream intelligible, desire is to be called the "dream-thought." It constitutes, along with the distortions that complicate it, the meaning of the dream: "Dreams . . . are not meaningless, they are not absurd; they do not imply that one portion of our store of ideas is asleep while another portion is beginning to wake. On the contrary, they are psychical phenomena of complete validity (*Vollgültiger*) – fulfillments of wishes; they can be inserted (*einzureihen*) into the chain of intelligible (*aus verständlichen*) waking mental acts: they are constructed by a highly complicated activity of the mind (*geistige*)."[8] Freud will again repeat at the end of chapter 6 that "two separate functions may be distinguished in mental activity during the construction of a dream: the production of the dream-thoughts, and their transformation into the content of the dream. The dream-thoughts are entirely rational and are constructed with an expenditure of all the psychical energy of which we are capable. They have their place among thought-processes that have not become conscious-processes from which, after some modification, our conscious thoughts, too, arise."[9]

One could not put it any better that, as regards its latent content, the dream-thought is homogeneous with all our other thoughts that come to language in the narrative consciousness that we draw from ourselves. Certainly the same text warns us (and the note added in 1925 strengthens this warning)[10] that the problem of the dream is not that of latent thoughts, but that of the dream-work by which these unconscious thoughts are transformed into the manifest content of the dream. This construction of the dream is "peculiar to dream-life and characteristic of it."[11] So it is here that a linguistic theory stands or falls. But at least it is not presumptuous to emphasize that dreams "concern themselves with attempts at solving the problems by which our mental life is faced."[12] For it is this homogeneity between the unconscious and the conscious that makes psychoanalysis itself possible inasmuch as the latent dream-thoughts, because they are thoughts, have a vocation for language.

[8] S.E. 4:122.
[9] S.E. 5:506.
[10] Ibid., 506n27.
[11] Ibid., 507.
[12] Ibid.

This semiotic character of the dream would be established on a solid foundation if it could be demonstrated that the dream-work itself brings into play processes that have their equivalents in the functioning of language. But Freud seems to discourage this undertaking by forcefully asserting that "dream-work is not simply more careless, more irrational, more forgetful, and more incomplete than waking thought; it is completely different from it qualitatively and for that reason not immediately comparable with it. It does not think, calculate, or judge in any way at all; it restricts itself to giving things a new form. It is exhaustively described by an enumeration of the conditions which it has to satisfy in producing its result."[13] The expression "dream-work" is there precisely to emphasize that it is a question of mechanisms whose description calls for a quasi-physical language: condensation is a kind of compression; displacement is a transference of intensity. No reader of Freud can escape the question whether this language must be taken literally or understood metaphorically. The linguistic reformulation of the theory is an attempt to interpret the energetic language in the second sense. If the energetic metaphors are inevitable, it is because the dream-work brings into play semiotic processes that have been desymbolized by the situation of repression. But these desymbolized processes remain nevertheless semiotic processes. Proof of this is the very possibility of the work of analysis which follows the reverse pathway of resymbolization and unfolds entirely within the setting of discourse. For example, condensation recovers its semiotic status of being a form of abbreviation (laconism) when analysis is applied to it, and relates the elements of the condensed representation to different trains of thought. Freud's insistence on the expression "train of thought" confirms that condensation is a condensation of thoughts, a case of over-determination, such that "each of the elements of the dream's content turns out to have been 'overdetermined' – to have been represented in the dream-thoughts many times over."[14] Condensation, therefore, is one vicissitude of representation, not a physical mechanism.[15] The elements retained in the abridged

---

[13] Ibid.

[14] Ibid., 283.

[15] "Not only are the elements of a dream determined by the dream-thoughts many times over, but the individual dream-thoughts are represented in the dream by several elements" (ibid., 284).

content constitute the nodal points toward which a large number of the dream-thoughts converge. What are condensed are significations, not things. The case where a person assumes the function of a collective image is the clearest example. It suffices that the associative chains succeed in dismembering the dream figure into its initial elements, bearing distinct names and capable of precise descriptions, for the condensation to be restored to its semiotic status as the multiple overdetermination of an element common to several associative chains.

The linguistic reinterpretation of displacement at first glance appears more difficult, inasmuch as displacement is a transference of psychical intensity and this transference of intensity immediately calls for an explanation of an economic type: To elude the censorship imposed by the resistance, an element far away from the affected interest and therefore from the prohibited representation receives the value that was originally placed on this representation. Therefore it is in terms of a transference of cathexis that the displacement allows itself to be expressed. And yet the displacement is not without a linguistic structure, as the reverse operation, which consists in re-establishing the distribution of elements as a function of a central point, a focal idea, attests. The discourse of the waking state, too, consists of a hierarchy of "topics," with dominant and secondary themes, relations of semantic distance, of proximity and distanciation, in what we could call the logical space of discourse.

These remarks, backed by the numerous examples of dreams analyzed by Freud in *The Interpretation of Dreams*, constitute a good introduction to recent attempts by some theoreticians to coordinate these linguistic aspects of the dream-work with the structures and processes contemporary linguistics has brought to light. In so doing, these authors have not only given us original but also liberating work as regards the prejudices that even Freud himself remained caught up in concerning the functioning of language. It seems true, for example, that Freud remained caught up in the idea that language consists of a nomenclature of words understood as labels, arising from the mnemonic traces left by the things represented. What is more, he was seduced by evolutionary theories that derived the origin of language from the expression of basic emotions. Thus he could think that the return from the dream to a more primitive ontogenetic and phylogenetic stage would guide language back to an equally more primitive stage where the words would still have antithetical significations reflecting the ambivalence of affects.[16]

Freud, it seems, knew nothing of the idea of language conceived of as a group of signifiers defined by their differences internal to the system. Nor did he seem to know the distinction between signifier and signified that characterizes the linguistic sign, or of the resources for dissociation, linguistic shifts, and substitution that this double-edged constitution offers. He apparently did not recognize the universal polysemy of words in natural languages or the exploitation of this fact in poetry and in jokes. He, who in the famous episode of the spool, saw the mastery of the lost object constituted in that game of presence and absence, did not have the semiotic theory to speak of this presence and absence. Freud, the master of the psychoanalytic interpretation of *Witz*, did not have an adequate linguistic model to account for this. Nor did he know of the covenant structure which the least exchange of speech represents, or of the symbolic order which each of us enters as soon as we speak and which has as its signified this very speech covenant. Nor, finally – and perhaps above all – did he recognize the rhetorical structures that govern the use of discourse in a situation.

I will insist only on this last point – that of the rhetorical resources of speech – because it is at this level that the progress of the science of language seems to reveal the deepest affinity with psychoanalysis's discovery – which both appears to be in advance of its own linguistic theory and in search of a more adequate one. From this point of view, one of the most noteworthy contributions of linguistics to psychoanalytic theory is certainly that of Roman Jacobson concerning metaphor and metonymy. This great linguist has shown that the opposition expressed at the level of two classical figures of rhetoric – the trope through resemblance and the trope through contiguity – in reality runs through every operation of language. Every linguistic sign implies two modes of arrangement: combination and selection. It is therefore possible to place all the phenomena which present aspects of either enchainment by contiguity or grouping together by similarity (every selection being made within a sphere of resemblance) on two orthogonal axes of combination and selection. Then to distinguish these two

[16] See "The Antithetical Meaning of Primal Words," S.E. 11:151–61.

families of operations, one speaks of the metonymic process and the metaphoric process. These operations take place on every level – phonological, semantic, and syntactic – leading to an opposition between personal styles, literary forms, plastic forms, and cinematographic forms. Jacobson also discerns this polarity in the unconscious symbolic process in the dreams that have been described by Freud. He suggests putting displacement (which would be metonymic) and condensation (which would be synecdochic) on the side of contiguity, and identification and symbolism on the side of similarity. If Jacques Lacan, on the contrary, apportions these polarities differently, boldly identifying displacement with metonymy and condensation with metaphor, these divergences are less important than the general attempt to break with the biologism and behaviorism attributed to post-Freudian psychoanalysis and to "return to Freud" by situating not only the analytic situation, but also the operations of the unconscious which the theory attempts to account for systematically, within the unique "field of speech and language."[17]

Having characterized the movement of the cure as the passage from empty speech – the empty speech of the analysand – to full speech – the "assumption by a subject of his history, insofar as it is constituted by speech addressed to another"[18] – Lacan does not hesitate in identifying the elaboration of the dream with its rhetoric: "Ellipsis and pleonasm, hyperbaton or syllepsis, regression, repetition, apposition – these are the syntactical displacements; metaphor, catachresis, autonomasia, allegory, metonymy, and synecdoche – these are the semantic condensations; Freud teaches us to read the intentions – whether ostentatious or demonstrative, dissimulation or persuasive, retaliatory or seductive – with which the subject modulates his oniric discourse."[19] The theory, consequently, should not be held to contradict the concrete discovery

---

[17] To recall the title of an important article by Jacques Lacan, "The Function and Field of Speech and Language in Psychoanalysis," in *Ecrits*, trans. Bruce Fink (New York: Norton, 2006), 197–268.

[18] Ibid., 213.

[19] Ibid., 221–2. As regards the symptom, he adds, "symptoms can be entirely resolved in an analysis of language, because a symptom is itself structured like a language; a symptom is language from which speech must be delivered" (223).

of psychoanalytic practice. We can say therefore that "the unconscious is that part of concrete discourse qua transindividual, which is not at the subject's disposal in reestablishing the continuity of his conscious discourse."[20] Also: "The unconscious is the chapter of my history that is marked by a blank or occupied by a lie; it is the censored chapter. But the truth can be refound; most often it has already been written elsewhere."[21] As for analytic method: "Its means are those of speech insofar as speech confers a meaning on the functions of the individual; its domain is that of concrete discourse qua field of the subject's transindividual reality; and its operations are those of history, insofar as history constitutes the emergence of truth in reality."[22]

What was said earlier in Freud's terms concerning the dream-thoughts now is supported by a global reinterpretation that there is thought wherever there is a symbolic organization. That part which is cut off from us is a slice of history which has already been interpreted: "What we teach the subject to recognize as his unconscious is his history – in other words, we help him complete the current historicization of the facts that have already determined a certain number of historical 'turning points' in his existence. But if they have played this role, it is already as facts of historical facts, that is, insofar as recognized in a certain sense or censored in a certain order."[23] This concept of a primary historicization permits the application of the laws of discourse and symbolization over the full extent of the psychoanalytic domain. This does not mean that everything in man is discourse, but that everything in psychoanalysis is speech and language.

Authors such as Marshall Edelson who follow Noam Chomsky rather than Saussure and Jacobson do not say anything really different. They only differ as to the linguistic model employed. Their claim is that there is more affinity between a transformational and generative linguistic model and the procedures of the unconscious than with a structural model. But their "Prolegomena to a Theory of Interpretation"[24] do not differ when it comes to considerations

---

[20] Ibid., 214.
[21] Ibid., 215.
[22] Ibid., 214.
[23] Ibid., 217.
[24] The title of Part I of Edelson's *Language and Interpretation in Psychoanalysis*.

regarding "Empty Speech and Full Speech in the Psychoanalytic Realization of the Subject."[25] The analyst is shown as listening to and at work interpreting phenomena of a semiotic nature while the analysand is caught up with the symbolic constructions of his childhood. What is new is the definition of the "linguistic competence" required for the deciphering of the semiotic edifices. This competence is described as the internalization of a set of transformations or rules that can be described within a theory of language and of symbolic systems. If we bring this assertion to bear on the problem that gives rise to our present discussion, namely, the possibility of furnishing a linguistic equivalent for what Freud described as a dream-work, we immediately see what can be seductive in borrowing a transformational model from Chomsky. The linguist, in effect, runs into a problem homologous to that of the psychoanalyst: how to account for the surface structure of a sentence with its ambiguities in terms of its deep structure. Just as condensed representation is the nodal point for several chains of thought, "an ambiguous sentence has one surface structure but as many different deep structures as it has senses."[26] Therefore it seems wholly appropriate to bring to light in terms of transformational linguistics the operations by means of which the dream-thoughts are transformed into an apparent content. This will be the case principally when the interpretation is applied to deviant forms that the user of language has recourse to in order to engender meaningful representations. But each deviant form presupposes a system of rules whose violation appears as appropriate. And psychoanalytic interpretation is the interpretation par excellence of significant deviances, comparable to the forms of "linguistic audacity" that characterize a poem.[27]

I will stop my summary of the linguistic reformulations of the theoretical apparatus of psychoanalysis here. What has been said should be sufficient to give an idea of the direction taken by the search for a point of contact between linguistics and psychoanalysis.[28]

[25] The title of Part I of Lacan's "The Function and Field of Speech and Language in Psychoanalysis."
[26] Edelson, *Language and Interpretation in Psychoanalysis*, 76.
[27] See Geoffrey Leech, *A Linguistic Guide to English Poetry* (London: Longman, 1969).
[28] The similarities between Lacan and Edelson, as I have indicated, are more important than their evident differences. For example, the role of

The Semiotic Dimension of the Image

The following reflections are centered on the notion of the image. They constitute a partial critique of the linguistic reformulations of psychoanalytic theory. The essential part of the preceding argumentation will be retained, but reoriented in a new direction. For one thing, it is a mistake to believe that everything semiotic is linguistic. Yet the theses referred to above always conclude by moving from the semiotic character of the described phenomena to their linguistic one. But it is also an error to believe that the image does not arise from the semiotic order. Unfortunately, the theories we have today hardly allow us to recognize this semiotic dimension, in that we remain the heirs of a tradition for which the image is a residue of perception or the trace of an impression. As a result, lacking a theory appropriate to the image, psychoanalytic theory seems to be stuck with the following disjunction: either it recognizes the function of the image in psychoanalysis, but misunderstands the semiotic dimension of its field, or it recognizes this semiotic dimension, but too quickly assimilates it to the realm of language. My own working hypothesis is that the universe of discourse appropriate to the psychoanalytic discovery is not so much a linguistic one as one of fantasy in general. Acknowledging this dimension of fantasy requires both a theory appropriate to the image and contributes to its establishment in the full recognition of its semantic dimension.

resemblance in what Edelson calls a "presentation" (following Susanne Langer) and which he opposes to "representations," leads him to write: "The psychoanalyst's skill in interpreting a presentation depends upon his sensitivity to the possibilities of metaphor, his responsiveness to resemblance and his capacity to detect patterns, arrangements, and significant forms" (*Language and Interpretation in Psychoanalysis*, 84). Then, using Kant's distinction between a "presupposition" (which is a part of the deep structure) and a "presumption" (which is something credited to the speaker by the auditor in a discourse situation), he remarks: "Here we are in the realm of what Katz terms *rhetoric*. The province of rhetoric is that meaning – which is other than the cognitive sense represented by the deep structure – conveyed by the choice of a particular surface structure" (ibid., 87). Obviously this latter remark is easily compared to Lacan's enumeration of the rhetorical figures brought into play by the unconscious.

I shall not take into account in my critique of the linguistic reformulations of psychoanalysis the reproach that is usually made against them of letting the dynamic and the economic aspects of unconscious phenomena fall away or their failure to say anything about the affects where the properly drive-like aspect of these phenomena is expressed non-linguistically. I shall suggest in concluding, however, that a theory of fantasy is perhaps more likely to account for the articulation of both the semiotic and the drive dimensions of psychoanalysis than is a linguistic theory. My critique, therefore, stays within the limits set by the theoreticians of the linguistic approach. I begin by accepting that the analytic technique is a technique that makes language its field of action and the privileged instrument of its efficacy. The difficulty does not concern the discourse within which the analytic process unfolds, but that other discourse which is slowly confirmed through this type of discourse and which it has to explicate, I mean the discourse about the complexes buried in the unconscious.[29] That these complexes should have an affinity for discourse, that they are sayable in principle is not to be doubted. Therefore the analytic situation itself establishes a semiotic aspect. Moreover, that the phenomena thus brought to light are governed by relations of motivation that take the place of what the natural sciences define as a causal relation, and that these relations are immediately constitutive of a history susceptible of being recounted, also is attested to by the narrative repetition that analysis produces. But none of this proves that what thus comes to language – or better, is brought to language – is or must be language. On the contrary, it is because the level of expression proper to the unconscious is not language that the work of interpretation is difficult and constitutes a veritable linguistic promotion.

The Image as Dream-Work

Freud directly addressed himself to this problem in section C of the sixth chapter of *The Interpretation of Dreams*, entitled "Die

---

[29] I borrow these terms from Emile Benveniste, "Remarks on the Function of Language in Freudian Theory," in *Problems in General Linguistics*, trans. Mary Elizabeth Meek (Coral Gables: University of Miami Press, 1971), 65–75.

Darstellungsmittel des Traums." The Standard Edition translates this as "The Means of Representation in Dreams." Freud begins with the fact that once the dream is interpreted it presents numerous logical relations, including antitheses and contradictions, but also conditions and consequences, logical relations that find appropriate expression in the syntax of our natural languages: if . . . then, because, identity, although, either/or. It is not an accident that dreams "have no means at their disposal for representing these logical representations between the dream-thoughts. For the most part dreams disregard all these conjunctions and it is the substantive content (*den sachlichen Inhalt*) of the dream-thoughts that they take over and manipulate. The restoration of the connections which the dream-work has destroyed is a task which has to be performed by the interpretative process."[30]

This incapacity of the dream to express logical relations is not a simple lack of the proper means. It is the counterpart of a positive feature that Freud calls "the psychical material (*psychisches Material*) out of which dreams are made."[31] This psychical material, which can be compared with the plastic arts of painting and sculpture, is nothing other than the image, but the image considered in its capacity to express or indicate plastically the dream ideas, as the term *Darstellung* (which originally signified *exhibitio*) conveys.[32] The dream-thoughts thus become (and are called) "dream-images."[33]

This exhibiting of the dream content in images, far from constituting a contingent feature of the dream-work, is in reality implied in the two major processes of condensation and displace-

---

[30] S.E. 5:312.

[31] Ibid.

[32] "But just as the art of Painting eventually found a way of expressing, by means other than the floating labels, at least the intention of the words (*die Redeabsicht*) of the Personages represented – affection, threats, warnings, and so on – so too there is a possible means by which dreams can take account of some of the logical relations between their dream-thoughts, by making an appropriate modification in the method of representation characteristic of dreams" (ibid., 313–14). A long enumeration follows of the various processes by means of which the different logical relations are figured in the dream.

[33] Depending on the context, the S.E. translates *Bild* by either image or picture. See, for example, ibid., 344, where both terms are used.

ment, for which we have attempted to give a linguistic and, more exactly, a rhetorical interpretation. As section D of this same chapter – "Considerations of Representability (*Darstellbarkeit*)" – establishes, these two processes work on the ruins of the logical relations and at the heart of the "pictorial" (*bildlich*) expression: "a thing that is pictorial (*das Bildliche*) is, from the point of view of a dream, a thing that is capable of being represented (*darstellungfähig*): it can be introduced into a situation in which abstract expressions offer the same kind of difficulties to representation in dreams as a political lead article in a newspaper would offer an illustrator."[34]

Here we are at the juncture of image and language, since on the one hand the creation of images consists in large part of a "visual representation"[35] of the dream processes, and on the other hand of a "pictorial language"[36] that uses concrete terms. It is with regard to this, moreover, that Freud comments on the kinship between the dream and wit,[37] as he did earlier with regard to the rebus and as he will do again a few lines later with regard to hieroglyphics. The concept of representability, therefore, designates a working level where the kinship between condensation, displacement, and disguise is affirmed and that joins the figured aspects of language to the unfolding of a spatial and visual spectacle. It is worth noting that condensation and displacement are mentioned in the same context (see the previous note) with regard both to words and visual images, as though these rhetorical figures and visual images belonged to the same realm of "representability." Yet ancient rhetoricians had already noticed that a figured language is one that gives a contour, a visibility to discourse. Consequently the problem is not so much that we find words in

[34] Ibid., 339–40.
[35] Ibid., 344.
[36] Ibid., 340.
[37] "In this way the whole domain of verbal wit is put at the disposal of the dream-work. There is no need to be astonished at the part played by words in dream formation. Words, since they are nodal points of numerous ideas, may be regarded as predestined to ambiguity; and the neuroses (e.g. in framing obsessions and phobias), no less than dreams make unashamed use of the advantages thus offered by words for purposes of condensation and disguise. It is easy to show that dream-distortion too profits from displacement of expression" (ibid., 340–1).

dreams and that the dream-work should be close to the "verbal wit" that governs jokes, but that language functions at a pictorial level that brings it into the neighborhood of the visual image and vice versa.

It seems to me that we should interpret what in the next section Freud calls "Representation by Symbols" in the same fashion. As is well known, Freud reserves the term symbol for representations that have a certain fixity ("like the 'gramma-logues' in short-hand")[38] and that belong to the oldest heritage of culture. This is why they are not peculiar to dreams but also may be found in folklore, popular myths, legends, in-words, popular wisdom, and current jokes. We can say that these symbols belong to the sphere of language if we mean by this not that they belong to the struc-ture of a natural language or to individual speech, but to the things said, which by an effect of sedimentation are assimilated to the code of the language and incorporated into the speech contract, to the point of becoming an integral part of what we call language in the broad sense of the term that encompasses its structure, the dynamism of speech, and the heritage of symbolism. But to recognize the linguistic character of symbolism – or what I would prefer to call its linguisticality, in order to emphasize that it is a question of a sedimented use of speech, which mimics the anonymous character of language – constitutes only half the truth. The problem of psychoanalysis begins with the private use by the dreamer of this public treasury of symbols. And it is here that the symbol, first inscribed in language in the sense just mentioned, now inscribes itself in the image. Freud says this not only in his title, "Representation by Symbols" (where the instrumental char-acter of the symbol in relation to the representation of the dream is made evident by the preposition *durch*), but also in the text: "dreams make use of this symbolism for the disguised representa-tion of their latent thoughts."[39] It is a question therefore of "indi-rect methods of representation."[40] In other words, the problem for interpretation is not the symbol's belonging to the verbal treasure of humanity, but its "pictorial" use by the dream. It is in this sense that the symbol is to be aligned with condensation, displacement,

[38] Ibid., 351.
[39] Ibid., 352.
[40] Ibid., 351.

figured language, and the visual image – all processes arising from the same "considerations of representability." Of course, without a knowledge of symbols on the psychoanalyst's part, hence without familiarity with the verbal treasure of a culture, the interpretation of the symbols in the dream is impossible. But it is their use in combination with other dream processes that allows them to be interpreted in a given situation. Thus, as Freud comments, they usually have more than one signification "and, as with Chinese script, the correct interpretation can only be arrived at on each occasion from the context."[41] So the dream does not contain raw fragments of cultural symbols. These are dramatized according to the need of the dream under consideration.[42] When such symbols belonging to the whole of humanity organize a dream we may speak not only of a representation by means of symbols, but also of a "typical dream."[43] But it is only through an abstraction from the individual history that makes singular use of such stereotypes that we can speak of typical dreams. In reality it is always about an individual dreamer that we say that it is he who puts together or exhibits the universal cultural motif. In this process of putting something together, the realm of the image and its employment in language is once again confirmed.[44]

[41] Ibid.

[42] This is why Freud warns us against any mechanical translation of symbols and against abandoning the associative technique of the dream in question. The translation of symbols must remain an auxiliary method (see ibid., 360). It is easy to see why this is so, since to do otherwise would be to deny the dream-work.

[43] "It would be possible to mention a whole number of other 'typical' dreams if we take this to mean that the manifest content is frequently to be found in the dreams of different dreamers" (ibid., 395).

[44] As regards the place of the subject matter of "typical dreams" in *The Interpretation of Dreams*, it is noteworthy that Freud treats their content not in the framework of the dream-work, but within the framework of the "material and sources of dreams" (ibid., 241ff.), hence before the sixth chapter on dream-work. There Freud extensively presents the oedipal dream in correlation with Sophocles' drama (260ff.). This confirms our thesis that the symbolism as such belongs to the dream material and not yet to the dream-work. (Freud even speaks of a primeval dream-material with regard to the points common to the drama and the dream, see 263). If the question of symbolism and with it that of the

I will conclude these remarks devoted to the image in *The Interpretation of Dreams* by emphasizing one fundamental characteristic of the image which is implicit in the whole analysis: the image is not a content, but a process. This is why I call this section "The Image as Dream-Work." The image, in effect, is not distinct from the dream-work; it is the very process of transformation of the dream-thoughts into the manifest content. This is why Freud speaks of "considerations of representability." It is a process, like Kant's schema, which is a general procedure for obtaining an image for a concept. This is the suggestion that I will pursue in the remainder of this essay by seeking to discover other aspects of the process of putting the dream-thoughts and symbols into an image as described in *The Interpretation of Dreams*.

The Image-Family

Until now our presentation has unfolded within the circle of the dream images. But the dream has made us constantly refer to other manifestations of the life of make-believe: folklore, legends, myths, literary fictions, works of plastic art (paintings and sculptures). In what sense must we assign them to one and the same level of psychical operations? More specifically, are there any common features of this level of operation that might be characterized as what I have called elsewhere "a space of fantasy"?[45]

typical dream occur a second time (in chapter 6, section D), it is from the point of view of the use of the symbolism and not of its content. This use rejoins the symbolism to the "means of representation," and therefore to the problematic of the image. That this distinction should be difficult to maintain in practice is attested to amply by the rejected anticipations of 6D in 5D and the embarrassed explanations of the section on typical dreams in chapter 5 (e.g., 241–2). The section on symbolism in chapter 6 was not added until 1914 and a part of the material from 5D was transferred to the new section. Thus the division we are considering there between the content and the use of symbols is in fact intentional and deliberate (see the editor's notes on xii and 242n1).

[45] This section draws on and abbreviates the analysis in "Psychoanalysis and Art," also in this volume. – Eds.

The unity of this space is not easily recognized due to the diversity of situations where it occurs (waking and sleeping), the diversity of levels of its efficacity (from hallucinations to the work of art), and the diversity of its media (language, sensory images, plastic works inscribed on canvas or in stone). Freud's vocabulary betrays this uncertainty. The term *Phantasieren*, for example – which we have not encountered to this point, having spoken so far only of the dream-images (*Traumbilder*) – oscillates between two uses. The first and more narrow use applies to the symbolic constructions of early childhood, also called "primitive scenes," which present themselves as true memories but which are largely fictive. It is this sense that Freud uses in section B of chapter 7 when he discusses "regression." Regression to the image is presented there as a quasi-hallucinatory revivification of perceptual images[46] and a re-emergence of the fantasies grafted onto infantile experience.[47] It is easy to see how the old psychology of the image as a revivification of a perceptive trace resists the psychoanalytic discovery of the constructed character of the phantasm. But it remains true that in these contexts the "fantasy" is closely bound to the scenario of the infantile scene. However, there is another use of the term *Phantasieren* which is given in the title of the short essay titled "Der Dichter und das Phantasieren" (1908), unhappily translated into English as "Creative Writers and Day-Dreaming."[48] The term *Phantasieren* there is not assigned simply to day-dreaming, but to the graduated scale of mental productions running from dream phantasms and neuroses at one extreme to poetic creations at the other, in passing through children's games, adults' day-dreams, heroic legends, and psychological novels. What unifies this field is, of course, the underlying common motivation, namely, the model of wish-fulfillment (*Wunscherfüllung*) furnished by the interpretation of dreams and analogically extended to these diverse mental productions. But this unity of motivation is not established unless we can identify the common imaginary mediation that is comparable to the process of the

---

[46] "In regression the fabric of the dream-thoughts is resolved into its raw material" (ibid., 542–3).

[47] "On this view a dream may be described as a substitute for an infantile scene modified by being transferred to recent experience" (ibid., 546).

[48] S.E. 9:141–54.

dream-work. So we must now attempt to identify the noteworthy features of this imaginary mediation.

We already know the first one: it may be called the characteristic of "figurability" if we recall the "considerations of representability" in *The Interpretation of Dreams*. But the creation of a sensory image proper to the dream is not the only expression of this figurability. We have seen that figured language, common to dreams and jokes, is equally part of this figurability. Language too is figurable. But figurability also applies to plastic representation. For example, "The Moses of Michelangelo" presents the equivalent of a figured discourse in stone.[49] This analysis, moreover, replaces the conflict incarnated in the stone by a discourse and thus leads back from the stone figure to the text of the book of Exodus, thereby revealing the fictive narrative common to both Scripture and the statue.[50]

This last remark leads us to a second characteristic of the fantastic as such, which is the basis for the analogy of its various incarnations. This is its character of being basically "substitutable." Here the semiotic character of the image comes to the forefront. An image has the sign's capacity to stand for, take the place of, replace something else. It is in this way that dreams are "typical." Not just, as we say, because they are common to several dreamers, but because their content is the structural invariant that allows a dream and a myth to stand for each other, as Freud discovered as early as the time of his self-analysis.[51] This moveable structure allows Freud in his interpretation of dreams to move smoothly from a dream image to a proverb, a quotation from a poet, a joke, a colloquial expression, a myth. And this equivalence between such different expressions allows us to return to our previous suggestion that the image in its dynamic function has an obvious kinship with the Kantian schema, which is not an "image" in the sense of a dead mental presence, but a procedure or method to provide images to concepts. In the same way, what we are calling the structural invariant is nothing other than the cross-

[49] S.E. 13:211–38.

[50] "What we see before us is not the inception of a violent action but what remains of a movement which has already taken place" (ibid., 229).

[51] Letter to Fliess, October 15, 1897, in S.E. 11:265.

reference from one variant to another, be it a dream, symptom, myth, or tale. It is one of the functions of the dream-work to make this invariant work in the way proper to the state of sleep, i.e., in the condition of a lack of inhibition. And it is the function of the work of interpretation to follow the inverse route of that taken by the dream-work, both works being guided by the dynamics of the schematic image.

I should like now to introduce a third feature beyond those of figurability and substitutability, a feature which is more suggested by the reading of Freud's writings than explicitly stated by him. If we return to the ambiguity of the word *Phantasieren* in German – an ambiguity reflected in Freud's use of the term – is it not true that it belongs to the fantastic as such to display several levels and to oscillate among them? At the bottom of the scale we have the infantile fantasy, in which the image is caught in the regressive movement described in chapter 6, section B, of *The Interpretation of Dreams*. Here the image has quasi-hallucinatory features, but at the same time presents the minimal factor of being a symbolic construction, what Lacan calls the primary historicization of the child's experience. At the top of the scale *Phantasieren* comes close to *Dichten*. It is, in one sense of this word, a fiction – in the sense of an invention embodied in stone or on canvas or in language. Whereas "the infantile scene is unable to bring about its own revival and has to be content with returning as a dream," the fiction has the public existence of a work of art or of language.[52] This polarity of imagination is exemplified in one place in Freud's essay "Leonardo da Vinci and a Memory of his Childhood."[53] The captive mode of *Phantasieren* finds expression in the fantasy of the vulture opening the infant's mouth with its tail. This fantasy displays its substitutive value in a series of equivalent pictures ranging from the image of the maternal breast to hieroglyphic writings and the mythical image of the phallic mother, or some infantile theory on sex, etc. The creative mode of *Phantasieren* finds expression in the invention – in the strong sense of the word – of the different expressions of the famous Leonardesque smile. Freud himself suggests "that in these figures Leonardo has denied (*verleugnet*) the unhappiness of his erotic life and has triumphed

[52] S.E. 5:546.
[53] S.E. 11:59–137.

over it in his art (*und künstliche überwinden*)."[54] If I am correct
in this interpretation of *Phantasieren*, then Freud has summarized
in this opposition between mere fantasy and creative work the
enigma of sublimation, which he did not think he had solved.[55]
But in any case, we are able here to duplicate the economic scale
from regression to sublimation with the scale of *Phantasieren* and
to display this scale within a unique space of fantasy.[56]

In conclusion, I want to emphasize once more that by under-
scoring the reference of psychoanalysis to this space of fantasy, I
do not intend to provide a refutation of the linguistic reformulations of psychoanalysis. What has to be preserved from them is
the emphasis on the semiotic dimension of the expressions of the
unconscious. Because we do not have a theory of imagination at
our disposal that does justice to this semiotic dimension, it is
natural that we tend to ascribe everything that is semiotic to language. But what is specific in the psychoanalytic discovery is that
language itself works at the pictorial level. This discovery is not
only a call for an appropriate theory of the imagination, but
already a decisive contribution to it.

[54] Ibid., 117.

[55] Cf. ibid., 136.

[56] In this essay I have made as little use of Freud's metapsychology as
possible to permit the psychoanalytic experience to correct the theory.
Can we not say, however, that Freud was well aware that language as
such was not the principal problem for psychoanalysis, and that precisely for that reason he spoke of the ideal representations of drives
(*Treib*) as a kind of *Vorstellung*? I take this expression, borrowed from
the German philosophical tradition, as one equivalent of what I here
speak of as the semiotic dimension, which is only partially linguistic
and fundamentally figurative, yet always meaningful. For a further
discussion of Freud's use of *Vorstellung*, especially in his metapsychology, see my *Freud and Philosophy: An Essay on Interpretation*, trans.
Denis Savage (New Haven: Yale University Press, 1970), 102–57, and
"Psychology and Art." It would be a decisive question for the metapsychology to know whether the recognition of an *imaginative* level
privileged in the procedures described by Freud does not make easier
the articulation of the economic and the semiotic perspectives, which a
purely linguistic theory seems to make largely incomprehensible.

Psychiatry and Moral Values

An investigation that would undertake to cover the entire field of problems posed by psychiatry with regard to ethics would unavoidably lose itself in generalities – not only because the problems and the schools of thought that can claim to be part of psychiatry are innumerable, but also because the ethical implications themselves are of such a diverse nature that they are practically incomparable. This is why I have deliberately chosen to limit this essay to one branch of psychiatry, psychoanalysis, and to one author, Freud. Two reasons govern this choice: first, it is Freud's work that exercises the greatest influence on contemporary culture at the popular as well as the scientific level of discussion; second, his work permits us to pose the problem of the relations between psychiatry and ethics in the most radical terms. At first glance the Freudian analysis of morality appears to be a traumatic negation of traditional moral beliefs. But the real problems, those that surpass ordinary banality, only take shape beyond this first shock. When we no longer resist, when we no longer seek to justify ourselves, we discover what is essential – namely, that we must not ask psychiatry and psychoanalysis for an alternative answer to unchanged questions, but for a new manner of asking moral questions.

A preliminary question is worth consideration: is psychiatry, and, above all, Freudian psychoanalysis competent to deal with ethics? Someone might object that Freud's writings on art, morals, and religion constitute extensions of individual psychology to group psychology and, beyond psychological phenomena, to a domain where psychiatry is no longer competent, the highest realm of human existence. Certainly it was during the last part of his life that Freud's great texts about culture accumulated: *The Future of an Illusion* (1927); *Civilization and Its Discontents* (1930); *Moses and Monotheism* (1937–39). But it is not a question of a belated extension from analytic experience to a general theory of culture. Already in 1908 Freud had written "Creative Writers and Day-Dreaming." *Delusions and Dreams in Jensen's "Gravida"* dates from 1907; *Leonardo da Vinci and a Memory of his Childhood* from 1910; *Totem and Taboo* from 1913; "The Moses of Michelangelo" from 1914; "Thoughts for the Times on War and Death" from 1915; "The 'Uncanny' " from 1919; "A Childhood Recollection from *Dichtung und Wahrheit*" from 1917; *Group Psychology and the Analysis of the Ego* from 1921; "A Neurosis of Demonical Possession in the Seventeenth Century" from 1923; and "Dostoevsky and Parricide" from 1928. The great "intrusions" into the domains of aesthetics, sociology, morality, and religion are strictly contemporary with texts as important as *Beyond the Pleasure Principle*, *The Ego and the Id*, and, above all, the "Papers on Metapsychology."

The truth of the matter is that these works are not just "applied" psychoanalysis, but psychoanalysis pure and simple.

How is this possible? What justifies psychoanalysis in speaking from its very beginning about art, ethics, and religion, not as a secondary extension of its task, but in conformity with its original intention?

The question is all the more legitimate in that the first intersection between psychoanalysis and a general theory of culture precedes all the works I have just cited and dates from the first interpretation of the Greek myth of Oedipus in a letter to Fliess of May 31, 1897: "Another presentiment, too, tells me, as I knew already – though in fact I know nothing at all, that I shall very soon discover the source of morality."[1] He clarifies this discovery in a second letter (October 15, 1897): "One single thought of general value has been revealed to me. I have found, in my own case too, falling in love with the mother and jealousy of the father, and I now regard it as a universal event of early childhood, even

[1] S.E. 1:252.

if not so early as in children who have been made hysterical. (Similarly with the romance of parentage in paranoia-heroes, founders of religions.) If that is so, we can understand the riveting power of Oedipus Rex, in spite of all the objections raised by reason against its presupposition of destiny; and we can understand why the later 'dramas of destiny' were bound to fail so miserably. . . . But the Greek legend seizes on a compulsion which everyone recognizes because he feels its existence within himself. Each member of the audience was once, in germ and in phantasy, just such an Oedipus, and each one recoils in horror from the dream-fulfilment here transplanted into reality, with the whole quota of repression which separates his infantile state from his present one."[2] In one fell swoop, Freud claims to have found the interpretation for a private dream and a public myth. From its very beginning psychoanalysis is both a theory of neurosis and a theory of culture.

Once again, how is this possible?

The principal answer is as follows. The object of psychoanalysis is not human desire as such – by which we mean wishes, libido, instinct, and eros (all these words having a specific signification in their specific contexts) – but human desire as understood in a more or less conflictual relation with a cultural world, whether this world is represented by parents – especially by the father – or by authorities, by anonymous external and internal prohibitions, whether articulated in discourse or incorporated in works of art or social, political, and religious institutions. In one way or another, the object of psychoanalysis is always *desires plus culture.* This is why Freud does not extend concepts that could have first been elaborated within a sort of neutralized cultural framework to cultural realities. Whether we consider *The Interpretation of Dreams* or the *Three Essays on the Theory of Sexuality*, the instinctual level is confronted from the very beginning by something like censorship, "dams," prohibitions, ideals. The nuclear figure of the father is merely the system's center of gravity. And even when we claim to isolate a human instinct, or a genetic phase of that instinct, we reach it only in the expressions of this instinct at the level of linguistic or prelinguistic signs and nowhere else. Analytic experience itself, insofar as it is an exchange of words

[2] Ibid., 265.

and silences, of speaking and listening, belongs to what we can call the order of signs, and as such becomes part of that human communication on which culture rests. This is why there exists a psychoanalytic institution in the proper sense of the word from the codification of the therapy session right up to the organization of psychoanalytic societies.

For these historical and systematic reasons, psychoanalysis is the theory of the dialectic between desire and culture. Consequently no human phenomenon is foreign to it to the degree that all human experience implies this dialectic.

The result of the unified structure of psychoanalytic theory is that it does not approach ethics as an isolated problem, but as a particular aspect of culture, itself considered as a whole. Psychoanalysis is a global theory that touches culture itself as a totality. The originality of Freudianism consists entirely in this. And it is by way of a global theory of culture that psychoanalysis takes up the phenomenon of morality.

An "Economic" Model of the Phenomenon of Culture

[What is "culture"?[3]

Let us first say negatively that there is no space here to oppose civilization and culture. This refusal to use a distinction that seems likely to become classic is itself very enlightening. There is not, on the one hand, a utilitarian enterprise meant to dominate the forces of nature, which would be civilization and, on the other hand, a disinterested, idealistic undertaking to realize values, which would be culture. This distinction, which may make sense from a point of view other than that of psychoanalysis, no longer holds as soon as we decide, to approach culture from the point of view of a balance sheet of libidinal investments and counter-investments.

[3] Some passages that follow repeat material drawn from Ricoeur's essay "Psychoanalysis and Contemporary Culture," in *The Conflict of Interpretations* (Evanston: Northwestern University Press, 1974), and *Freud and Philosophy: An Essay on Interpretation*, trans. Denis Savage (New Haven: Yale University Press, 1971). We indicate these passages in brackets. The section here comes from "Psychoanalysis and Contemporary Culture," 124–30. – Eds.

This economic interpretation dominates all Freud's discussions regarding culture.

From this point of view the first phenomenon to be considered is coercion, because of the renunciation of instincts it implies. It is on this note that *The Future of an Illusion* opens. Culture, Freud notes, began with the prohibition of the oldest desires: incest, cannibalism, murder. And yet coercion does not constitute the whole of culture. Illusion, whose future Freud is examining, finds its place in a larger cultural task for which prohibition is merely the hard outer shell. Freud delineates the core of the problem with three questions: To what point can we diminish the burden of the instinctual sacrifices imposed on human beings? How to reconcile them to those renouncements that are unavoidable? How, beyond this, to offer individuals satisfying compensations for these sacrifices? These questions are not, as we might first believe, questions raised about culture; instead they are what constitute it. What is in question in the conflict between prohibition and instinct is this triple problematic: the diminution of the instinctual burden; reconciliation with the unavoidable; and compensation for sacrifice.

What are these questions if not those of an economic interpretation? Here we reach the unitary point of view that not only binds together all Freud's essays on art, morality, and religion, but that also connects "individual psychology" and "group psychology," and roots them in the "metapsychology."

This economic interpretation of culture is displayed in two moments, especially well illustrated in *Civilization and Its Discontents*. First, there is everything that we can say without having to resort to the death instinct. Then there is what we cannot say without making this instinct intervene. Short of this point of inflection that opens it to the tragic within culture, the essay advances with a calculated simplicity. Culture's economy appears to coincide with what we could call a general "erotics." The goals sought by the individual and those that animate culture appear as sometimes converging, sometimes diverging figures of the same Eros: The "process of civilization is a modification which the vital process experiences under the influence of a task that is set it by Eros and instigated by Ananke – by the exigencies of reality; and . . . this task is one of uniting separate individuals into a community bound together by libidinal ties."[4] Therefore it is the same "erotics" that binds groups together and that brings an individual to look for pleasure and flee suffering – the triple suffering that the world, his body, and other human beings inflict upon him. Culture's development is like the growth of an individual from infancy to adulthood, the fruit of Eros and Ananke, of love and work. It is the fruit of love more than of work, however, because the necessity to be united in work to exploit nature is insignificant compared to the libidinal tie that unites individuals into a single social body. It seems then that it is the same Eros that animates the search for individual happiness and that means to unite human beings into ever larger groups.

But the paradox quickly appears: as a struggle against nature, culture gives human beings the power heretofore conferred on the gods, but this resemblance to the gods leaves them unsatisfied: the discontent of civilization. Why is this? We can undoubtedly account for some of the tensions between the individual and society solely on the basis of this general "erotics," but we cannot account for the more serious conflict that makes culture tragic. It is easy, for example, to explain that family ties resist being extended to larger groups. For every adolescent the passage from one circle to the other necessarily appears as rupturing the oldest and the narrowest bond. We understand, too, that something about feminine sexuality resists this transfer of the privately sexual to the libidinal energies of the social tie. We can go even further in the direction of conflicting situations without encountering radical contradictions. Culture, we know, imposes sacrifices on the enjoyment on all sexuality – through its prohibition of incest, censorship of infantile sexuality, supercilious channeling of sexuality into the narrow ways of legitimacy and monogamy, imposition of the imperative to procreate, and so forth. But however painful these sacrifices may be and as unavoidable as these conflicts may be, they still do not constitute a true antagonism. The most we can even say is that, on the one hand, the libido resists with all its inertial force the task that culture imposes upon it to abandon all its previous positions, and, on the other hand, that society's libidinal ties feed on the energy deducted from sexuality threatening it with atrophy. But all this is so little "tragic" that we might

[4] S.E. 21:134.

even dream of a sort of truce or settlement between the individual libido and the social bond.

So the question arises again: why do human beings fail to be happy? Why are they unsatisfied insofar as they are cultural beings?

It is here that Freud's analysis changes direction: Consider what is laid down for human beings: an absurd commandment, love their neighbor as themselves; an impossible demand, love their enemies – a dangerous order that squanders love, rewards the wicked, and leads to loss for anyone imprudent enough to apply it. But the truth that is hidden behind this unreasonable imperative is the unreasonableness of an instinct that escapes a simple erotics:

> The element of truth behind all this, which people are so ready to disavow, is that men are not gentle creatures who want to be loved, and who at most can defend themselves if they are attacked; they are on the contrary, creatures among whose instinctual endowments is to be reckoned a powerful share of aggressiveness. As a result, their neighbor is for them not only a potential helper or sexual object, but also someone who tempts them to satisfy their aggressiveness on him, to exploit his capacity for work without compensation, to use him sexually without his consent, to seize his possessions, to humiliate him, to cause him pain, to torture and to kill him. *Homo homini lupus.*[5]

The instinct that so perturbs the relation of one human being to another and that requires society to rise up as an implacable dispenser of justice is, as we will have recognized, the death instinct, the primordial hostility of human beings toward other human beings.

With the introduction of the death instinct, the whole economy of the essay is recast. While the "social erotics" could consistently appear to be the extension of the sexual erotics, either as a displacement of its object or a sublimation of its goal, the splitting of Eros and Death in two on the plane of culture can no longer appear as the extension of a conflict that could be better understood on that of the individual. On the contrary, it is the tragic in culture that serves as the privileged revealing of an antagonism that remains silent and ambiguous at the level of an individual life

[5] Ibid., 111.

and psyche. To be sure, Freud had forged his doctrine of the death instinct as early as 1920 (in *Beyond the Pleasure Principle*), without accentuating the social aspect of aggressiveness, and within an apparently biological framework. But it remained something like an adventurous speculation, despite the experimental support for the theory (repetition neurosis, infantile play, the tendency to relive painful episodes, and so forth). By 1930, Freud saw more clearly that the death instinct remained a silent instinct "in" the living being and that it only became manifest in its social expression as aggressiveness and destruction. It is in this sense that I said above that the interpretation of culture becomes what reveals a fundamental instinctual antagonism.

Thus in the second half of Freud's essay we see a sort of rereading of the theory of instincts starting from their cultural expression. We also understand better why the death instinct, in the psychological scheme of things, is both an unavoidable inference and a difficult-to-isolate experience. We never grasp it except in conjunction with Eros. Eros utilizes it by diverting it from one person to another. It becomes mingled with Eros when it takes the form of sadism, and we find it working against the individual himself through masochistic satisfaction. In short, it only betrays itself when mixed with Eros, sometimes by doubling object-libido, sometimes by overloading narcissistic ego-libido. It is unmasked and revealed as anti-culture. Thus there is a progressive revelation of the death instinct across the three biological, psychological, and cultural levels. Its antagonism is less and less silent as Eros serves first to unite the individual to himself, then the ego to its object, and finally to bind individuals into ever larger groups. In repeating itself from level to level, the struggle between Eros and death becomes more and more manifest and attains its full meaning only at the level of culture:

> This aggressive instinct is the derivative and the main representative of the death instinct which we have found alongside Eros and which shares world-dominion with it. And now, I think, the meaning of the evolution of civilization is no longer obscure to us. It must present the struggle between Eros and Death, between the instinct of life and the instinct of destruction, as it works itself out in the human species. This struggle is what all life essentially consists of, and the evolution of civilization may therefore be

simply described as the struggle for life of the human species. And it is this battle of the giants that our nurse-maids try to appease with their lullaby about Heaven. *Eiapopeia von Himmel!*[6]

But this is not all, for in the last chapters of *Civilization and Its Discontents*, the relation between psychology and the theory of culture is completely reversed. At the beginning of this essay it was the libido's economy, borrowed from the metapsychology that served as guide in elucidating the phenomenon of culture. Then, with the introduction of the death instinct, the interpretation of culture and the dialectic of instincts were seen as referring to one another in a circular movement. With the introduction of a feeling of guilt, it is now the theory of culture, through a kind of recoil, that serves as the basis for psychology. Indeed, the feeling of guilt is introduced as the "means" by which civilization holds aggressiveness in check. This cultural interpretation is pushed so far that Freud can affirm that the express intention of his essay was "to represent the sense of guilt as the most important problem in the development of civilization" and to show, moreover, why the progress of civilization must be paid for by a loss of happiness due to the reinforcement of this feeling. He quotes the famous words of Hamlet in support of this conception: "Thus conscience does make cowards of us all . . ."[7]

If, therefore, the sense of guilt is the specific means by which civilization holds aggressiveness in check, it is not surprising that *Civilization and Its Discontents* should contain the most developed interpretation of this feeling, whose substance, however, is fundamentally psychological. But the psychology of this feeling is possible only if we begin with an "economic" interpretation of culture. From the point of view of individual psychology, the feeling of guilt appears to be merely the effect of an internalized, introjected aggressiveness that the superego has taken over in the form of a moral conscience and that it turns back against the ego. But its whole "economy" appears only when the need for punishment is placed within a cultural perspective: "Civilization, therefore, obtains mastery over the individual's dangerous desire for aggression by weakening and disarming it and by setting up an

[6] Ibid., 122.
[7] Ibid., 134.

agency within him to watch over it, like a garrison in a conquered city."[8]

Thus the economic, and, if I may say so, the structural interpretation of the feeling of guilt depends upon a cultural perspective, and it is only within the framework of the structural interpretation that the diverse partial genetic interpretations elaborated during different periods by Freud concerning the murder of the primeval father and the instituting of remorse can be situated and understood. Considered by itself, this explanation remains somewhat problematic because of the contingency it introduces into the history of a feeling that is also presented as having the characteristics of "fatal inevitability."[9] However, the contingent character of this development, as it is reconstituted by the genetic explanation, is attenuated as soon as the genetic explanation itself is subordinated to the structural, economic interpretation:

> Whether one has killed one's father or has abstained from doing so is not the really decisive thing. One is bound to feel guilty in either case for the sense of guilt is an expression of the conflict clue to ambivalence, of the eternal struggle between Eros and the instinct of destruction or death. This conflict is set going as soon as men are faced with the task of living together. So long as the community assumes no other form than that of the family, the conflict is bound to express itself in the Oedipus complex, to establish the conscience and to create the first sense of guilt. When an attempt is made to widen the community, the same conflict is continued in forms which are dependent on the past; and it is strengthened and results in a further intensification of the sense of guilt. Since civilization obeys an internal erotic impulsion which causes human beings to unite in a closely-knit group, it can only achieve this aim through an ever-increasing reinforcement of the sense of guilt. What began in relation to the father is completed in relation to the group. If civilization is a necessary course of development from the family to humanity as a whole, then – as a result of the inborn conflict arising from ambivalence, of the eternal struggle between the trends of love and death – there is inextricably bound up with it an increase of the sense of guilt,

[8] Ibid., 123–4.
[9] Ibid., 132.

which will perhaps reach heights that the individual finds hard to tolerate.[10]]

Examining these two texts has not yet told us anything specific about ethics, but a framework has been assembled wherein the ethical problem can be posed in new terms drawn from the economic function of culture considered as a whole. We can say two contrary things about this theory of culture. On the one hand, to the degree that all processes of culture are viewed from the economic point of view, we can say that psychoanalysis is a reductive theory. I will return to this interpretation at the end of this essay. But we must also say in an opposite sense that the supremacy of the economic point of view could be established only through the intermediary of an interpretation of cultural phenomena that gives a voice, an expression, a language to forces that themselves are mute. The conflicts among instincts that are at the root of these cultural phenomena can only be approached within the cultural sphere where they find an indirect expression. The economics then passes through a hermeneutics. It will be important that these two conceptions remain opposed to each other to the end of our discussion.

The Economy of Ethical Phenomena

It is now possible to deal directly with the interpretation of moral phenomena in Freudian theory. By understanding them in a new way, psychoanalysis may well change our "lived" moral experience. But as I said at the beginning of this essay, when psychoanalysis turns its gaze toward morality, it is experienced by the uninitiated as trauma and aggression. Let us therefore pass through this wasteland in Freud's company.

We shall consider in succession the clinical-descriptive, the genetic-explanatory, and finally the economic-theoretical level, where we shall rejoin the level attained straightaway in the preceding analysis of the global phenomenon of culture.

1. If we limit ourselves to the properly descriptive level, Freud's discovery about morality consists essentially in applying to ethical

---

[10] Ibid., 132–3.

phenomena the instruments that had proved themselves in the description of such pathological phenomena as obsessional neurosis, melancholy, and masochism. This is what allows extending concepts forged in the clinic such as cathexis, repression, and defense mechanisms to this new order of phenomena. Morality then appears as annexed to the pathological sphere. But to assure this extension of descriptive concepts forged in contact with dreams and neuroses, it was also necessary to extend the unconscious character of the sphere of the repressed to that repressing agency Freud calls the superego. This is why Freud adds a new topography (id, ego, superego) to his first topography (unconscious, preconscious, conscious) which allows him to account for the fundamentally unconscious character of the processes by which the agency of repression itself is constituted. The new agencies required to take up the ethical phenomenon are not so much places as roles in a "personology." Ego, id, and superego are expressions that denote the relation of the personal to the anonymous and suprapersonal in the founding of the ego. The very question of the ego is a new question with respect to the question of conscious awareness dealt with in *The Interpretation of Dreams*. To become an ego is different from becoming conscious, that is, lucid, present to oneself, and attentive to reality. Becoming an ego has to do rather with the alternative of being dependent or autonomous. This is no longer a phenomenon of perception (either internal or external perception), but of strength or weakness, that is, of mastery. According to the title of one of the chapters of *The Ego and the Id*, the second topography has its end in "The Ego's Relations of Dependence" (chapter 5). These relations of dependence are master-slave relations: dependence of the ego on the id; dependence of the ego on the world; dependence of the ego on the superego. Through these alienated relations a personology is outlined. The role of the ego, carried by the personal pronoun, is constituted in relation to the anonymous, the sublime, and the real.

These new considerations, which are not contained in the trilogy unconscious-preconscious-conscious, may be introduced in a properly descriptive fashion. What in effect, from a properly clinical point of view, is the superego? Freud gives a very revealing synonym for it in the third chapter of *The Ego and the Id*. He says, "ego ideal or superego."[11] The *New Introductory Lectures on Psychoanalysis* is more specific: "But let us return to the super-ego. We have allotted to it the functions of self-observation, of conscience, and of [maintaining] the ideal."[12]

[By self-observation Freud means the split experienced as a feeling of being observed, watched, criticized, condemned: the superego manifests itself as an eye and a watchful gaze.

The moral conscience, in turn, designates the severity and cruelty of this experience. It resists our actions like Socrates' demon, which says "No," and condemns us after the action. Thus not only is the ego watched, it is also mistreated by its inner and superior other. We need not emphasize that these two features of self-observation and condemnation are in no way borrowed from a Kantian style of reflection on the condition of the good will and the a priori structure of obligation, but from clinical experience. This split between the observer and the rest of the ego is revealed in a greatly exaggerated way in the delusion of being observed, and melancholy declares its cruelty.

As for the ideal, it is described as follows: the superego "is also the vehicle of the ego ideal by which the ego measures itself, which it emulates and whose demand for ever greater perfection it strives to fulfill."[13] At first glance it may seem that no patho-logical model presides over this analysis. Is it not a question here of moral aspiration, of the desire to conform to, of forming oneself in the image of, of having the same content as a model? The cited text does permit such an analysis. But Freud is always more attentive to the constraining character of the responses that the ego gives to the demands of the superego than to its spon-taneity. Moreover, when placed with the two preceding features, this third characteristic takes on a coloration that we can readily call pathological in both the clinical and the Kantian sense of the word. Kant spoke of the "pathology of desire"; Freud speaks of the "pathology of duty" in its modes of observation, condem-nation, and idealization.][14]

[11] S.E. 19:27.
[12] S.E. 22:66.
[13] Ibid., 64–5.
[14] *Freud and Philosophy*, 184–5. – Eds.

[The pathological approach reveals the initial situation of morality as alienated and alienating. A "pathology of duty" is just as instructive as a pathology of desire. In the final analysis it is no more than a prolongation of the latter. In effect, the ego oppressed by the superego is in a situation vis-à-vis this internal stranger analogous to the ego confronted by the pressure of its desires. Because of the superego we are "foreign" to ourselves. Thus Freud speaks of the superego as an "internal foreign territory (*inneres Ausland*)."[15]]

[We must not ask of psychoanalysis what it cannot give: the origin of the ethical problem, its founding principle; but what it can give: the source and the genesis of this problem. The difficult problem of identification has its roots here. The question is how can I become myself, beginning from another, such as the father? The advantage of a thought that begins by rejecting the primordial character of the ethical ego is that it displaces our attention to the process of internalization by which the external becomes internal. That way not only a proximity to Nietzsche is discovered, but also the possibility of a confrontation with Hegel and his concept of the doubling of consciousness by which it becomes self-consciousness. Certainly by rejecting the primordial character of the ethical phenomenon, Freud can only encounter morality as the humiliation of desire, as prohibition and not as aspiration. But the limitation of his point of view is the counterpart of its coherence. If the ethical phenomenon first appears in a wounding of desire, it is justifiable by a general erotics, and the ego, prey to its diverse masters, again falls under an interpretation bound up with an economics.][16]

So runs the clinical description of the moral phenomenon.

This description, in turn, calls for an explanation that can only be genetic. For if moral reality presents characteristics so markedly inauthentic, it must be treated as derived and not as original. ["Since [the superego] goes back to the influence of parents, educators and so on, we learn still more of its significance if we turn to those who are its sources."[17] This declaration from the *New*

---

[15] Ibid., 57. [The bracketed text comes from *Freud and Philosophy*, 185–6. – Eds.]

[16] *Freud and Philosophy*, 186. – Eds.

[17] Ibid., 67.

Introductory Lectures is a good expression of the function of genetic explanation in a system that does not recognize either the original character of the cogito or its ethical dimension. Genetic explanation takes the place of a transcendental foundation.

It would be fruitless to argue that Freudianism in its basic intention is anything other than a variety of evolutionism or moral geneticism. Nevertheless, a study of its texts does allow us to affirm that having begun dogmatically, Freudianism does not cease to render its own explanation more problematic to itself as it carries it out.

For one thing the proposed genesis does not constitute an exhaustive explanation. The genetic explanation reveals a source of authority – the parents – that merely transmits a prior force of constraint and aspiration. The text cited above continues, "A child's superego is in fact constructed on the model not of its parents but of its parents' superego; the contents which fill it are the same and it becomes the vehicle of tradition and all the time-resisting judgments of value which have propagated themselves in this manner from generation to generation." Therefore, it would be fruitless to seek a full justification for moral judgments within genetic explanation. Their source is somehow given in the world of culture. The genetic explanation only circumscribes the earliest phenomenon of authority without really exhausting it.][18]

2. Genetic explanation depends on the convergence of ontogenesis and phylogenesis, in other words, on the convergence of the psychoanalysis of the infant and that of primitive societies.

[One thing that strikes every reader of Freud's first writings is the sudden lightning flash of his discovery of the Oedipus complex, which was simultaneously recognized as being both an individual drama and the collective fate of humanity, both a psychological fact and the source of morality, both the origin of neurosis and the origin of culture. The Oedipus complex receives its intimately personal character from the discovery that Freud made through his own self-analysis. But at the same time its general character is suddenly glimpsed in the background of this individual experience.][19] If his self-analysis unveils the striking effect, the compulsive aspect of the Greek legend, the myth, in return, attests to the

[18] *Freud and Philosophy*, 186–7. – Eds.
[19] Ibid., 188. – Eds.

fatality that adheres to the individual experience. Perhaps it is within this global intuition of a coincidence between an individual experience and universal destiny that we must look for the real motivation (which no anthropological investigation could exhaust) of all the Freudian attempts to articulate the ontogenesis – that is, the individual's secret – in terms of the phylogenesis, our universal destiny. [The scope of this universal drama is apparent from the beginning. It is attested to by the extension of the interpretation of *Oedipus Rex* to the character of Hamlet: if "the hysteric Hamlet" hesitates to kill his mother's lover, it is because within him lies "the obscure memory that he himself had meditated the same deed against his father because of his passion for his mother."[20] This is a brilliant and decisive comparison, for if Oedipus reveals the aspect of destiny, Hamlet reveals the aspect of guilt attached to this complex. It was not by accident that as early as 1897, Freud was citing Hamlet's words, "Thus conscience does make cowards of us all . . ." about which he remarks, "His conscience is his unconscious feeling of guilt."

Now what gives the individual's secret a universal destiny and an ethical character, if not the passage through institutions? The Oedipus complex is the dream of incest when "incest is antisocial and civilization consists in a progressive renunciation of it."[21] Thus the repression that belongs to everyone's history of desire coincides with one of the most formidable cultural institutions, the prohibition of incest. The Oedipus complex posits the great conflict between civilization and instincts that Freud never stopped commenting on from "'Civilized' Sexual Morality and Modern Nervous Illness" (1908) and *Totem and Taboo* (1913), to *Civilization and Its Discontents* (1930), and *Why War?* (1933). Repression and culture, intrapsychical institution and social institution, coincide in this exemplary point.][22]

Can phylogenesis be carried beyond ontogenesis? We might think so from reading *Totem and Taboo* (I am thinking here of

[20] Sigmund Freud, *The Origins of Psycho-analysis; Letters to Wilhelm Fliess, Drafts and Notes, 1887–1902*, ed. Marie Bonaparte, Anna Freud, and Ernst Kris; trans. Eric Mosbacher and James Strachey (New York: Basic Books, 1954), 224.

[21] Ibid., 210.

[22] *Freud and Philosophy*, 190–1. – Eds.

the section dealing with taboos: Chapter 1, "The Horror of Incest," and Chapter 2, "Taboo and Emotional Ambivalence"). As is well known, the kernel of Freud's explanation is constituted by bringing together the incest prohibition as established by anthropology and the Oedipus complex as it comes from clinical study of obsessional neurosis. But, in truth, *Totem and Taboo* just provides the occasion for a psychoanalytic interpretation of anthropology in which psychoanalysis rediscovers what it already knew, although now on the scale of human history.

The guiding thread of the analogy between the history of an individual and the history of the species is furnished by [the structural kinship between taboos and neurotic obsessions. The former function as a collective neurosis, the latter as an individual taboo. Four characteristics assure this parallel: "(1) the fact that the prohibitions lack any assignable motive; (2) the fact that they are maintained by an internal necessity; (3) the fact that they are easily displaceable and that there is a risk of infection from the prohibited object; and (4) the fact that they give rise to injunctions for the performance of ceremonial acts."[23] But the most important reason for putting these two together is constituted by the analysis of emotional ambivalence. We can say that taboo serves as a guideline. The taboo is both attractive and repulsive. This double emotional structure of desire and fear strikingly illumines the psychology of temptation and recalls Saint Paul, Saint Augustine, Kierkegaard, and Nietzsche. Taboo puts us in a place where the forbidden is attractive because it is forbidden, where the law excites concupiscence: "the basis of taboo is a prohibited action, for performing which a strong inclination exists in the unconscious."][24] Emotional ambivalence appears, then, as the common ground of and awareness of the taboo (and of remorse), on the one hand, and the moral imperative as it has been formalized by Kant, on the other.

[Did Freud think he had explained conscience through emotional ambivalence? Some texts, which surreptitiously transform the analogy into a direct filiation, do suggest this. But ambivalence is just the way in which we experience certain human relations,

---

[23] S.E. 13:28–9.
[24] Ibid., 32. [The bracketed text is from *Freud and Philosophy*, 202. – Eds.]

once the prohibition has been posited that follows from the appearance of a bond higher than desire: The father figure in the Oedipus complex and the passage from biological relations to "group kinship" in totemic organizations require an already existing authority. Up to this point *Totem and Taboo* clarifies the emotional expression of this authority more than its ultimate origin. But the psychology of temptation, to which the theme of emotional ambivalence belongs, only makes more evident the lack of an original dialectic of desire and law. What is left unspoken in these two chapters is the existence of institutions as such.

In order to fill this gap Freud had to posit a real Oedipus complex at humanity's origin, an original parricide whose scar all subsequent history bears.][25]

I shall not consider here the details of the Freudian myth of the first murder of the father figure which brings into play not only an old-fashioned anthropological apparatus but also a reconstruction of totemism itself that surpasses the phenomenon of taboo properly speaking. But at the completion of this reconstitution of origins, [the problem of institutions reappears in full force. In mythical terms, how could the prohibition against "fratricide" arise from a "parricide"? By unmasking the father figure in the alleged totem, Freud has only made more acute the problem that he wanted to resolve, namely, the ego's adoption of external prohibitions. Certainly without the horde's jealousy of the father there is no prohibition, and without the "parricide" there would be no stopping of the jealousy. But these two ciphers of jealousy and parricide are still ciphers for violence. Parricide puts a stop to the jealousy, but what prevents the repetition of the crime of parricide? This was already Aeschylus's problem in the *Orestia*, as Freud is quick to acknowledge. Remorse and obedience after the crime allow us to speak of a covenant with the father, but at most this explains only the prohibition against killing, not the prohibition against incest. That requires another covenant, a covenant among the brothers. By this pact they decide not to repeat their jealousy of the father; they renounce that violent possession that was the motive for the murder: "Thus the brothers had no alternative, if they were to live together, but – not, perhaps, until they had passed through many crises – to institute the law against

[25] *Freud and Philosophy*, 204–5. – Eds.

incest, by which they all alike renounced the women whom they
desired and who had been their chief motive for dispatching their
father."[26] And a little further on: "In thus guaranteeing one another's lives the brothers were declaring that no one of them must be
treated by another as their father was treated by them all jointly.
They were precluding the possibility of a repetition of their father's
fate. To the religiously based prohibition against killing the totem
was now added the socially based prohibition against fratricide."[27]
With this renunciation of violence under the goad of discord, we
are given all that is necessary for the birth of institutions. The
true problem of law is fratricide, not parricide. With the symbol
of the pact among the brothers, Freud has met the true requirement for analytical explanation of the problem of Hobbes, Spinoza,
Rousseau, and Hegel: the change from war to law. The question
is whether that change still belongs to an economics of desire.][28]

3. We are now ready to take the last step, that is, integrating
the clinical description and the genetic explanation in an economic point of view such as I have presented it at the beginning
of this essay at the level of the global phenomenon of culture.

What is an economic explanation of morality?

Its task is to account for what has until now remained external
to desire as a "differentiation" of the instinctual substratum; in
other words, to make the historical process of the introjection of
authority correspond to the economic process of the distribution
of cathexes. It is this differentiation, this modification of instincts,
that Freud calls the "superego." In these terms [this new economic
theory is much more than a translation of a collection of clinical,
psychological, and anthropological material into a conventional
language. It is charged with resolving a hitherto insoluble problem
on both the descriptive and the historical planes. The fact of
authority has constantly appeared as the presupposition of the
Oedipus complex as applied to either an individual or a group.
Authority and prohibition must be introduced in order to pass
from individual or collective prehistory to the history of the adult
and the civilized person. The entire effort of the new theory of
agencies is to inscribe authority within the history of desire, to

[26] Ibid., 144.
[27] Ibid., 146.
[28] *Freud and Philosophy*, 210–11. – Eds.

make it appear as a "difference" within desire. The institution of the superego is the answer to this perplexity. The relationship between the genetic and economic points of view is therefore reciprocal. On the one side, the new theory of agencies indicates the recoil of the genetic point of view and the discovery of the Oedipus complex on the first system. It provides a conceptual structure to the genesis that at least allows posing the central problem in systematic terms, even if it does not resolve this problem: the promotion of the sublime at the heart of desire. If the Oedipus drama is the pivot point of this institution, it comes down to a question of putting the Oedipus complex and the advent of the superego into relation and of stating this relation in economic terms.][29]

One important concept plays a decisive role in accomplishing this: the concept of identification.

We can follow its development from the *Three Essays on the Theory of Sexuality* (more precisely the section added in 1915), where identification is compared to idealization; then in the article "Mourning and Melancholia," where identification is conceived as a reaction to the loss of the beloved object through internalization of the lost object; to *Group Psychology and the Analysis of the Ego*, where the intersubjective character of identification comes to the fore: "Identification is known to psychoanalysis as the earliest expression of an emotional tie with another person." This is how chapter 7 titled "Identification" begins. Not just the relation to another as a model is emphasized, but this relation itself divides into a wish *to be like* and a wish *to have* and *to possess*.

> It is easy to state in a formula the distinction between an identification with the father and the choice of the father as an object. In the first case one's father is what one would like to *be*, and in the second he is what one would like to *have*. The distinction, that is, depends upon whether the tie attaches to the subject or to the object of the ego. The former kind of tie is therefore already possible before any sexual object-choice has been made. It is much more difficult to give a clear metapsychological representation of the distinction. We can only see that identification endeavours to

---

[29] *Freud and Philosophy*, 212–13. – Eds.

mould a person's ego after the fashion of the one that has been taken as a model.[30]

Freud never more forcefully expressed the problematic and the non-problematic character identification.

Freud brings these properly economic discoveries together in the synthesis of *The Ego and the Id*. The question that dominates its third chapter is: [how can the superego, which from a historical point of view stems from parental authority, derive its energies from the id according to an economic point of view? How can the internalization of authority be a differentiation of intrapsychical energies? The overlapping of these two processes, belonging to two different planes from a methodological point of view, explains how what is sublimation from the point of view of effects, and introjection from the point of view of method, can be likened to "regression" from an economic point of view. This is why the problem of "replacement of an object-cathexis" by an identification is taken in its most general sense as a kind of algebra of placements, displacements, and replacements. So presented, identification appears as a postulate in the strong sense of the term, a demand that we must accept from the beginning. Consider the following text:

> When it happens that a person has to give up a sexual object, there quite often ensues an alteration of his ego which can only be described as a setting up of the object inside the ego, as it occurs in melancholia; the exact nature of this substitution is as yet unknown to us. It may be that by this introjection, which is a kind of regression to the mechanism of the oral phase, the ego makes it easier for the object to be given up or renders that process possible. It may be that this identification is the sole condition under which the id can give up its objects. At any rate the process, especially in the early phases of development, is a very frequent one, and it makes it possible to suppose that the character of the ego is a precipitate (*Niederschlag*) of abandoned object-cathexes and that it contains the history of those object-choices.[31]

[30] S.E. 18:106.
[31] S.E. 19:29.

Thus the abandonment of the object of desire, which initiates sublimation, coincides with something like a regression. This is a regression, if not in the sense of a temporal regression to an earlier stage of the libido, at least in the economic sense of a regression from object-libido to the narcissistic libido, considered as a reservoir of energy. If the transformation of an erotic object choice into an alteration of the ego is really a method of dominating the id, the price that must be paid is as follows. "When the ego assumes the features of the object, it is forcing itself, so to speak, upon the id as a love-object and is trying to make good the id's loss by saying, 'Look, you can love me too – I am so like the object!' "[32]

We are now prepared for the generalization that will henceforth dominate the problem:

> The transformation of object-libido into narcissistic libido which thus takes place obviously implies an abandonment of sexual aims, a desexualization – a kind of sublimation, therefore. Indeed, the question arises, and deserves careful consideration, whether this is not the universal road to sublimation, whether all sublimation does not take place through the mediation of the ego, which begins by changing sexual object-libido into narcissistic libido and then, perhaps, goes on to give it another aim.][33]

Freud's whole effort from here on is to make the identification with the father of individual and collective prehistory a part of the theoretical schema of identification through abandoned object cathexes. I shall not consider his theoretical elaboration of this since it no longer concerns the ethical implications of psychoanalysis. It will suffice to have shown, on the plane of doctrine, the convergence among (1) a clinical description of morality, (2) a genetic explanation of this information, and (3) an economic explanation of the processes implied by this genesis.

Ethics and Psychoanalysis

The preceding analyses bring us to the threshold of the crucial question: can we speak of a psychoanalytic ethics? The answer

---

[32] Ibid., 30.
[33] Ibid. [*Freud and Philosophy*, 222–3. – Eds.]

must be frankly and clearly negative if by ethics we mean a pre-
scribing of duties, either old or new. But this negative response to
a question that has not itself been affected by psychoanalysis does
not exclude our asking whether its critique of morality does not
imply a new way of thinking about ethics.

But first we must consider more fully the negative response.
That psychoanalysis prescribes nothing follows first from its theoretical status, then from its discoveries concerning morality, and
finally from its character insofar as it is a therapeutic technique.

First, the theoretical status of psychoanalysis prevents it from
becoming prescriptive. The Freudian interpretation of culture,
taken overall, and of ethics considered in particular, implies a
limitation of a certain kind. Psychoanalytic explanation, we have
seen, is essentially an economic explanation of the moral phenomenon. Its limit results from its very project of understanding
culture from the point of view of its emotional cost in pleasures
and pains. Therefore, we cannot expect anything else from this
enterprise than a critique of authenticity. Above all, we cannot
ask it for what we might call a critique of foundations. This is a
task for another method, another philosophy. Psychoanalysis as
psychoanalysis is limited to unmasking the falsifications of desire
that inhabit the moral life. We have not founded a political ethic,
or resolved the enigma of power, because we have discovered – as,
for example, in *Group Psychology and the Analysis of the Ego*
– that the tie to the chief mobilizes an entire libidinal cathexis
with a homosexual characteristic. Nor have we resolved the
enigma of the authority of values when we have discerned the
father figure and an identification, as fantastic as it is real, with
him in the background of moral and social phenomena. The
legitimation of a phenomenon such as power or value is something
else. So is what we make of the emotional cost of experience, the
sum of pleasures and pains in our lives. And because psychoanalysis cannot pose the question of moral legitimation, it must limit
itself to merely marking the place of a phenomenon as important
as that of sublimation, in which an axiological point of view is
mixed with an economic one. In sublimation, instinct is working
on a higher level, although we must say that the energy invested
in new objects is the same energy that was formerly invested in a
sexual object. The economic point of view accounts for this connection only as being based on energies, not for the new value

promoted by the process of abandoning one thing and relating to another. The difficulty by speaking of socially acceptable goals and objects is put off, for social utility is a veil of ignorance thrown over the problem of value raised by sublimation. So psychoanalysis gives no access to the problem of value, of its ground, its radical origin, because its economic point of view is just that, economic. Its strength is that of suspicion, not of justification, of legitimation, still less of prescription.

Second, the discoveries of psychoanalysis about morality are what prohibit it from moralizing. In a sense close to that of Nietzsche in the *Genealogy of Morals*, the exploration of conscience's archaisms reveals that man is wrongly accused in the first place. This is why it is fruitless to ask psychoanalysis for an immediate ethics without moral conscience first having changed its position as regards itself. Accusation itself has to be accused.

Hegel saw this before Nietzsche and Freud. In criticizing the "moral vision of the world" in chapter 6 of *The Phenomenology of Spirit*, he denounced the "judging conscience" as denigrating and hypocritical. It should recognize its own finitude, its equality with the judged conscience, so that the "forgiveness of sins" might be possible through the knowledge of a reconciled self. But unlike Nietzsche and Hegel, Freud does not accuse accusation. He understands it and in understanding it he makes its structure and strategy public. A genuine ethics, one where the cruelty of the superego would yield to the severity of love, is possible in this direction. But first it would be necessary to learn in depth that the catharsis of desire is nothing without the catharsis of the judging conscience.

The fundamentally non-ethical character of psychoanalysis results not only from its theoretical status, or even from its discoveries concerning morality, but also from its technique in that it is therapeutic. This therapy implies in principle the neutralization of the moral point of view. In the essay titled "Remembering, Repeating, and Working Through," Freud insists that psychoanalysis is not just, or not even principally, a purely intellectual interpretation, but work against resistances and a "handling of" the forces released by transference. Not only does psychoanalytic explanation have an economic character, its treatment itself is an economic operation. This economic work Freud calls *Durcharbeiten*:

This working-through of the resistances may in practice turn out to be an arduous task for the subject of the analysis and a trial of patience for the analyst. Nevertheless it is a part of the work which effects the greatest changes in the patient and which distinguishes analytic treatment from any kind of treatment by suggestion.[34]

In another essay, "On Beginning the Treatment," Freud attaches this handling of resistances to the handling of transference: the name "psychoanalysis" applies only "if the intensities of the transference have been used for the overcoming of resistances."[35]

This struggle against resistances and by means of transference brings us to the decisive insight that the sole ethical value that is thereby brought into play is veracity. If psychoanalysis is a technique, it is not included in the cycle of techniques of domination; it is a technique of veracity. What is at stake is self-recognition and its itinerary runs from misunderstanding to recognition. In this regard it has its model in the Greek tragedy *Oedipus Rex*. Oedipus's fate is to have already killed his father and married his mother. But the drama of recognition begins beyond this point, for this drama consists entirely in his recognition of the man whom earlier he had cursed: "I am that man. In a sense I always knew it, but in another sense I didn't; now I know who I am." Beyond this, what can the expression "technique of veracity" signify? First, that it takes place entirely in the realm of speech. Therefore, we are faced with a strange technique. It is a technique based on its requiring work and on its commerce with emotional energies and mechanisms belonging to the economy of desire. But is it a unique kind of technique in the sense that it only grasps or handles those energies through their meaning effects, through the work of talking about them? So what is in question in analysis is the access to a true discourse, which is certainly something different from social adaptation, talk of which all too quickly leads to overthrowing the scandal of psychoanalysis in order to make it socially acceptable. For who knows where a true discourse may lead as regards the established order, that is, for the established disorder?

If, therefore, veracity is the sole ethical value implied by its analytic technique, psychoanalysis is led to practice what we could

[34] S.E. 12:155–6.
[35] Ibid., 143.

call a suspension of the ethical as regards the rest of moral philosophy. But an ethics that is reduced to veracity is not nothing.
It contains the seeds of new attitudes, drawn from the putting
aside of dissimulation.

To be sure, the vulgarization of psychoanalysis does tend to
lead to a sort of babbling about anyone and everyone's libido,
which has nothing to do with "working through," with the work
of truth. The vulgarization of the results of psychoanalysis, apart
from its technique and its work, even tends to induce reductive
schemes and to authorize saying the first thing that comes to mind
about all the eminent expressions of culture: "Now we know that
all the works of culture are nothing but . . ." Psychoanalysis in
this sense reinforces what Max Weber called "disenchantment"
(*Entzauberung*). This is true, but this is the price modern culture
must pay for a better understanding of itself. Whether we like it
or not, psychoanalysis has become one of the means through
which our culture seeks to understand itself. And it is unavoidable
that we should become aware of its significance only through the
truncated representations that are allowed by the narcissism of
our resistance. Misunderstanding is the unavoidable path to
understanding.

This same misunderstanding inclines popular consciousness to
look for a system of justifications for moral positions in vulgarized
psychoanalysis, positions that have not undergone its questioning
in their depths, even though psychoanalysis wanted to be precisely
a tactic for unmasking every justification. Thus some want it to
ratify education without restraints – because neurosis comes from
repression – and see in Freud a discreet apologetic for and cam-
ouflaging of a new Epicureanism; others, taking their stand on
the theory of stages of maturation and integration, and on the
theory of perversions and regressions, utilize it to the profit of
traditional morality – did not Freud define culture as the sacrific-
ing of instincts? Once set off on this way, nothing stops us from
psychoanalyzing psychoanalysis itself: did not Freud publicly
provide a "bourgeois" justification for the discipline of monogamy, while secretly providing the "revolutionary" justification
for orgasm? But the consciousness that poses this question, and
that attempts to enclose Freud within this ethical either-or, is
a consciousness that has not undergone the critical test of
psychoanalysis.

The Freudian revolution is its diagnostic technique, its cold lucidity, its laborious search for truth. It is a mistake to attempt to change its science into a form of preaching; a mistake to ask ourselves whether it is the scientist or the Viennese "bourgeois" trying to justify himself who speaks of perversion and regression; a mistake to suspect him – in order to blame him or commend him – of slipping approval of an unacknowledged Epicureanism under the diagnosis of the libido, when he really only turns the unpitying gaze of science on the sly conduct of moral man. Here is our misunderstanding: Freud is heard as though he were a prophet, even though he speaks as an unprophetic thinker. He does not bring a new ethic, but he does change the awareness of those for whom the ethical question remains open. He does so by changing our knowledge of our consciousness and by giving us the key to some of its ruses. Freud can indirectly change our ethics because he is not directly a moralist.

For my part, I would say that Feud is too tragic a thinker to be a moralist. Tragic in the sense of the Greeks. Instead of turning us toward heartrending options, he makes us look at what he himself calls the "hardness of life," following the German poet Heine. He teaches us that it is difficult to be human. If from time to time he seems to be pleading for the diminution of instinctual sacrifice through an easing of social prohibitions or for an acceptance of this sacrifice in the name of the reality principle, it is not because he believes that some sort of immediate diplomatic agreement is possible among the clashing agencies. Rather he waits for a total change of consciousness that will proceed from a wider and better articulated understanding of the human tragedy, without worrying about drawing its ethical consequences too soon. Freud is a tragic thinker because human situations for him are unavoidably conflictual situations. Lucid understanding of the necessary character of these conflicts constitutes, if not the last word, at least the first word of a wisdom that would incorporate the instruction of psychoanalysis. It is not by accident that Freud – naturalist, determinist, scientist, child of the Enlightenment – kept returning to the language of tragic myths: Oedipus and Narcissus, Eros, Ananke, Thanatos. We have to assimilate this knowledge to reach the threshold of a new ethic, which we should stop trying to derive directly from Freud's works, an ethic that must be prepared for slowly and over time through the fundamentally non-ethical instruction of psychoanalysis. The self-awareness that analysis offers modern people is difficult to bear and painful because of the narcissistic humiliation it inflicts on us – but at this price, it rejoins that reconciliation whose law was pronounced by Aeschylus: "wisdom comes through suffering."

The Atheism of Freudian Psychoanalysis

That Freud is one of the great atheists of contemporary culture is beyond doubt. One need only to read *The Future of an Illusion*, *Civilization and Its Discontents*, *Moses and Monotheism*. It is more important to determine what kind of atheism gets expressed here, and above all what its actual relation to psychoanalysis properly speaking is.

As concerns the first point, the Freudian critique of religion does not belong exactly to the positivist type of such critiques. To be sure, religion is, to Freud's eyes, an illusion that ought to be replaced by science. But this positivism is something Freud shared with most of the scientists of his generation. It is more interesting to compare him to the critique of religion one finds in Feuerbach, Nietzsche, and Marx. For all these thinkers, the case against religion passes through the detour of a critique of culture. They all make use of a genesis or a genealogy, to use the Nietzschean term, which consists in discovering the source of an illusion, of a fabricating function in the hidden moments of consciousness. The psychoanalytic critique of religion falls under this new type of critique. The illusion it claims to unmask does not resemble error in an epistemological sense, or a conscious, deliberate lie, in the moral sense of the word. It is a production of meaning whose key escapes the one who carries it out and that requires a special technique of deciphering or decryption. This exegesis of "false consciousness" requires a technique of interpretation more akin to philology and the criticism of texts than to physics or biology. This is why the atheism that follows from it does not have the same basis as does the one coming from materialistic science or from an empirically based logical positivism. It is rather a question of a reductive hermeneutics applied to the "meaning effects" belonging to the world of culture. In this regard, the Freudian psychoanalysis of religion is much closer to the genealogy of morals in a Nietzschean sense or even to the theory of ideologies in a Marxist one than to August Comte's critique of theology and metaphysics.

The kinship with Feuerbach, Marx, and Nietzsche runs even deeper. For them, the reduction of illusions is just the reverse side of a positive enterprise of liberation and, in that way, an affirmation of human beings as human. In different manners and by apparently opposed ways, these masters of suspicion propose bringing to light a human power that was displaced and lost in an alien transcendence. Whether it be a matter of a Marxist leap from the rule of necessity to that of freedom by means of a scientific comprehension of the laws of history, the contemplation of fate and the eternal return in Nietzsche, or the passage from the pleasure principle to the reality principle in Freud, the project is the same: to reveal human beings to themselves, as a power of affirmation, of the creation of meaning.[1] In relation to this project, however close, interpretation, under its negative aspects, is just the ascetic moment that human desire has to pass through before being restored to its proper grandeur.

It is by means of this distant goal, which the exercise of suspicion and the technique of interpretation apply to, that Freud most profoundly touches modern people. It is not only, nor even principally, a new kind of therapy that he brings, but a global interpretation of the phenomena of culture and religion as part of culture. With him, our culture proceeds to its self-analysis. It is this great event that we have to make sense of and judge.

The Legitimacy of a Psychoanalysis of Religion

What, then, is the relation of this critique of religion to psychoanalysis properly speaking? We might be tempted to try to avoid

[1] See "Formulations on the Two Principles of Mental Functioning," S.E. 12:218–26.

this critique by refusing to give any credit to psychoanalysis in this regard. Is it not above all else an explanation and a means of therapy applicable only to dreams and neuroses, that is, to human beings' "inner life," to what lies behind it or under it? By what right does psychoanalysis speak as well of art, morals, religion? Faced with this objection, it seems to me that we must affirm three things, all of equal strength. First, the competence of psychoanalysis extends to the whole of human reality; second, it reaches even to religion as a phenomenon of culture; and third, as psychoanalysis, it is necessarily iconoclastic.

Psychoanalysis applies to the whole of human reality: we would be making a serious error about its significance if we assigned desire to it as its sole domain or object. Desire, for Freud, always stands in an antagonistic relation with other factors that place it straightaway into a cultural situation. What is "censorship" in the theory of dreams, if not a cultural factor playing an inhibiting role as regards our "oldest desires"? In this way, dreams, in their dynamism, uncover the same factors that ethnology finds regarding the prohibition of incest.[2] The superego represents, internal to the individual psyche, the social function of prohibition, a model that makes possible the education of desire.[3] More precisely, the father, as the bearer of language and culture, is at the center of the oedipal drama, whose stakes are precisely the entry of desire into a cultural realm.[4] In this way a vast domain is outlined which we can call the semantics of desire. Everything in a way stems from it, inasmuch as culture is itself a complex form of this semantics of desire.

We can see then in what legitimate sense psychoanalysis can speak, as psychoanalysis, about religion. It takes it up as one of the dimensions of culture.[5] Culture is considered in economic terms; that is, from the point of view of the affective cost in terms of pleasure and displeasure, satisfaction and privation, to which

---

[2] See Claude Levi-Strauss, *The Elementary Structures of Kinship*, trans. James Harle Bell, John Richard von Sturmer, and Rodney Needham (Boston: Beacon, 1969).

[3] *The Ego and the Id*, S.E. 19:12–66.

[4] On the identification of the father, besides the essay cited in the preceding note, see *Group Psychology and the Analysis of the Ego*, S.E. 18:105–7.

[5] See chapters 1 and 2 of *The Future of an Illusion*, S.E. 21:5–14.

human desire relates in multiple ways. It forbids and it consoles. It forbids incest, cannibalism, murder. In this sense it demands an instinctual sacrifice on the part of the individual. Yet, at the same time, its true raison d'être is to protect us against nature. In this respect, it proposes lowering the cost of the instinctual sacrifices imposed on human beings, reconciling individuals with those renouncements that are unavoidable, offering them satisfying compensations for these sacrifices. It is in this sense that culture is a consolation. Religion, considered as one form of cultural grandeur, is the supreme instrument of this asceticism and this reconciliation. It is in this double sense that it deals with desire and fear – the fear of punishment and the desire for consolation. Its true face is that of consolation. Religion is the highest response that human beings find in culture for the harshness of life: their powerlessness against the crushing forces of nature, sickness, and death; their powerlessness to master the relation of one human being to another, which remains destined to result in hate and war; their powerlessness to master the instinctual forces that threaten them from within or to satisfy the implacable teacher that takes on the figure of the superego. The consolation of religion is the answer to all the harshness of life.

Yet if psychoanalysis deals with religion as a cultural factor, its attitude is necessarily iconoclastic, independently of the faith or non-faith of the psychoanalyst. The psychoanalyst does not talk about God, but about the god of human beings. For the analyst, religion is the illusion that belongs to the strategy of desire. Psychoanalysis is well armed to take up cultural phenomena as a whole and the religious phenomenon in particular from the angle of the semantics of desire. It possesses an initial model with which he looks for analogous forms in the other registers of human existence. This model is that of the dream, or more exactly the pair dream-symptom. In its most elementary form it presents the process of "wish fulfillment" (*Wunscherfüllung*).[6] This process applies to all the phenomena of culture insofar as one can consider them as analogical extensions of the disguised accomplishment of repressed desires, in the mode of a substituted realization.

[6] See *The Interpretation of Dreams*, S.E. 5:550–72.

The Great Themes of the Freudian Critique
of Religion

Let us consider this critique in greater detail in order to be able to grasp its points of insertion into the practice and theory of psychoanalysis.

We can distinguish several layers of interpretation: At a first level, the critique rests on a certain number of more or less strict analogies to phenomena arising in the psychoanalytic clinic; at a second level, the critique makes recourse to a genesis with a historical-cultural character and to a reconstruction of the origins of humanity; at a third level, the one where the religious phenomenon actually functions, one tries to establish the economic sum of the set of phenomena that have been considered in turn on the individual and the collective planes.

Freud's first attack can be found in his essay from 1907 titled "Obsessive Actions and Religious Practices."[7] Religious practice, and more precisely the observance of a ritual, is compared term by term with obsessional neurosis. There is the same concern on both sides to respect the details of the ritual, the same attention not to leave anything out, the same conscious torment when some fragment has been omitted, and finally, the same defensive and protective character toward the ceremony with regard to a threat of punishment coming from elsewhere. It is important to understand this parallelism. We must not forget that Freud is also the one who discovered that the ceremonies of the obsessed person have a meaning. Therefore it is in terms of meanings that the comparison works. In the first place, it signifies that human beings are capable both of religion and neurosis, to such an extent that their analogy can constitute an actual reciprocal imitation: "In view of these similarities and these analyses," writes Freud, "we might go so far as to consider obsessional neurosis as the counterpart of religion and to describe this neurosis as a private religious system, and religion as a universal form of obsessional neurosis."[8] As can be seen, this formula has more than one meaning. Religion is what can be caricatured in an obsessional

[7] S.E. 9:117–27.
[8] Ibid., 126–7.

neurosis. "Obsessive neurosis presents the tragic-comic caricature of a private religion."[9] The question remains whether this caricature realizes the deepest intention of religion or only its degradation and regression, where it begins to lose the meaning of its symbolism. But this is something that psychoanalysis as such cannot decide.

From this 1907 essay to *Moses and Monotheism* in 1939, the search for analogies is pursued in many directions. For example, *Totem and Taboo* conceives of the projection of the omnipotence of desire onto divine figures using the model of paranoia. This archaic religion corresponds to the narcissistic age of the libido. And this problem of projection is at the center of the Freudian theory of "illusion." Indeed, at the same time that the ideals imposed by the parental authority and those that succeed it get internalized, desire projects onto a transcendent region the source of prohibition and, perhaps even more, of consolation. Everything gets organized here around the parental core, the nostalgia for the father. Humans' god, the idol of their desire, is the enlarged figure of a father who threatens, who forbids, who gives the law and the names, who institutes the order of things and the order of cities, who compensates and consoles, who reconciles human beings with the harshness of life.

But the interpretation cannot stop at this level: First of all, because the analogy remains indeterminate and, according to Freud, has to be taken as one of identity. Yet clinical experience cannot prove this. Above all, there remains a gap between the private character of the neurotic's religion and the universal one of the neurosis of religious humanity. Hence it is the function of the phylogenesis not only to consolidate the analogy into an identity, but also to account for the differences at the level of the manifest contents. This is why throughout his life, from *Totem and Taboo* in 1912 to *Moses and Monotheism* written in 1937–8, Freud made recourse to an ethnological explanation whose task it was to provide the equivalent, in the dimension of the human species as a whole, of the Oedipus complex whose importance to the personal mythology of his patients clinical experience demonstrated. It was in this way that Freud was led to reconstitute what we could call a myth of origins, basing himself on the ethnology

[9] Ibid., 119.

of his day and the classic works from the beginning of the century about totemism, then later on some works devoted to the origins of Jewish monotheism. Freud asks just one thing from these works: the more or less probable confirmation that humanity had passed through an original drama – more precisely a criminal episode – that constitutes the core of the Oedipus complex of humanity. At the origin of history, a cruel father must have been killed by his sons acting together. The social institution properly speaking issued from this agreement among the brothers. But the murder of the father left a deep wound that required a reconciliation with the image of the injured father. The retrospective obedience to the father's law will be one of the elements of this reconciliation, the other one consisting in the commemoration of repentance by means of the totemic meal, wherein will be repeated in a disguised form both the murder of the father and the establishing of the reconciliation with his internalized and sublimated image.[10]

In *Moses and Monotheism*, Freud looks for another murder, that of a prophet, which would be for monotheistic religions what the murder of the primitive father had been for totemism. The Jewish prophets then will be the artisans of a resurgence of the Mosaic god. Beneath the features of an ethical god the traumatic event itself returns. The return to the Mosaic god would thus be at the same time the return of a repressed traumatism. In this way we reach the point where a resurgence on the plane of representations and a return of the repressed on the emotional plane coincide. The murder of Christ will be in turn another reinforcement of the memory of origins. At the same time, Freud takes up again his old hypothesis of the revolt of the sons. The redeemer must have been the principal guilty party, the leader of the band of brothers, just like the rebellious hero in Greek tragedy: "for he was the resurrected Moses and behind him the returned primal father of the primitive horde, transfigured and, as the son, put in the place of the father."[11]

With this concept of the "return of the repressed," we reach the third level of Freudian interpretation, the properly economic one. In *The Future of an Illusion* and *Civilization and Its Discontents*, Freud tries to place this genesis of an illusion, both

[10] See chapter IV of *Totem and Taboo*, S.E. 13:100–61.
[11] *Moses and Monotheism*, S.E. 23:90.

as regards individuals and history, in the cultural process as we have described it above: to diminish the charge of instinctual sacrifices imposed on human beings; to reconcile individuals with those renunciations that are unavoidable; to offer them satisfactory compensations for these sacrifices. The figure of the father, as it reappears through the mechanism of the return of the repressed, becomes the pivot point of "consolation." Because human beings are always helpless as a child, they remain prey to a nostalgia for the father. And if all distress is nostalgia for the father, all consolation is a reiteration of the father. Child-like people, confronted with nature, forge gods for themselves in the image of the father. The genetic explanation is in this way incorporated into an economic one. The analogy established on the plane of clinical practice between the traumatic neurosis revealed by the history of the child's development and what Freud has called the universal obsessional neurosis of humanity is transposed to the plane of the economic balance sheet. Early traumatism, defense, latency, explosion of the neurosis, partial return of the repressed, all these make up not just the descriptive and clinical analogy but also the functional and economic one. Hence the specifically psychoanalytic interpretation of religion: its hidden meaning is the nostalgia for the father.[12]

The Value and Limits of a Psychoanalysis of Religion

To conclude, I propose outlining the broad lines of a discussion that might bring together psychoanalysts, philosophers, and theologians. There would have to be first a preliminary discussion concerning the limits in principle of a psychoanalysis of culture. But, however important it might be, this discussion should not take the place of a mutual questioning about what lies behind this.

To begin this first discussion, about method, it should be agreed that psychoanalytic interpretation cannot be taken as excluding other interpretations not so much concerned with reducing or destroying as with understanding and restoring symbolic contents

[12] Cf. *The Future of an Illusion*, S.E. 21:22–4.

on the mythic-poetic level as genuine. The limits of Freudian interpretation are not to be sought on the side of the object, for nothing is inaccessible to it, nor, of course, forbidden to it. Its limit lies on the side of its point of view and model. On the side of its point of view: every human reality, every sign, every meaning is apprehended from the angle of the semantics of desire, that is, in terms of the economic balance sheet of pleasure and displeasure, satisfaction and frustration. Here lies its initial decision, also its competence. As for its model, it is posited from the start: it is *Wunscherfüllung*, wish-fulfillment, for which the dream and neurotic symptom are the first illustrations. It is assumed that the whole of human reality will fall under psychoanalytic interpretation insofar as it offers analogies to this primitive achievement. This is what grounds both the validity and the limit of validity of a critique of religion.

If we apply this criterion of validity to the particular analyses that Freud devotes to religion, we can say the following:

(1) At the level of clinical practice, the analogy between religious phenomena and pathological phenomena must remain what it is: a mere analogy whose ultimate meaning remains in suspense. Human beings are capable of neurosis just as they are capable of religion, and vice versa. But what does this analogy signify? Psychoanalysis does not know the answer to this as analysis. It has no means to decide if faith is only this, if ritual is originarily, in its primordial function, obsessional ritual, if faith is only consolation as in the model of childhood. It can present its caricature to religious people. But it leaves them the charge to meditate on the possibility that they do not resemble their contorted double. The value of its analogy, and therefore also the limits of this analogy, seem to me to turn on one critical point: is there in the affective dynamism of religious belief something that goes beyond its own archaism?

(2) At the level of the genealogy of religion, by way of ethnology, another locus of indecision appears: is the fantasy of the murder of the father that Freud discovers at the source of the figure of the gods merely the vestige of a traumatic memory, an actual "primitive scene," or a symbol capable of providing a first layer of meaning to the imagination devoted to the question of origins, but also more and more detached from its function of

infantile and quasi-neurotic repetition, one more open to an investigation into the fundamental meaning of human destiny? Freud sometimes came up against this non-vestigial make-believe, the bearer of new meaning. Not, it is true, when he was talking about religion, but when he was talking about art. An artist like Leonardo da Vinci showed himself capable of transfiguring the vestiges of the past and, with a traumatic memory, of creating a work in which his past was both "disowned and surpassed by art" (*verleugnet und künstlerisch überwunden*).[13] Why does the "transfiguration" of the primitive figure of the father not include the same ambiguity, the same double valence of oneiric resurgence and cultural creation? Can one and the same fantasy not carry two opposed vectors? A regressive vector that enslaves it to the past and a progressive one that makes it a detector of meaning. This is the way that needs to be explored. Is not what gives force to a religious symbol its taking up the fantasy of a primitive scene to convert it into an instrument of discovery and an exploration of origins? By their symbolic representations, human beings speak of the founding of their humanity. Through its vestigial function, the symbol shows an imagination of origins at work concerning which we can say that it is "historial," *geschichtlich*, because it speaks of an advent, of a coming into being, but not "historical," *historisch*, because it has no chronological signification.

(3) The properly economic interpretation of the religious phenomenon, as a "return of the repressed," poses the ultimate question: Is religion the monotonous repetition of its own origins, a sempiternal going over and over the ground of its own archaism? For Freud, there is no history of religion. The task here would be to show by what education of desire and fear religion surmounts its own archaism. This ascending dialectic of affects would have to be laid out along with a parallel dialectic of the fantasy. But then it would be necessary to take into account the texts in which and through which religious human beings have "formed" and

---

[13] "It is possible that in these figures Leonardo has denied [*verleugnet*] the unhappiness of his erotic life and has triumphed over it in his art [*und künstlerisch überwunden*], by representing the wishes of the boy, infatuated with his mother, as fulfilled in this blissful union of the male and female natures." *Leonardo da Vinci and a Memory of His Childhood*, S.E. 11:117–18.

"educated" their beliefs. It is not possible to do a psychoanalysis of belief without passing through the interpretation of the "scriptures" in which the object of belief announces itself. And there is hardly any need to say that *Moses and Monotheism* is in no way at the level of an exegesis of the Old Testament. This is why it has no chance of encountering those creations of meaning through which religion distances itself from its primitive model.

However, I do not want to end with these objections by which the reader runs the risk of setting aside the instruction and harsh schooling through which faith can pass under the guidance of Freud and psychoanalysis. We are far from having incorporated the truth of what Freud has to say about religion. He has already reinforced the unbelief of unbelievers; he has hardly begun to purify the faith of believers.

There are two points where we still have something to learn from Freud. The first has to do with the relation of religion to prohibition, the second its relation to consolation. We will not recover the properly biblical dimension of sin so long as we have not liquidated in ourselves what remains of the archaic, the infantile, the neurotic in a "feeling of guilt." Guilt is a trap, an occasion for falling backward, for getting stuck in the pre-moral, for stagnating in our archaisms. Nowhere is it more necessary to pass through a "destruction" in order to recover the genuine sense of sin. Cannot the Freudian critique of the superego lead us back to the Pauline critique of the Law and of works? The result would be that the central figure of religion, which psychoanalysis tells us stems from the prototype of the father, will not be able to carry out its conversion, in the direction of the actual father of Jesus Christ, so long as it has not itself passed through all the degrees corresponding to those of guilt, from fear conveyed through taboos to the sin of injustice, in the sense of the Jewish prophets, and even up to the sin of the righteous, that is, up to the evil of self-righteousness in the Pauline sense of this term.

But perhaps it is in the order of consolation that the lesson of psychoanalysis has not yet been seen. There are in fact two types of consolation, inextricably mixed together: the infantile and idolatrous form, that professed by Job's friends, and, on the other hand, the consolation based on the spirit, which is not narcissistic or based on self-interest, which is not a protection against the calamities of existence nor a refuge against the harshness of life.

This consolation is accessible only through an extreme obedience to reality. It comes through mourning the loss of the first consolation. Anyone who will have gone to the end of this movement will have truly assumed the Freudian iconoclasm into their own movement of faith.

Psychoanalysis and the Work of Art

Opponents of psychoanalysis concur in reproaching it for reducing art and aesthetic creation. An attentive reader of Freud's writings should instead, it seems to me, puzzle over Freud's modesty, his protests of incompetence, his admissions of failure, and, finally, his insistence on stressing the limits of psychoanalysis when applied to art.

Such warnings abound in the last chapter of *Leonardo da Vinci and a Memory of His Childhood*: pathography, it is stated, does not propose to explain the great man's work, and of course no one can be reproached for not delivering what was never promised. The proposed goal lies in explaining Leonardo's inhibitions in his sexual life and in his artistic activity. As for the artist's talent and his capacity for work, these are too intimately tied to sublimation. For this reason we must admit that the essence of the artistic function must remain psychoanalytically inaccessible to us. In short, if psychoanalysis does not explain to us why Leonardo was an artist, it at least allows us to understand the manifestations and the limits of his art.

These are not merely isolated reservations; they can also be found in an *Autobiographical Study*, in *Civilization and Its Discontents*, in the *Outline of Psycho-Analysis*. It is repeatedly asserted in different forms that the aesthetic evaluation of a work of art as well as an explanation of artistic talent are not psychoanalytic tasks.

These persistent precautions should make us stop and think.[1] My investigation aims at measuring their true importance. My inquiry will consider the hypothesis that the admission of an inherent limit in applying psychoanalysis to art is purely tactical, meant only to lower the resistances of a listener or a reader unfamiliar with psychoanalysis to an explanation which, in fact, leaves no remainder. I would like to demonstrate the insufficiencies of arguments supporting this thesis and to seek in Freud's own metapsychoanalysis the reasons for his scruples. I shall thus not consider arguments foreign to Freud's own work but shall limit myself to an internal approach.

I

An initial argument could perhaps be drawn from the strategic function performed by elements borrowed from art in the most incontestable of psychoanalytic works, *The Interpretation of Dreams*. Far from psychoanalysis being constituted without any reference to works of art and then "applied" to them later, the comparison between dreams, symptoms, folktales, and myths is absolutely primitive and organically tied to the central demonstration of the *Traumdeutung*. This parallelism is quite astonishing: from the outset, Freud's fundamental discovery in his self-analysis is placed under the aegis of a hero of Greek legend whose existence is, for us, purely literary. Oedipus exists only in *Oedipus Rex*, a character drawn by Sophocles and nothing more. In this way, an individual drama is at once identified and named through the mediation of a figure which poetry first set up as a mythical paradigm. Of course, it is not the poetic, literary, aesthetic aspect of

---

[1] Do not the introductory declarations of "The Moses of Michelangelo" (1914; S.E. 13:211–36), which we must not forget, was first published anonymously, refer to the same caution? "I may say at once that I am no connoisseur in art, but simply a layman. I have often observed that the subject-matter of works of art has a stronger attraction for me than their formal and technical qualities, though to the artist their value lies first and foremost in the latter. I am unable rightly to appreciate many of the methods used and the effects obtained in art. I state this so as to secure the reader's indulgence for the attempt I propose to make here" (211).

the figure of Oedipus that fascinated Freud, but the "subject-matter" and the identical nature of the content signified by the myth and that revealed by self-analysis. At the very least, one aesthetic feature is relevant: the universality attached to literary fiction. So if the myth is not dealt with as fiction, its meaning does allow a particular psychological fact to bear directly the seal of a universal structure. This is expressed in the very name given to the experience discovered along the strict path of self-analysis, which from now on will bear a Greek name.[2]

This demonstrative schema functions only if, implicitly, one grants that the work of art has the same explanation as the dream. Or, more precisely, it is necessary that dreams and works of art be reciprocally paradigmatic in a demonstration that is strictly circular. This is possible if they occupy the role of some model from different points of view: the dream, from a genetic point of view; the work of art, from a structural one.

Indeed, on the one hand, dream analysis provides the key for interpreting the derivation of meaning, in accordance with the formula that gives chapter 3 of *The Interpretation of Dreams* its title: "a dream is the fulfillment of a wish."[3] The formula itself summarizes a series of propositions: dreams have a meaning; this meaning calls for a precise type of decoding, detail by detail; the latent meaning is separated from the apparent meaning by a work – the "dream-work" – which brings together the relations of force and the relations of meaning, as is expressed in the notions of displacement, condensation, representability, secondary revisions;

---

[2] The letters to Fliess attest to the primitive origins of this parallelism: "One single thought of general value has been revealed to me. I have found in my own case too, falling in love with the mother and jealousy of the father, and I now regard it as a universal event of early childhood. . . . If that is so, we can understand the riveting power of *Oedipus Rex*, in spite of all the objections raised by reason against its presupposition of destiny; and we can understand why the later 'dramas of destiny' were bound to fail so miserably. . . . Each member of the audience was once, in germ and in phantasy, just such an Oedipus, and each one recoils in horror from the dream-fulfillment here transplanted into reality, with the whole quota of repression which separates his infantile state from his present one." Letter to Fliess, Oct. 15, 1897, S.E. 1:265.

[3] S.E. 4:122.

and finally, desires represented in dreams in a disguised manner are the oldest desires, archaic and infantile.

This is what is paradigmatic in dreams and this is what is analogically transposed from the dream to the work of art.

The structural aspect, however, is no less important than the genetic one. We could neither identify nor name a psychical production, if we were not able to detect an invariant to serve as a prime analogon for its diverse variants. It is here that the work of art provides an exemplarity all its own: if self-analysis revealed the "riveting power," the "compulsion" of the Greek legend, in turn the elevation of the intimate personal complex to the level of poetic fiction placed the seal of universality on an experience that would otherwise remain particular, incommunicable, and ultimately silent. The individual secret is a universal fate; for this reason, it can be stated. It has already been stated.

What is at stake in this circular relation is thus much more than the possibility of articulating a theory of culture based on the semantics of desire;[4] it is the possibility of rendering the genesis itself intelligible. The *Three Essays on Sexuality* reveal the fundamentally "historical" aspect of human sexuality, tied to the successive constitutions by which it passes from "stage" to "stage." This "historicity" – which the theory of stages will continue to develop in the course of successive editions of the *Three Essays* – holds within it a serious threat to the scientific character of psychoanalysis. How could the "history" of desire be told if it were not put into forms capable of being fixed in cultural denominations? Genesis must then indeed be based on structure if it is to be an explanation, that is, if it is to make us understand.

[4] It is this aspect that I developed in *Freud and Philosophy*, part 2, "The Interpretations of Culture," in the section titled "The Analogy of the Work of Art" (163–77). This is why the passage to institutions and, with this, the ethical character that becomes part of this universal fate, are strongly emphasized here. The connection between ontogenesis and phylogenesis appeared to me in particular as a means of proving that psychoanalysis is from the outset a theory of culture, because its object is not brute wishes but wishes in a cultural setting. In the present essay, I should like to return to an even more primitive problem, which concerns the very intelligibility of analytic experience. This is why I have insisted on the structural function of literary fiction in relation to the genetic function of analytic interpretation.

This can be shown by a careful study of the instance of literary examples in the *Traumdeutung*. Literary fictions – and among them, the Oedipus tragedy – are evoked in reference to a very special category of dreams, which Freud calls "typical dreams."[5] Among these dreams of universal signification, Freud cites dreams of nudity and exhibition and dreams of the death of close relatives. Unlike the dreams analyzed in the earlier sections, which Freud says constitute a dream-world constructed by each person "according to his individual peculiarities and so make it unintelligible to other people," these dreams have "the same meaning for everyone."[6] Now these are also dreams where the associative method proves particularly inadequate and sterile. It is precisely for these dreams that literature offers a meaningful schema, a sort of double check easier to read than the dream itself. This is possible because the forces of inhibition which are responsible for distorting the dream have been partially eliminated in the literary work for reasons that will be apparent later. This is true in the case of Hans Christian Andersen's story *The Emperor's New Clothes*, which provides a less distorted version of the dream of nudity with its apparent bizarre characteristics.[7] And as the myth of Paradise, where Adam and Eve are naked, has the same root meaning, and since, on the other hand, the fantasy itself appears naked in the perversion termed *exhibitionism*, a series can be formed from dreams, folktales, myths, and symptoms. This series is structured by the invariant we call "typical" dreams and which also forms the meaning of the tale, of the myth, and of the symptom. We shall return later to an important aspect of this structure, namely, the fact that the invariable is nothing other than the cross-reference from one variant to the other: dream, symptom, myth, tale. For the present, let us content ourselves with recognizing the

[5] S.E. 4:241–76.

[6] Ibid., 241.

[7] Speaking of dreams of nakedness, where the dreamer is embarrassed and the spectators are strangely indifferent, Freud observes: "We possess an interesting piece of evidence that the dream in the form in which it appears – partly distorted by wish-fulfillment – has not been rightly understood. For it has become the basis [*die Grundlage*] of a fairy tale which is familiar to us all in Andersen's version, *The Emperor's New Clothes*" (ibid., 243).

way in which the genesis is reinforced by the structure through the mediation of poetic fiction.[8]

Indeed, it is this very reciprocal relation between individual genesis and universal type that permits the connection of dreams of the death of a close relative, dreams accompanied by deep grief, to the Oedipus legend. Before he even mentions Sophocles' tragedy, Freud insists on "the obscure information which is brought to us by mythology and legend from the primeval ages of human society."[9] Out of this obscure information there progressively appears "an unpleasing picture of the father's despotic powers and of the ruthlessness with which he made use of it. Kronos devoured his children, just as the wild boar devours the sow's litter; while Zeus emasculated his father and made himself ruler in his place."[10] Freud is able to pass from this mythological notation to the analysis of some dreams of adult neurotics in analysis about death. And this is because, for him, there is no line of demarcation between the normal and the pathological. At most, neurotics present "on a magnified scale" the same feelings of love and hate as do most children.[11] This is why one can follow the inverse path, from the symptom toward the legend: "This discovery is confirmed by a legend that has come down to us from classical antiquity: a legend whose profound and universal power to move can only be understood if the hypothesis I have put forward in regard to the psychology of children has an equally universal validity. What I have in mind is the legend of King Oedipus and Sophocles' drama which bears his name."[12]

---

[8] Freud is content to note: "There can be no doubt that the connections between our typical dreams and fairy tales and the material of other kinds of creative writing are neither few nor accidental. It sometimes happens that the sharp eye of a creative writer has an analytic realization of the process of transformation of which he is habitually no more than the tool. If so, he may follow the process in a reverse direction and so trace back the imaginative writing to a dream" (ibid., 243). For example, the legend of Ulysses as he appears to the eyes of Nausicaa and her maidservants is reconverted into a familiar dream by Gottfried Keller in "Der grüne Heinrich" (ibid., 246).

[9] Ibid., 256.

[10] Ibid.

[11] Ibid.

[12] Ibid., 261.

It is thus the psychology of children that furnishes the core of the argument, provided that it has "universal validity." But it is the legend and its literary elaboration that provide the evidence for this. The explanation is thus perfectly circular: psychoanalysis brings out "the particular nature of the material" – which a bit further on is called "the primaeval dream-material"; but it is the tragedy which makes it speak: "There must be something which makes a voice within us ready to recognize the compelling force of destiny in the *Oedipus*. . . . His destiny moves us only because it might have been ours – because the oracle laid the same curse upon us before our birth as upon him. . . . Our dreams convince us that that is so."[13] The drama's superiority in regard to dreams consists only in that it "shows" us our desires as they are both realized and punished. But the drama, in its turn can be traced back to the dream, as was the case in the Andersen fairy tale. In Sophocles' tragedy itself, the myth's meaning is mirrored in a dream which occurs as a quotation; Jocasta herself consoles Oedipus with these words:

> Many a man ere now in dreams has lain
> With her who bare him. He hath least annoy
> Who with such omens troubleth not his mind.[14]

But the role of literary fiction is not only that of revealing the universality of a structure; it also allows us to specify in what the structural invariant consists. It is not an atemporal essence but the law governing a series, the law of constructing cross-references from one variant to the other. We have already seen, in connection with the "typical" dream of nudity, how the meaning of the dream was repeated in different ways in the fairy tale, the myth, and the perverse symptom. Within the sphere of fiction the same kinds of cross-references occur: the "type" signified by a dream refers to various poetic creations which can be arranged according to a scale of distortion, following the degree to which repression has altered the basic readability. In this way, the structural kinship between *Hamlet* and *Oedipus*, perceived as early as the period of the letters to Fliess, is founded both on the identity "of the same

[13] Ibid., 262.
[14] Lewis Campbell translation, ll.982ff., quoted in S.E. 4:264.

material" and on "the whole difference in the mental life of these two widely separated epochs of civilization: the secular advance of repression in the emotional life of mankind."[15] In *Hamlet*, the repression is so accentuated that it is only from the hero's inhibitions that one can then move back to the oedipal core – namely, that Hamlet is unable to accomplish the prescribed vengeance "on the man who did away with his father and took that father's place with his mother, this man who shows him the repressed wishes of his own childhood realized."[16]

It is not the accuracy of Freud's interpretation of *Hamlet* that I am concerned with here, but its strategic function in his demonstration. It aims at strengthening the invariability of the "type" by relating the difference in regard to another version of the same symbol to forces that cause the identity in meaning to be dispersed under various disguises. At the same time, this identity exists nowhere but in the correlation, not only of the dream fantasy and the literary drama but also of different cultural expressions of the same theme.

It is this thematic unity of works of art, dreams, and symptoms that gives the present argument its force and inclines some to consider Freud's scruples, mentioned earlier in this essay, to be only simulated. The strict parallelism implied in the circular argumentation of the *Traumdeutung* makes it very plausible that Freud's reservations are only a clever tactic for dealing with the resistances of a nonanalytic public.

However, this argument by itself is not decisive. And this for one important reason. The purely strategic – and if one may say so, simply apologetic – use of literary examples, of poetic fictions, in a work expressly dealing with the interpretation of dreams, precisely excludes treating cultural works according to their specific nature, that is, as artistic creations. On the contrary, only their libidinal origin is taken into consideration, what above we called the "material" (*Rohstoff*), "the primaeval dream-material" from which the legend arose. Now Freud's scruples, we remember, concerned the formal and aesthetic qualities of the work as a creation. We thus cannot confine ourselves to the first argument.

---

[15] "In the *Oedipus* the child's wishful phantasy that underlies it is brought into the open and realized as it would be in a dream" (ibid.).
[16] Ibid., 265.

II

A second argument against the actual sincerity of Freud's modest claims in regard to the application of psychoanalysis to art can be drawn from the few studies in which works of art no longer serve only as supporting examples but are analyzed in themselves. These essays seem to justify the assertion that these works are analogues to dreams and to symptoms and that the analogy itself is based in the fantasmatic structure common to the series of analogues. Indeed, the analogy is not a vague resemblance but a constructed kinship.

Let us see, then, how Freud marks out what I shall call the space of fantasy in general and distributes the figures of fantasy within this homogeneous setting.

The short essay *Der Dichter und das Phantasieren* (1908), translated into English under the title "Creative Writers and Day-Dreaming,"[17] prepares the reader for this unitary vision of the entire field of *das Phantasieren* by ordering along a graduated scale diverse mental productions, whose extreme forms seem to lack any common measure: the fantasies of the dreamer and of the neurotic at one end of the spectrum; poetic creations, which the layman attributes to a "separate personality," at the other end of the spectrum. The distance between them can be reduced if one can insert suitable intermediaries between the opposing terms. This is the tactic employed by this clever little essay. The intermediary degrees considered here are children's games and adult's day-dreams (*Tagträume*). Then come folktales, where the hero portrays "his majesty the Ego, the hero alike of every day-dream and of every story."[18] Then come psychological novels, which are related to the egocentric type by a series of gradual transitions until one reaches the point where the author appears to be the spectator of his characters' actions. The continuity of these transitions allows the extension, step by step, of the model of *Wunscherfüllung* (wish-fulfillment) provided by the interpretation of dreams. The critical difference between the work of art and the fantasy does not, then, reside in the instinctual "material"

[17] S.E. 9:143–53.
[18] Ibid., 150.

(*Rohstoff*) employed but in the technique by means of which the writer obtains the effect produced on his reader. While the day-dream causes shame only in the dreamer and makes him tend to hide his fantasies from others, the artist creates pleasure out of what should repel us or leave us cold.

How? All *ars poetica*, Feud tells us, is contained in the techniques by which the artist manages to seduce us by offering us an "increment of pleasure," a purely formal pleasure, belonging to the very representation of fantasies. This "incentive bonus" – technically termed "fore-pleasure" – allows us to take pleasure in the liberation of psychic forces which find their fantasmatic expression in the work. "We give the name of an *incentive bonus*, or a *fore-pleasure*, to a yield of pleasure such as this, which is offered to us so as to make possible the release of still greater pleasure arising from deeper psychical sources."[19]

This distinction between the thematic and the technical allows the difference between the fantasy and the work of art to be included in the sphere of the *Phantasieren* (which I am calling here "fantasy in general"). And this distinction does not cast "technique" outside the space of fantasy, to the extent that the theory of "fore-pleasure" itself arises out of the common economy that presides over the release of tensions coming from the unconscious sphere, which will later be called the "id." But, as early as the *Three Essays on Sexuality*, the theory of the "incentive bonus" is solidly anchored in the first theory of instinctual drives. As in the series of maneuvers that bring the complete sexual act to its term, aesthetic pleasure serves to set off deep-seated discharges. This connection between technique and the hedonistic thus keeps the work of art within the sphere of wish-fulfillment. At the same time, it reveals what is essential to Freud's strategy as he confronts the great enigma of creativity. Unable to be worked out as a whole, it is dissolved bit by bit. After isolating the thematic, one steps around the obstacle of creation by replacing it with the question of the effect produced on the art lover, and one links the technique to the effect of pleasure. The problem is thus kept within the bounds of the range of the economy of desire.

It was in *Jokes and their Relation to the Unconscious* (1905) that Freud first transposed his concept of the economy of fore-

[19] Ibid., 153.

pleasure from the theory of instinctual drives to aesthetics.[20] Jokes indeed have the advantage of presenting for analysis a precise pleasure-effect, for it is pinpointed by the release of laughter. As such, the purely verbal techniques of *Witz* present nothing strikingly new in regard to what the analysis of the dream-work had brought to light: condensation, displacement, representation by the contrary, etc.; nothing new except an emphasis that the very notion of "dream-work" did not allow to be foreseen, in the sense of a correspondence between these procedures and certain rhetorical figures. This more or less linguistic interpretation of the "distortion" performed by the dream-work unquestionably allows the entire field of verbal productions to be annexed to the domain of fantasy. But it is in particular by reason of its contribution to an economic theory of laughter that the essay on *Witz* assures the continuity among all the phenomena belonging to the space of fantasy. The pure technique using words, characteristic of *Witz*, gives the mind a surface pleasure that serves as a release for forces that are hidden in the obscene, aggressive, or cynical modalities of word play. The pleasure taken in word play, as a work on the body of the word, is in itself a minimal pleasure, tied to the saving of psychical work which is realized in condensation, displacement, etc. In this way, the pleasure derived from nonsense frees us from the restrictions that logic inflicts on our thought and lightens the yoke of every intellectual pursuit. But if this pleasure is minimal, as are the savings it expresses, it still has the remarkable power of contributing, in the form of a bonus, to the erotic, aggressive, or skeptical tendencies.

Thus the puzzle of aesthetic technique fades out of sight if it is considered not from the perspective of the creator but from that of the effect produced on the public. At the same time, this weakens the objection that could be drawn from the fact that the author cannot be submitted to analytic investigation because he is unable to contribute by his associations – and especially through the work of transference – to clarifying the energies freed by his own imaginative creation. For if the author is out of reach, the art lover who experiences the pleasure-effect produced by the work of art is accessible to analytic investigation. He is in the position of the nocturnal dreamer and of the day-dreamer.

[20] S.E. 8.

Once the space of fantasy has been delimited by this initial work of circumspection, it is then possible to determine the features of the space of fantasy that guarantee the homogeneity of the phenomena placed under this common heading. I should like to stress two of these features which, in Freud's work, determine *Phantasieren* in its very essence.

The first is discussed within the framework of the dream-work, in chapter 6 of the *Traumdeutung*, under the heading "Considerations of Representability" (*Rücksicht auf Darstellbarkeit*).[21] It is the third operation of the dream-work, after condensation and displacement. This operation consists in substituting for a verbal expression of a given thought a "pictorial" expression. But the figurability of this *Darstellbarkeit* exceeds representability in visual images, for it extends to the verbal images themselves, which, by reason of this figurative capacity, are restored to their full polysemic resources and to the entire range of their ambiguities. This causes Freud to say that language is here carried back to the ancient richness of hieroglyphic writing.[22] This representability – something like an aptitude for *staging* – is treated elsewhere under the title of "formal" regression (in order to distinguish it from "temporal" regression and "topological" regression);[23] that is, it is treated as the regression of logical links moving toward concrete and figurative expression. Its kinship with hieroglyphic writing allows us, in turn, to extend to the nonverbal aspects of dreams the notion of a "text" which covers the entire field of what is figurable. It is this "textual" aspect, in the extended sense of the word, that is implied when we apply to dreams, in all of their figurative aspects, the metaphor of censorship, whose initial use referred to the "blotting out" of correspondence, newspapers, and literary texts in general by a political authority with an essentially repressive function. Figurability, however, attests to the nonverbal character of the dream-work, even in its properly

---

[21] S.E. 5:339–49.

[22] "Yet, in spite of all this ambiguity, it is fair to say that the productions of the dream-work, which it must be remembered, *are not made with the intention of being understood*, present no greater difficulties to their translators than do the ancient hieroglyphic scripts to those who seek to read them" (ibid., 341).

[23] Ibid., 548.

verbal expressions. When it utilizes language, it continues to be nonverbal to the extent that its writing is more hieroglyphic than phonetic.

This nonverbal or preverbal character of the figurative text of dreams explains the ease with which one can, without leaving the space of figurative fantasy, move to more plastic expressions, as, for instance, in the case of examples borrowed from statuary.

We find this in the essay "The Moses of Michelangelo."[24] The marble statue of *Moses*, sculpted by Michelangelo for the church of San Pietro in Vincoli in Rome, is treated in this way as a fantasy objectified in stone. The puzzle it offers to our understanding and the effect it produces on our sensibilities are treated in terms of the enigma and the affective effect that a dream produces in "staging" itself. In both cases, it is the "intention" of the artist and of the dreamer that is to be discovered by way of analysis. "To discover his intention, though, I must first find out the meaning and the content of what is represented in his work; I must, in other words, be able to *interpret* it."[25] The work of stone and the work of words (it is not by chance that *Hamlet* is evoked once more in this context), to the extent that they are different modalities of the same fundamental figurability, give rise to the same need – "the need of discovering in it some source of power beyond them [the impressive thoughts and the splendor of language] alone."[26] It is not surprising therefore that a statue should be treated exactly like a dream. In both cases interpretation involves the same attention to unnoticed details, the same sort of separate treatment – analytic in the strict sense of the word – of each of these details taken in themselves, especially those that are disregard or ignored ("the rubbish-heap, as it were, of our observations").[27] For example, the position of Moses' right-hand finger in relation to the draping of his beard, the position of the tablets of the Law upside down and balancing on an edge. In this way, little by little, the figure of a compromise is drawn between opposing movements that took place the instant before and of which there remain only vestiges in the present position: "What we see

[24] S.E. 13:211–36.
[25] Ibid., 212.
[26] Ibid., 213.
[27] Ibid., 222.

before us is not the inception of a violent action but the remains of a movement that has already taken place."[28]

What follows in the essay confirms that the statue can and must be deciphered like a "text." Freud returns here to a written text, the book of Exodus, in order to measure the differences between Michelangelo's stone text and that of Scripture. The meaning of Michelangelo's work lies in the difference between the two texts, one depicting a hero in the throes of violent anger, the other daring to create "a different Moses . . . one superior to the historical or traditional Moses."[29] What is more, the interpretation can go so far as to grasp the realization, not only in terms of its difference in regard to an earlier textual and scriptural model, but its difference in regard to the idea that analysis reconstructs. Freud hazards this conclusion: "In his creations Michelangelo has often enough gone to the utmost limit of what is expressible in art; and perhaps in his statute of Moses he has not completely succeeded, if his purpose [*seine Absicht*] was to make the passage of a violent gust of passion visible in the signs left behind it in the ensuing calm."[30] Moving back in this way from the realization to the intention, analysis can retranslate the intention into words: "But why should the artist's intention not be capable of being communicated and comprehended in *words*, like any other fact of mental life?"[31] It is this verbal translation of a plastic figure that emerges in the words that sum up the essay: "And so he carved his Moses on the Pope's tomb, not without a reproach against the dead pontiff, as a warning to himself, thus, in self-criticism, rising superior to his own nature."[32]

These successive translations from writing into a message in stone, and then again from stone into discourse, are produced within the same space of fantasy on the basis of the figurability common to its different expressions.

This last remark leads us to the second characteristic of the fantastic as such, which founds the analogy of its various incarnations. This is its character of being basically substitutive, that is,

[28] Ibid., 229.
[29] Ibid., 223.
[30] Ibid., 236.
[31] Ibid., 212.
[32] Ibid., 234.

of a sign's capacity to hold for, to take the place of, to replace something else.

This substitutive character is implied in the psychoanalytic notion of "meaning"; to say that dreams have "meaning" is not to designate what they mean in appearance but to point to the latent meaning that is to be reconstructed from them. This is why it is necessary to interpret: "for 'interpreting' a dream implies assigning a 'meaning' to it that is, replacing [*ersetzen*] it by something which fits into the chain of our mental acts as a link having a validity and importance equal to the rest."[33]

Interpretation, though, does no more than follow the inverse route of that taken by the dream-work. The latter fulfills a wish only by dissimulating its object under a substituted object. For this reason, the symptomatic value of dreams is due entirely to the absolutely primitive substitutability of the sign-effect. Transposition, deformation, distortion – all effects that are included in the German expression *Traumentstellung* ("distortion" in English) – are grounded in this capacity of a sign to replace something else, principally, other signs. The relation hiding–showing, which is essential to the idea of "the disguised fulfillment of a repressed wish," is a result of this substitution by which the "same meaning" is preserved in the "other" meaning. Displacement and condensation are just the mechanisms by which substitution renders itself unrecognizable, without canceling the chain of meanings. And the whole psychoanalytic analytic maneuver is built upon a substitution in the opposite direction: How, Freud asks at the beginning of the essay on "The Unconscious," do we arrive at knowledge of the unconscious? His answer: "It is of course only as something conscious that we know it, after it has undergone transformation [*Umsetzung*] or translation [*Übersetzung*] into something conscious."[34]

Substitution takes on the precise form given to it by psychoanalysis when it is combined with the preceding feature, staging, which is essential to the figurability of dreams. More precisely, it is when dreams refer back to some infantile scene that figurability and substitutability combine their effects: "On this view a dream might be described as a *substitute* [*Ersatz*] *for an infantile scene*

[33] *Interpretation of Dreams*, S.E. 4:96.
[34] S.E. 14:166.

modified by being transferred onto a recent experience. The infantile scene is unable to bring about its own revival and has to be content with returning as a dream."[35]

In the figurable-substitutable character of fantasies, we grasp the most important feature of the Freudian "fantastic." The most primitive possibility of the work of art is contained in this, at first disconcerting, discovery that we are never dealing with signs that would give us the thing itself, but with signs that are already signs of signs.

In order to understand this, we must go back to what Freud calls primal repression, which means that every observable repression, to which we are able to relate this or that distortion, is already a subsequent repression, "after the fact" (*nachträglich*) in relation to the *Urverdrängte* that is always posited behind "proper" [*eigentlich*] repression. Because of this, we never witness an initial substitution, and analysis is compelled to move among signs of signs. Of course, psychoanalysis must posit at the level of theoretical concepts, and consequently at the level of metapsychological construction, something like an initial psychic "presentation" of drives, a primordial "holding for." In his writings on metapsychology, Freud creates to this end the concept of *Repräsentanz* – a technical term, here translated as *presentation* (*representation* in the Standard Edition). At the beginning of the essay on "The Unconscious," we read: "We have learnt from psychoanalysis that the essence of the process of repression lies not in putting an end to, in annihilating, the idea which represents an instinct [*den Trieb repräsentierende Vorstellung*], but in preventing it from becoming conscious."[36]

This absolutely primitive linking of force and meaning is presupposed by every "transposition" and every "translation" from the unconscious to the conscious. But it is presupposed only as a theoretical construction which allows psycho-*analysis* to be *psycho*-analysis, that is, always to deal not with instincts – presumed biological realities – but with the "representatives of instinct," whether these representatives be "ideas" or "affects." The decisive fact is that psychoanalysis moves, has always moved, among the "mental derivatives [*psychische Abkömmlinge*] of the repressed

---

[35] *The Interpretation of Dreams*, S.E. 5:546.
[36] S.E. 14:166.

representative."[37] The notion of primal repression is there to remind us that we are always in the mediate, in the already expressed, the already said: "The second stage of repression, *repression proper*, affects mental derivatives of the repressed representative, or such trains of thought [*Gedankenzüge*] as, originating elsewhere, have come into associative connection with it."[38] It is therefore because analysis knows only secondary distortions that it also knows only signs of signs. Communication between the systems *Ucs.*, *Pcs.*, *Cs.*, can only be deciphered inside the signifying architecture of the derivatives: "In brief, it must be said that the *Ucs.* is continued into [*setzt sich in*] what are known as derivatives."[39] "Formation substitutives," "symptoms," "return of the repressed" are so many different vicissitudes which guide the play of substitutions. The possible combinations revealed here are immense: among the "derivatives" of the *Ucs.*, some present both the superior organization of the *Cs.* system and the specific laws of the *Ucs.* system. These hybrid formations we know well: they are the fantasies of the normal individual and of the neurotic, but they are also the highly complex substitutive formations with which the artist plays.

If we apply these remarks from the metapsychology to the notion of the psychic text proposed above, then it must be said that psychoanalysis knows only "translations" of texts, different versions for which we can provide from no original text. Being in some sense primitive, substitution is the very fabric of the "fantastic."

In this respect, so-called childhood memories provide the best example of this fantastic constitution, and prefigure works of fiction. The very expression "infantile scene," which we borrowed earlier from the *Traumdeutung*, expresses the twofold character of figurability and distortion in the very play of theatrical exposition. No formation demonstrates better what the fantasy's construction "after the fact" consists of than does the "screen-memory." Through its character of being already substituted, this memory belongs to the "fantastic." The poetic imagination has no need to be grafted onto memory; it is already at

[37] Ibid., 148.
[38] Ibid.
[39] Ibid., 190.

work there. Between *Dichten* and *Phantasieren* the link is absolutely primitive.

On the basis of this analysis, the position that can be taken against the irreducibility of the work of art is clear. The same interplay of figurability and substitution already at work in dreams and memory continues in aesthetics. Is this not what was presupposed above by the work of interpretation when it referred back from a dream to a fairy tale, from a fairy tale to a myth, in order to go back to a perverse symptom? Was not this cross-reference from one level to the other based upon the eminently substitutable character of fantasy in general? Furthermore, is not the deciphering itself entirely reducible to this interplay of references?

There is no doubt that this is one of the most decisive implications of the Freudian understanding of fantasy for the theory of art. The possibility of treating a work of art as a dream is based on the possibility of substituting one for the other. The admirable short essay, "Das Unheimliche" (1919) – "The 'Uncanny'" – draws, in this respect, the ultimate consequences of the absolutely homogeneous nature of the fantastic resulting from the mutual substitutability of these expressions.[40] Hoffmann's "Fantastic Tales" can be treated like a dream because tales and dreams stand for one another. In this way, the tale "Der Sandmann" – "The Sandman," who tears out the eyes of little children, throws them in his sack, and carries them to the moon as fodder for his hook-beaked young – is the equivalent of a dream. The fear expressed here is a substitute for something else, namely, the fear of castration; and this substitution becomes "intelligible as soon as we replace the Sand-Man by the dreaded father at whose hands castration is expected."[41]

Dreams and fairy tales are thus substitutable, just as in a dream and in a fairy tale castration and tearing out eyes are substitutable, just as in the story of the child Nathaniel, the father and Coppelius "represent the two opposites into which the father-imago is split by his ambivalence [the child's feelings]; whereas the one threatens to blind him – that is, to castrate him – , the other, the 'good' father, intercedes for his sight."[42] The equivalence of the modes of

[40] S.E. 17:219–56.
[41] Ibid., 232.
[42] Ibid., 232n.

the fantastic (dream and fairy tale) is made possible by reason of the constitutive substitution of the fantasy (tearing out eyes/punishing). The "uncanny" effect this tale produces comes from an affective material no different from that produced by the return of the repressed in dreams: something that is at once most "familiar" (*heimlich*) to us because most personal, and at the same time seems "strange" (*unheimlich*), for it has become foreign to us.

We should go perhaps even further. This primordial substitutability belonging to fantasy would explain not only that dreams, tales, myths, and symptoms can be exchanged one for another, but that humanity has to create works of art just as it has to dream. If substitution is indeed the essence of the fantastic, mankind had to try to structure its fantasies because of the impossibility of an absolutely original return of the repressed. If a primal "presentation" is impossible, if a lived restitution is impossible, is the only way to rediscover one's childhood, which is behind one, to create it before oneself, in a work?

This final consequence also marks the return of our initial qualms. They concerned two points: aesthetic technique and artistic talent. To what extent have they been removed? As for the first one, we can say that the difficulty was circumvented, not resolved. The effect on the spectator of the technique of "fore-pleasure" is acknowledged, but this technique itself continues to be impenetrable. Psychoanalysis shows in what way dreams and works of art are substitutable; their essential dissymmetry is yet to be understood. It is one thing to fantasize at night in dreams. It is something else again to produce a lasting object – a sculpture, painting, or poem – the sole reality that can take the place of that absent original, what we call the impressions of early childhood. It is here that our qualms in regard to the first point are extended to the second one: for if the artist makes a lasting work, it is because he is successful in structuring his fantasies outside of himself. In what can this talent possibly consist?

If we keep this question in mind, we can see that an essay like "The Moses of Michelangelo" succeeds to the extent that this question is bracketed. It is indeed remarkable that the statute is treated as an object isolated from the rest of Michelangelo's work and from the great text of his life. It is compared only to the corresponding biblical text, which is itself isolated from its context (and in addition, in the appendix of 1927, to the *Moses* of Nicolas de Verdun – that is, to another variant of the archetypical Moses, caught here at the very moment when the storm of passions is being unleashed and not, as in Michelangelo's *Moses*, at the moment when the calm has returned after the storm). Psychoanalysis succeeds, then, to the extent that it can delimit the structural unity of a "type" (here, the "type" Moses) and can make this unity pass through its diverse textual variants. Freud's scruples begin short of – and beyond – the case in which the individuality of a variant is to be carried back to the creative genius of an extraordinary personality.

But perhaps it is the question itself that should come under suspicion.

III

Here, a third argument takes over: if, in the texts we have just examined, Freud does not directly undertake a study of the enigma par excellence, of artistic creation, it will be held that this is because the theme of "talent," of "genius," or of "creation" is not at bottom aesthetical but theological. And along with this, that it belongs to a hidden ideology, whose privileged cultural expressions arise from a cultural sphere other than art, one that Freud has indeed marked out elsewhere, in his writings on religion. The very idea of a creator, in effect, conserves a religious resonance, perhaps even in the most rationalistic of minds. It is in the rationalistic mind that this theological ideology finds its final refuge: Is not the creator the father of his works, and thus a father figure? As Sarah Kofman writes in *The Childhood of Art*, it is only in a theological conception of art that one can posit "a free conscious subject, the father of his works as God is of creation."[43]

Freud's scruples, which we referred to at the beginning of this essay, attest to his having accepted, if not in what he does at least in what he says, the ideology of genius. Yet the strategic function of his qualms is revealed when we read that to shatter the idol of the artist, the hidden figure of the father, is, in the final analysis,

[43] Sarah Kofman, *The Childhood of Art: An Interpretation of Freud's Aesthetics*, trans. Winifred Woodhull (New York: Columbia University Press, 1988), 20.

"to accomplish a murder, that of the artist as genius, as great man."[44] This is why the application of psychoanalysis to art encounters the strongest of resistances. Freud's scruples are meant to take this resistance into account. But in order to unmask such resistance, it is only necessary to "read Freud's texts on art in accordance with a method of deciphering that he himself has taught, by distinguishing between what he says and what he actually does in his discourse."[45] Reading Freud's text with a suspicious eye would then not risk being arbitrary, but would conform to the prototype found in Freud's own writings on religion. These texts can then be shown to contain the key to a self-critique which, applied to the texts on art, would put an end to the sort of self-censure that continues to function there, whether sincerely or as a trick.

In the light of texts such as *The Future of an Illusion*, *Civilization and Its Discontents*, and *Moses and Monotheism*, the cult of the genius in art indeed appears to be cut from the same instinctual fabric as does that of the religious genius. In both instances, over-evaluating the father in early childhood, rivaling him, repressing the murder-wish directed toward him, and finally internalizing his figure, all lead to the same kind of disguised sublime figures. The principal difference between the cult of art and the religion of the father lies in the fact that the artistic phase corresponds to the narcissistic stage, and the religious phase to that of the cathexis of the libido, to the fixation of the parents – to employ the progressive schema of *Totem and Taboo* (which speaks not of the artistic phase but of the animist phase). This parallelism would thus make art "the last bastion of narcissism."[46]

This argument has the advantage of revealing how dangerous it can be to apply psychoanalysis to art. To destroy the idea of genius is to repeat the murder of the father. At the same time, "The Moses of Michelangelo" can no longer remain unrelated to *Moses and Monotheism*. By analyzing Michelangelo's statue, does Freud not commit, in regard to the great sculptor's genius, the same murder that formerly the Hebrews committed in regard to the great prophet? Nor can we leave aside the claims of veneration

[44] Ibid., 26.
[45] Ibid., 35.
[46] Ibid.

addressed to the "good nature" that resides in creators of art and the attack against the same idea of the "good nature" of benevolent providence, when this idea is professed by a religious mind. No, we cannot fail to transfer to the aesthetics of genius Freud's own statements in "The Economic Problem of Masochism," in which the terms Nature, God, and Providence are replaced by *Logos* and *Ananke*.[47]

This form of argumentation is certainly one of the strongest to be directed against an interpretation that would take literally the most modest of Freud's statements concerning psychoanalysis's "application" to art. Yet it does not appear to me to entirely resolve the problem.

If, indeed, the ideology of genius prevents a scientific explanation of artistic talent, we cannot simply set it aside in order to account completely for the phenomenon of aesthetic creation. I would say, on the contrary, that it is by raising the hypothesis of the ideology of genius that Freud exposes the true difficulty, the one that concerns the destiny of the instinctual drives in the case of aesthetic activity. In fact, as soon as the investigation is directed along this path, we quickly will discover that his qualms expressed in regard to aesthetic creation coincide quite precisely with those that Freud expresses elsewhere on the subject of the psychoanalytic treatment of the instinctual vicissitude he calls "sublimation."

This is what is shown by the text I have held in reserve until now: *Leonardo da Vinci and a Memory of his Childhood*.

We cannot say of this text what was said above about "The Moses of Michelangelo," namely, that it avoids the problem of creation by substituting for it the analysis of a fantasy objectified in stone, nor that it replaces the problem of creation with that of the effects produced on the art lover. The problem of creation and creator is instead placed at the center of this work, and the constellation of fantasies, memories, and creations at the periphery of the instinctual core of the man Leonardo.

It is precisely by doing this that Freud comes in contact with the two enigmas of creation and sublimation, which resemble one another and form a pair. What is it about Leonardo that has puzzled most critics? Not so much his genius as the fact that for

[47] S.E. 19:168.

him investigation replaced creation, that his interest was increasingly directed toward science, that even in his artistic activity he was so peculiarly slow and intermittent – even negligent – in his work, and finally that he was indifferent to the outcome of this or that work. In considering the artist's inhibitions and Leonardo's distance from sexuality and from his own homosexuality, kept from any possible realization, Freud confronts the problem which, to my mind, guarantees the complete coherence of this brief work: the problem of converting libido into sublimated energy. Sublimation is proposed here as the third vicissitude of infantile sexual investigation during the period when repression puts an end to the first attempts at intellectual independence; alongside neurotic inhibition and obsession, where thought becomes entirely sexual, there is a third type, "the rarest and most perfect" one; here, "the libido evades the fate of repression by being sublimated from the very beginning into curiosity and by becoming attached to the powerful instinct for research as a reinforcement."[48] It is this capacity to sublimate the greater part of his libido into an instinct for research that makes Leonardo the "the prototype of all later intellectual work directed towards the solution of problems."[49]

If we continue to keep in mind this relation established initially between the peculiar modality of creation in Leonardo and the general problem of sublimation as the fate of instinct, what follows in Freud's work can be seen at once to form a coherent whole. The second and third chapters deal with the fantasy that gives the work its title "a memory of [Leonardo's] childhood," but they include no references to, no mention of, Leonardo's paintings. This point is of the greatest importance for an understanding of Freud's work. For here it is not a question of creation or of sublimation. The entire analysis unfolds within the space of figurability and of substitution by which we earlier characterized the fantastic as such. The "memory," as we know, is the famous vulture opening the infant's mouth with its tail. This memory is treated as a construction "after the fact," cast back into childhood. It serves as a link to an entire series of "translations" which reveal nothing other than the capacity for substituting the figures

[48] S.E. 11:80.
[49] Ibid., 79n.

of fantasy for one another, not to mention the oneiric, or mythical, or literary modality of them. The "translations" are mutually equivalent in regard to the meaning content: the fantasy of passive homosexuality is traded for the image of the maternal breast; the mother is replaced by the vulture in the hieroglyphic writing of the Egyptians; in its turn, the maternal vulture, which according to legend is impregnated by the wind, is traded for the husbandless mother of Leonardo's early childhood. The circle formed by these translations can indeed sometimes pass through a private fantasy – which Freud does not hesitate to call the "real content of the memory"; sometimes through a mythical symbol – the goddess Mut, image of the phallic mother; and, finally, to close the circle through a fantasy tied to an infantile sexual theory, the infantile hypothesis of the maternal penis: In all this, Freud does nothing more than transfer to Leonardo's "case" the most confirmed psychoanalytic theories regarding the laws of fantasy.[50]

In this way, until a work has been brought into play, we remain inside a system of pure equivalents, moving from Leonardo's "memory," to homosexual dreams, to the imaginative structure of the first infantile theories on sex, to the mythical representation of the phallic mother. Something new appeared when, beginning with chapter 4, an aesthetic object was introduced: the *Mona Lisa*'s smile, which is also repeated in the smile of the *Madonna and Child with St. Anne* and in all the "Leonardesque" smiles. In one sense – the meaning which the theme of the fantastic has revealed up to now – the *Mona Lisa*'s smile is interchangeable with the fantasy about the vulture: "it was his mother who possessed the mysterious smile – the smile that he had lost and that had fascinated him so much when he found it again in the Florentine lady."[51] In this sense, it is his mother's smile, the memory of which was awakened by the Florentine lady, that is painted on the canvas; it is the smile which, during the period when the *Madonna and Child with St. Anne* was painted, "drove him at

[50] On two occasions, Freud even makes Leonardo's unconscious speak through the psychoanalytic translation: "That was a time when my fond curiosity was directed to my mother and when I still believed she had a genital organ like my own" (ibid., 98). And: "through this erotic relation to my mother . . . I became a homosexual" (ibid., 106).
[51] Ibid., 111.

once to create a glorification of motherhood, and to give back to his mother the smile that he had found in the noble lady."[52]

This is why Freud can say that "the picture contains the synthesis of the history of his childhood: its details are to be explained by reference to the most personal impressions in Leonardo's life."[53]

So runs the interpretation within the limits of Freud's theory of fantasy, marked by the dual traits of figurability and substitutability. The equivalence of the painted smile and the fantasy of the vulture seems perfect: the "same" infantile impression engenders both: Leonardo "strove to reproduce the smile with his brush, giving it to all his pictures."[54]

But there follows immediately a slight adjustment that undercuts the equivalence: "It is possible that in these figures Leonardo has denied the unhappiness of his erotic life and has triumphed over it in his art, by representing the wishes of the boy, infatuated with his mother, as fulfilled in this blissful union of the male and female natures."[55] These words alone – *denied* and *triumphed over* – express, in regard to the work itself, the enigma of sublimation in the dynamics of instinctual drives. In regard to the work, sublimation signifies that the fantasy and the painting are not interchangeable: We can go from the work to the fantasy; we cannot find the work in the fantasy. What is expressed in economic terms in the first chapter as the libido replacing "its immediate aim by other aims which may be valued more highly and which are not sexual," is expressed in objective terms as the elevation of the fantasy to a work.[56] Transposing the famous saying *wo es war, soll ich werden* – "where id was, must ego be" – I am tempted to say, where there was the fantasy of the vulture, there must come to be the mother's smile as a pictorial work. The enigma of the *Mona Lisa*'s smile is not the fantasy of the vulture. For the painted smile does not repeat any real memory, not that of the lost mother nor that of the Florentine lady whose encounter triggered the regression to the childhood memory and kindled a new erotic flare-up, more powerful than his inhibitions. The

[52] Ibid., 112.
[53] Ibid.
[54] Ibid., 117.
[55] Ibid., 117–18.
[56] Ibid., 78.

celebrated smile – the Leonardesque smile – is a figurative innovation in relation to any repetition of fantasies. The work of art is
not limited to exhibiting the object of a desire; for the kisses of
the first mother, the lost mother, are themselves lost insofar as
they are real memories; the fantasy is always a substitute for
something absent that is signified; its sole presence is that created
by the painter; the true smile, which will be sought in vain, is not
behind us, in some actual event that could be relived, it is in front
of us, on the painted canvas.[57]

The entire theoretical enigma of sublimation is concentrated
here in the passage from a simple "mental derivative" – the fantasy
– to a work which now exists as one of our cultural treasures.
Leonardo's brush does not re-create the memory of his mother; it
creates it as a work of art, by creating the smile as seen by
Leonardo.

It is no longer possible, therefore, to set in opposition here what
Freud does and what he says. He makes an actual difficulty of
interpretation coincide with a theoretical difficulty of his metapsychology. It was, in fact, the underlying difficulty in the previous analyses as well. Why were *Oedipus Rex* and *Hamlet*, as
poems, capable of impressing the seal of universality on a dream,
even on a "typical" one? Why, if not because dreams, the typical
and sterile products of our nights, have already been "denied" and
"overcome" in a lasting creating of our days? Sublimation had
therefore been anticipated in the universalizing function of the
aesthetic model of dreams. The meaning of dreams is not only
less hidden here, and for this reason more readable, but is produced as meaning in a space other than the space of fantasy, that
is, in the space of culture.

[57] On this point, I have nothing to change from the analysis I proposed
in *Freud and Philosophy*: "The Gioconda's smile undoubtedly takes us
back to the childhood memory of Leonardo da Vinci, but this memory
only exists as a symbolizable absence that lies deep beneath Mona Lisa's
smile. Lost like a memory, the mother's smile is an empty place within
reality; it is the point where all real traces become lost, where the abolished confines one to fantasy. It is not therefore a thing that is better
known and that would explain the riddle of the work of art; it is an
intended absence which, far from dissipating the initial riddle, increases
it" (173–4).

That sublimation itself continued to be a great enigma to Freud is abundantly confirmed by his continuing allusions to this problem. The first of the *Three Essays on Sexuality* characterizes sublimation by the deviation of the libido's goal rather than by the substitution of the object. As he proceeds, he attaches to it the notion of the bonus of seduction and of fore-pleasure, whose use in aesthetics we saw earlier. But he then admits in the same essay: "But we must end with a confession that very little is as yet known with certainty of these pathways, though they certainly exist and can probably be traversed in both directions."[58] In the third essay, which compares sublimation to repression, Freud says expressly that these are processes "of which the inner causes are quite unknown to us."[59] And in his essay "On Narcissism," sublimation is contrasted with rather than compared to idealization.[60] The more Freud distinguishes sublimation from other mechanisms, particularly from repression and even from reaction-formation, the more its own mechanism remains unexplained: It is a displacement of energy but not a repression of it; it indeed appears to be related to an aptitude with which the artist is particularly gifted.

At the time of *The Ego and the Id*, the emphasis is placed on the conversion of object-libido into narcissistic libido and on desexualization; such desexualization, he adds, is "a kind of sublimation, therefore. Indeed, the question arises, and deserves careful consideration, whether this is not the universal road to sublimation, whether all sublimation does not take place through the mediation of the ego, which begins by changing sexual object-libido into narcissistic libido and then, perhaps goes on to give it another aim."[61] As we see, sublimation is as much the heading of a problem as the name of a solution.

Faced with such difficulties, one understands that Freud must be taken literally precisely when he says, in his *Leonardo*: "Since artistic talent and capacity are intimately connected with sublimation we must admit that the nature of the artistic function is also inaccessible to us along psychoanalytic lines."[62] But by recognizing

---

[58] S.E. 7:206.
[59] Ibid., 239.
[60] S.E. 14:73–102.
[61] S.E. 19:30.
[62] S.E. 11:136.

that psychoanalysis has real limits, the philosopher who reflects and meditates on them at the same time discovers what such limits mean for a theory that unceasingly advances on the unknown: These limits are not fixed boundaries; they are as movable as the investigation itself and, in this sense, are indefinitely surmountable.

Life: A Story in Search of a Narrator

That life should have something do with narration has always been known and said. We speak of the story of a life to character-ize the interval between birth and death. Yet this assimilation of a life to a story does not just happen. It is even a banal idea that needs to be subjected to critical doubt, where such doubt is a result of the knowledge acquired in the past few decades concerning narrative and narrating – knowledge that seems to remove the story from life as lived, confining it to the realm of fiction. We shall begin by passing through this critical zone with an eye to rethinking in a different way this all too rudimentary and all too direct relation between a story and a life, to show how fiction helps to make life, in the biological sense of the word, a human life. We shall want to apply to the relation between narrative and life the Socratic maxim that an unexamined life is not worth living.

I will take as my starting point for crossing this critical zone one critic's statement that stories are told and not lived; life is lived and not told. In order to clarify this relation between living and recounting I suggest that we first investigate the act of narrating itself.

The theory of narration I am going to refer to here is quite recent, since in its elaborated form it hails from the Russian and Czech formalists of the twenties and thirties and from the French structuralists of the sixties and the seventies. But it is also a very old theory, one that I find prefigured in Aristotle's *Poetics*. It is true that Aristotle knew only three literary genres: epic, tragedy, and comedy. But his analysis was already sufficiently general and formal to allow room for modern transpositions. For my part, I want to retain from Aristotle's *Poetics* his central concept of emplotment (in Greek: *muthos*), which means both "fable" (in the sense of a make-believe story) and "plot" (in the sense of well-constructed one). It is this second aspect of Aristotle's *muthos* that I will take as my guide and from this concept of "plot" I want to draw all those elements able later to help us toward a reformulation of the relation between life and narrative.

What Aristotle refers to as a plot is not a static structure, but an operation, an integrative process, one that, I hope to show, is completed only in the reader or spectator, that is, in the living receiver of the told story. By an "integrative process" I mean the work of composition that confers on the narrated story an identity that we can call a dynamic one. What is recounted is this or that story, as one complete story. It is this structuring process of emplotment that I want to examine in the next section.

Emplotment

I shall define the operation of emplotment in the broad sense as a synthesis of heterogeneous elements. A synthesis of what kinds of elements? In the first place, it is a synthesis of multiple events or incidents and the complete story. From this first point of view the plot has the power to draw a single story out of the multiple incidents or, if you prefer, by transforming the manifold incidents into one story. In this respect, an event is more than a mere occurrence, something that just happens. It is what contributes to the progress of the story just as it contributes to its beginning and its ending. Because of this, we can say that the narrated story is always more than a simple serial or successive enumeration of the order of the incidents or events that it organizes into an intelligible whole.

But the plot is also a synthesis from a second point of view. It brings together components as heterogeneous as encountered but unwanted circumstances; agents of actions and those who passively undergo them; accidental or expected encounters; interactions that place the actors in relations ranging from conflict to cooperation; means that are more or less in agreement with their ends; and, finally, unintended results. Bringing together all those factors in a single story makes the plot a unity that we could say is concordant and discordant at the same time (which is why I like to speak of discordant concordance or concordant discordance). We gain some understanding of such composition through the act of following a story. To follow a story is a very complex operation, one guided by expectations concerning what comes next, expectations that we adjust in light of the unfolding of the story, right up to its conclusion. I will note in passing that retelling a story is a better way of revealing this synthetic activity at work in the composition, in that we are less captivated by the unexpected aspects of the story and more attentive to the way in which it moves toward its conclusion. Finally, the plot is a synthesis of the heterogeneous in a still more profound sense, which will serve below to characterize the temporality proper to every narrative composition.

We can say that we find two kinds of time in every told story: on the one hand, a discrete, open-ended, and theoretically endless succession of incidents (we can always ask: and then what? and then?); on the other, the told story presents another temporal aspect characterized by integration, culmination, and the ending thanks to which the story gains a configuration. I would say in this sense that to compose a story is, from the temporal point of view, to draw a configuration from a succession. We already can surmise the importance of this characterization of stories from the temporal viewpoint, in that, for us, time is both that which passes and flees and that which endures and remains. But we shall come back to this below. Let us be content for now with our characterization of the told story as a temporal totality and of the poetic act as the creation of a mediation between passing time and time as enduring. If we were to speak of the temporal identity of a story, we would have to characterize it as something that endures and remains across that which passes away.

From this analysis of a story as a synthesis of the heterogeneous, we can retain three features: the mediation exercised by the plot between multiple incidents and the story; the primacy of concordance over discordance; finally, the competition between succession and configuration.

I would like next to present an epistemological corollary to this thesis regarding emplotment considered as a synthesis of the heterogeneous. This corollary has to do with the status of the intelligibility that ought to be given to the configuring act. Aristotle did not hesitate to say that every well-told story *teaches* something. Furthermore, he said that stories reveal *universal* aspects of the human condition and that, in this sense, poetry is *more philosophical* than the history of historians, which is overly dependent on life's anecdotal aspects. Whatever we might say about the relation of poetry and historiography, it is certain that tragedy, epic, and comedy – to mention only the genres known to Aristotle – develop a kind of intelligence we could call narrative intelligence, which is much closer to practical wisdom and moral judgment than to science and, more generally, to the theoretical use of reason.

This can be shown quite easily. Ethics as conceived of by Aristotle and as it can still be understood, as I shall show in other lectures, speaks abstractly of the relation between "virtues" and the "pursuit of happiness." It is the function of poetry, in its narrative and dramatic forms, to propose to the imagination for meditation sample cases which constitute thought experiments by means of which we learn to connect the ethical aspect of human behavior with happiness and unhappiness, fortune and misfortune. By means of poetry, we learn how changes in fortune result from this or that behavior, as presented through the plot of a narrative. It is thanks to the familiarity we have acquired with modes of emplotment learned from our culture that we learn to link the virtues or, rather, the excellences, to happiness and unhappiness. These "lessons" from poetry constitute the universals Aristotle spoke about, but they are universals of a lower degree than those of logic and of theoretical thought. Nevertheless, we must speak of "intelligence," but in the sense that Aristotle gave to *phronēsis* (which gets translated into Latin as *prudentia*). In this sense, I would like to speak of a "phronetic intelligence" in order to distinguish it from theoretical intelligence. Narrative belongs to the former, not to the latter.

This epistemological corollary of our analysis of the plot itself has numerous implications concerning the efforts of contemporary narratology to elaborate a genuine science of narrative. I will say that all these undertakings, which are entirely legitimate in my view, are justified only as a kind of simulation of a narrative intelligence always already there, a simulation that puts into play deep structures unknown to those who tell stories or who follow stories, but which place narratology at the same level of rationality as that of linguistics and the other sciences of language. To characterize the rationality of contemporary narratology by its ability to simulate in a second-order discourse what we already understood a story to be when we were children is not meant to discredit these modern efforts, but merely to situate them accurately within the degrees of knowledge.

I could just as well have looked for a model of thought more modern than Aristotle's; for example, the relation Kant establishes in the *Critique of Pure Reason* between the schema and the categories. Just as for Kant the schema points to the creative focal point of the categories, and the categories designate the ordering principle of the understanding, emplotment constitutes the creative focal point of a story, and narratology constitutes the rational reconstruction of the rules underlying poetic activity. In this regard, it is a science with its own requirements. What it seeks to reconstruct are all the logical and semiological constraints, along with the transformation laws, that preside over the working of the narrative. My thesis, therefore, does not express any hostility toward narratology; it is limited to saying that narratology is a second-order discourse that is always preceded by a narrative intelligence which issues from the creative imagination.

From here on, my analysis will stay at the level of this first-order narrative intelligence.

However, before moving on to the question regarding the relation between stories and life, I would like to pause to consider a second corollary that will set us on the way toward the reinterpretation of this very relation.

There is, I will say, a life of narrative activity inscribed in the "traditionality" characteristic of the narrative schema.

To say that the narrative schema has its own history and that this history possesses all the characteristics of a tradition is in no way meant to defend an idea of tradition understood as an inert transmission of dead sediment. On the contrary, it is meant to point to tradition as a living transmission of an innovation that can always be reactivated by a return to the most creative moments of poetic composition. This phenomenon of traditionality is the key to the functioning of narrative models and, consequently, to identifying them. The constitution of a tradition rests in effect on the interaction between the two factors of innovation and sedimentation. To sedimentation we ascribe those models that in retrospect constitute the typology of emplotment that allows us to arrange in order the history of literary genres. But we must not lose sight of the fact that these models do not constitute eternal essences, but rather derive from a sedimented history whose genesis has been lost sight of. But if this sedimentation does enable us to identify a work as being, for example, a tragedy, a *Bildungsroman*, a social drama, etc., the identification of a work by way of the sedimented models found in it is not exhaustive. This identification must also take into account the opposite phenomenon of innovation. Why?

Because the models themselves have arisen from a prior innovation, they provide a guide for further experimentation in the narrative domain. The rules change under pressure of innovation, but they change slowly and even resist change in virtue of the sedimentation process. This is why innovation remains the opposite pole to tradition. There is always room for innovation inasmuch as whatever was produced, by the *poiesis* of making the poem, is always a singular work, *this* work. The rules constitute a kind of grammar governing the composition of new works, new before becoming typical. Every work is an original production, a new being within the realm of discourse. But the opposite is no less true. Innovation remains a rule-governed strategy. The work of the imagination does not start from nothing. In one way or another it is linked to models received through tradition. But it can enter into a variable relation to these models. The range of solutions lies for the most part between the two poles of servile repetition and calculated deviation, passing through every degree of rule-governed deformation. Folk tales, myths, and traditional narratives in general stay closer to the pole of repetition. This is why they are the privileged realm of structuralism.

But as soon as we move beyond the domain of these traditional narratives, deviance prevails over rules. The contemporary novel, for instance, can in large measure be defined as an anti-novel, inasmuch as it is the rules themselves that have become the object for new experimentation. Whatever may be the case for this or that work, the possibility of deviance is included in the relation between sedimentation and innovation that constitutes tradition. The variations between these two poles confer on the productive imagination a historicity of its own and keep the narrative tradition alive.

From Narrative to Life

We can now attack directly our paradox for today that stories are told, life is lived. An abyss seems to open up between fiction and life.

To bridge this abyss, it seems to me, a serious revision of both terms of the paradox is necessary.

Let us stay for the moment on the side of the narrative, hence that of fiction, and let us see how it leads back toward life. My thesis here is that the process of composition, of configuration, does not complete itself in the text but in the reader and, under this condition, it makes possible the reconfiguration of life through the narrative. More precisely, I will say that the sense and the reference of a story well up from the intersection of the world of text and the world of the reader. Thus the act of reading becomes the crucial moment of our entire analysis. Reading's ability to transfigure the experience of the reader rests on this capacity of narrative.

Allow me to insist on the terms I just used: the world of the reader and the world of the text. To speak of the world of the text is to emphasize the feature of every literary work to open up a horizon of possible experience, a world which it might be possible to inhabit. A text is not an entity closed-in on itself. It is the projection of a new universe, distinct from the one in which we live. To appropriate a work through reading it is to unfold the implicit horizon of the world that embraces the action, the characters, and the events of the story told. The result is that through their imagination readers belong to both the horizon of experience of the work and that of their own real action. Our horizon of expectation and our horizon of experience continually meet and fuse. Gadamer speaks in this sense of a "fusion of horizons" essential to the act of understanding a text.

I am well aware that literary criticism is careful to maintain the distinction between the inside of a text and its outside. It prefers to look upon every exploration of a text's linguistic universe as foreign to its aims. Text analysis should therefore stop at the border of the text and deny itself any departure from the text. I will say here that this distinction between outside and inside is an invention of the method of textual analysis itself, and does not correspond to the reader's experience. This opposition results from the extrapolation to literature of the characteristic properties of the kind of unit linguistics works with: phonemes, lexemes, words. For linguistics the real world is extra-linguistic. Reality is not contained within the dictionary or in grammar. It is precisely this extrapolation from linguistics to poetics that seems to me open to criticism. It is the methodological decision, belonging to structural analysis, to deal with literature in terms of linguistic categories that imposes the distinction between inside and outside.

From a hermeneutic point of view, that is, from the point of view of the interpretation of literary experience, a text has an entirely different meaning than that which structural analysis borrowed from linguistics recognizes in it. This meaning mediates between human existence and the world, between human beings, between a human being and him- or herself. The mediation between a human being and the world is called referentiality; that between human beings is communicability; that between a human being and him- or herself is self-understanding. A literary work includes these three dimensions of referentiality, communicability, and self-understanding. The work of hermeneutics thus begins where linguistics stops. It seeks to discover new features of non-descriptive referentiality, non-utilitarian communicability, and non-narcissistic reflexivity engendered by the literary work. In a word, hermeneutics turns on the hinge connecting the (internal) configuration of a work and the (external) re-figuration of a life.

In my opinion, everything said earlier concerning the dynamics of composition proper to literary creation is nothing but a lengthy preparation for understanding the real problem, i.e., that of the dynamics of transfiguration proper to the work. In this regard, emplotment is the joint work of the text and the reader. It is necessary to follow, to accompany the configuration, to actualize its capacity of being followed, for the work to have a configuration within its own borders. To follow a story is to reactualize the configuring act that gives it form. It is also the act of reading that accompanies the interplay between innovation and sedimentation, the play with narrative constraints, with the possibilities of deviation, even the battle between the novel and the anti-novel. In the end, it is the act of reading that completes the work, which transforms it into a guide for reading, with its zones of indetermination, its latent richness for interpretation, its ability to be reinterpreted in ever new ways within historical contexts that themselves are always new.

At this stage of our analysis we begin to catch sight of how narrative and life can be reconciled to each other, for reading itself is already a way of living in the fictitious universe of the work. In this sense we can already say that stories are told but also lived in imagination.

But we must now correct the second term of the alternative, what we call "life." We must put in question the false assumption that life is lived and not told.

With this in mind, I would like to insist on the pre-narrative capacity of what we call a life. What has to be called into question is the too simple equating of life and narrative. A life is no more than a biological phenomenon so long as it is not interpreted. And in this interpretation fiction plays a considerable mediating role. To pave the way toward this new phase in our analysis we must attend to the mixture of doing and undergoing, of action and suffering that makes up the very fabric of life. It is this mixture that narrative seeks to imitate in a creative way. In fact, in my reference to Aristotle I left out the definition he gives to "narrative." It is, he says, the imitation of an action, *mimēsis praxeōs*. Therefore we need first to look for the handholds that narrative can find in the actual experience of acting and suffering; that which in this experience requires insertion in narrative and perhaps expresses a need for it.

The first anchorage we find for narrative intelligibility in actual experience is the very structure of human acting and suffering itself. In this regard, human life differs profoundly from animal life and all the more so from mineral existence. We understand what action and passion are in virtue of our ability to utilize in a meaningful way the entire network of expressions and concepts that natural languages offer us for distinguishing "action" from merely physical "movement" and from psycho-physiological "behavior." For example, we understand the meanings of project, goal, means, circumstances, and so on. All these notions taken together make up the network of what we could call a *semantics of action*. And we rediscover in this network all the components of narrative that appeared earlier under the heading of a synthesis of the heterogeneous. In this regard our familiarity with the conceptual network of human action is of the same order as the acquaintance we have with the plots of the stories known to us. It is the same phronetic intelligence that presides over the understanding of action (and of passion) and over that of a narrative.

The second anchorage that the narrative proposition finds in our practical understanding resides in the symbolic resources of the practical realm. This is a feature that will govern which aspects of doing, of being able to do, and of knowing-how-to-do are put to use in the poetic transposition.

If indeed action can be narrated, it is because it is already articulated through signs, rules, and norms. It is always symbolically mediated. This characteristic of action has been strongly emphasized by cultural anthropology. If I speak more precisely of a "symbolic mediation," I do so in order to distinguish among cultural symbols those which underlie action to the point of constituting its primary meaning, before the autonomous wholes connected with speaking and writing get detached from this practical level. We would find them again were we to discuss ideology and utopia. Here I shall limit myself to what we could call implicit or immanent symbolism, in contradistinction to such explicit or autonomous symbolism. What characterizes the implicit symbolism of action is that it constitutes a context for the description of particular actions. In other words, it is as a function of some symbolic convention that we are able to interpret a given gesture as signifying this or that meaning; the same arm movement can, depending on the context, be understood as a greeting, as hailing a taxi, or as casting a vote. Before being subjected to interpretation, these symbols are the interpretants internal to an action. In this way symbolism confers a first readability on action. It makes action a quasi-text for which the symbols furnish the rules of significance, as a function of which some act of behavior can be interpreted.

The third anchorage of narrative in life lies in what we may call the pre-narrative quality of human experience. Thanks to it we have the right to speak of life as of an incipient story, and thus of life as an activity and a passion in search of a narrative.

Understanding an action is not limited to familiarity with its symbolic mediations, it extends so far as the recognition of temporal structures in the action that call for narration. It is not by accident or by mistake that we are accustomed to speak of stories that happen to us or stories we are caught up in or quite simply of the story of a life.

Someone will object here that my entire analysis rests on a vicious circle. If every human experience is already mediated by all sorts of symbolic systems, it also already mediated by all kinds of stories we have heard. How then can we speak of a narrative quality of experience and of human life as an incipient story, since we have no access to the temporal drama of existence outside of the stories told to their subject by others than ourselves?

To this objection I would oppose a number of situations that, in my opinion, compel us already to ascribe to experience as such something like a virtual narrativity which does not proceed from a projection, as it is said, of literature on life, but which constitutes a genuine demand for narrative. It was to characterize these situations that I introduced the expression "pre-narrative structure of experience."

Without leaving behind everyday experience, are we not inclined to see certain chains of episodes of our life as as-yet-untold stories, stories that ask to be told, stories that offer anchorages for narrative? I am not unaware how incongruous it sounds to speak of an as-yet-untold-story. Are not stories told, by definition? This is not disputable so long as we are talking about actual stories. But is the notion of a potential story unacceptable?

I want next to consider two less common situations in which the expression "as-yet-untold story" imposes itself on us with surprising force. The patient who addresses him- or herself to a psychoanalyst presents him with bits and pieces of lived histories, dreams, "primitive scenes," conflicting episodes. We can rightly say that the goal and outcome of analytic sessions is that the person analyzed draws from these bits and pieces a narrative that is both more bearable and more intelligible. This narrative interpretation of psychoanalytic theory implies that the story of a life proceeds from untold and repressed stories in the direction of stories that the subject can be responsible for and take as constitutive of his or her personal identity. It is the search for this personal identity that guarantees the continuity between the potential or virtual story and the express story for which we assume responsibility.

There is another situation where the idea of an as-yet-untold story seems to fit. It is the case when a judge tries to understand an accused person on trial by unraveling the knot of complications in which the suspect is caught up. We can say that this individual appears to be "entangled" in the stories that happen to him before any of these stories are told. This "entanglement" thus appears as a pre-history of the story told, whose beginning remains to be chosen by the narrator. The pre-history of the story is what connects it to a larger whole and gives it a background. This background is built from the ongoing, continuous overlapping of every lived story. The stories that get told must emerge from this background. And with this emergence the implied subject also emerges. The major consequence of this existential analysis of human beings as entangled in stories is that the telling is a secondary process grafted onto our "being entangled in stories." Narrating, following, and understanding stories are only the continuation of such untold stories.

From this twofold analysis we learn that fiction, particularly narrative fiction, is an irreducible dimension of self-understanding. If it is true that fiction can only be completed in life, and that life cannot be understood other than through stories we tell about it, then we are led to say that an *examined* life, in the sense we borrowed earlier from Socrates, is a *narrated* life.

What is a narrated life? It is a life in which we rediscover all the fundamental structures of narrative referred to above, and principally, the interplay of concordance and discordance which seemed to us to characterize a narrative. There is nothing paradoxical or outrageous about this conclusion. If we open Saint Augustine's *Confessions* at Book XI, we discover a description of human time that corresponds completely to the structure of discordant concordance that Aristotle, some centuries earlier, had discerned in poetic composition. In this famous treatise on time, Augustine sees time as being born from the unceasing dissociating of the three aspects of the present: expectation, which he calls the present of the future; memory, which is the present of the past; attention, which is the present of the present. Whence the instability of time; better, its ceaseless disassociation. This is why Augustine can define time as a distending of the soul, *distentio animi.* It consists in the permanent contrast between the instability of the human "present" and the stability of the divine "present," which embraces past, present, and future in the unity of creative vision and action.

In this way, we are led to juxtapose and confront Aristotle's notion of plot and Augustine's definition of time. We could say that in Augustine discordance wins out over concordance; hence the wretchedness of the human condition. For Aristotle, concordance wins out over discordance; hence the incomparable value of narrative to bring order to our temporal experience. But we must not push this opposition too far, since for Augustine himself there would be no discordance if we did not tend toward a unity of intention, as the simple example of reciting a poem demonstrates: When I am about to recite the poem it is wholly present in my mind; next, as I am reciting it, its parts pass one after the other from the future to the past, crossing through the present, until finally, the future being exhausted, the whole of the poem has become past. It is necessary therefore that a totalizing intention guides my inquiry so that I feel the more or less cruel bite of time that continues to scatter my soul by turning expectation, memory, and awareness into discordance. If therefore in the lived experience of time discordance wins out over concordance, the latter should still be the permanent object of our desire. We can say the opposite for Aristotle. Narrative, we said, is a synthesis of the heterogeneous. But there is no concordance without discordance. Tragedy is exemplary in this regard: no tragedy without reversals, without unexpected blows, without terrible and pitiful events, without a great flaw committed in ignorance or by mistake rather than through evil-mindedness. If therefore concordance wins out over discordance, what makes up narrative is the battle between them.

Let us apply to ourselves this analysis of the discordant concordance of narrative and the concordant discordance of time. It seems that our life, embraced in a single glance, appears to us as the field for a constructive activity, drawing upon the narrative intelligence through which we attempt to recover, and not simply to impose from the outside, the narrative identity that constitutes us. I emphasize this expression "narrative identity," because what we call subjectivity is neither an incoherent succession of events nor an immutable substance incapable of becoming. It is exactly the kind of identity that narrative composition alone can create by means of its dynamism.

This definition of subjectivity in terms of narrative identity has numerous implications. In the first place, it is possible to apply to ourselves the play of sedimentation and innovation that we recognized at work in every tradition. Similarly, we do not stop reinterpreting the narrative identity that constitutes us in light of stories handed down to us by our culture. In this sense, our self-understanding presents the same features of traditionality as does the understanding of a work of literature. In this way we learn to become the narrator of our own story without completely becoming the author of our life. We could even say that we apply to ourselves the concept of the narrative voices that make up the symphony of great works, of epics, tragedies, dramas, and novels.

The difference is that in these works it is the author who has disguised himself as the narrator and who wears the masks of his many characters, among them, the dominant narrative voice telling the story we read. We can become the narrator of ourselves, imitating these narrative voices, without becoming our own author. That is the great difference between life and fiction. In this sense, it is certainly true that life is lived and its story told. An unbridgeable distinction remains, but it is partly abolished by the power we have to apply to ourselves the plots we have received from our culture and to try out in this way the different roles assumed by favorite characters in the stories we love best. It is in this way, by means of imaginative variations on our ego, that we try to apply a narrative understanding to ourselves, the only kind of understanding that escapes the pseudo-alternative of pure change and absolute identity. Between them lies a narrative identity.

Allow me to say in conclusion that what we call the subject is never given at the start. Or, if it were so given it would run the risk of reducing itself to a narcissistic, self-centered, and avaricious ego, from which precisely literature can deliver us. So, what we lose on the side of narcissism, we regain on the side of our narrative identity. In the place of an ego enchanted by itself is born a *self*, instructed by cultural symbols, first among which are the stories passed down in the literary tradition. These stories confer a nonsubstantial but narrative unity on us.

Narrative: Its Place in Psychoanalysis

My reflection on the place of narrative or, better, of the narrative function in psychoanalysis was born from the encounter between two independent lines of thought. On the one side, the working of the narrative function: At this level, I did not take psychoanalysis into account, since I was thinking about a kind of creation that is aware of itself, rightly or wrongly, hence one that is planned, willed, in some way, either as history or as fiction. My working hypothesis about narrativity not only did not owe anything to psychoanalysis, it is not assumed to add anything whatsoever to it. It has to do with the learned art of composing narratives.

However, at the end of my inquiry, I came upon the notion of a narrative identity by which I meant the crossroads or intersection between two ways of narrating. One is historical, and takes account of documents; the other is fictional, and is an exploration of something make-believe. The notion of narrative identity I proposed is a kind of "mixture" of the historical and fictional modes of narrative. At the end of this work I proposed the following hypothesis. Our understanding of ourselves is a narrative understanding, that is, we cannot grasp ourselves outside of time, and hence outside of some narrative. There is an equivalence therefore between what I am and the story of my life.

In this sense, this narrative dimension is constitutive of our self-understanding. It possesses the double character of being historical and fictional at the same time: On the one side, memory is also the set of documents that I possess about my own existence (my family photos, birth certificate, and the stories about my origins all belong to the order of historical knowledge, which is a knowledge based on documentation). On the other, I may also say that the narrative I make about myself is the story of my life since I can try out different plots regarding my existence. Therefore, self-understanding by way of narrative – and there are not any other ways – is a good example of the intersection of the two large forms of narrative: history and fiction. In self-understanding they join together. Moreover, what are we interested in in history? A better understanding of the different humanity's cultural and spiritual dimensions. For if nothing human is alien to me, these are my possibilities that I can explore by means of history. In this sense, history and fiction cooperate to make up self-understanding. This was my first line of thought.

The second line came from my increasing dissatisfaction regarding Freudianism. By Freudianism I mean the metapsychological doctrine as presented starting from the *Outline* in 1894, then moving on to chapter 7 of *The Interpretation of Dreams* and the well-known essays on metapsychology, where we find the article on the unconscious, the article on the instinctual drives, and so on, up to the last systematic writings: *The Ego and the Id* and *Beyond the Pleasure Principle*, followed by *Moses and Monotheism* and *Civilization and Its Discontents*. If I speak of a theoretical dissatisfaction, this is because I became more and more convinced that Freudian theory is discordant with its own discovery and that there is more in this Freudian discovery than in the theoretical discourse Freud offers regarding it.

In saying this I am in complete agreement with Jürgen Habermas and others, as well as with a number of English-speaking interpreters of psychoanalysis. They all see a growing gap between its theory – which is ultimately based on a mechanistic model, an economic one, hence an energetic one, which completely misses the key dimension of Freud's discovery – and its practice. Currently, I am trying to reinterpret psychoanalysis by taking as my starting point, not the theory, but what happens in analytic experience itself, that is, what happens in the relation between analysand and analyst, in particular in the transference phase. I am cautious about this since if one has some relation to the theoretical writings without having experienced the practice, it is imprudent to speak of the analytic experience. Hence it is from a distance that I say all this and I await the corrections of those who do practice psychoanalysis. Yet Freud's writings, insofar as they do convey something of his experience, do present testimony about his practice that we can oppose to his theorizing.

Drawing on this testimony and that of other psychoanalysts whom I admire (Pierre Aulagnier, the Mammonis, and others), I would like to reintroduce the narrative element into the structure of the analytic experience, by showing how it introduces itself into what I will call the criteriology of the analytic fact. I do so, it seems to me, not against this experience, but as pressured to do so by it.

What is it that distinguishes the analytic fact from all other facts? Four elements, I will say, the narrative one being the fourth element.

First, the analytic experience is possible only on the condition of presupposing that the deepest affects are not foreign to language (what Freud calls libido as, for a long time, Jung did too). This is very important if we are to introduce a narrative element, which is one of language. I will say that the fundamental hypothesis of psychoanalysis is that the affective, the emotional depth of a human being, however deeply it may lie hidden – and admitting the Freudian theory of repression – however repressed it may be, retains a kinship with language.

To put it in more philosophical language, human *pathos* has a profound affinity with the human *logos*, and this is what makes human desire human and not animal. Human sexuality is human and not animal because, precisely, it passes through language. We can say with Hegel that, passing through a demand and a quest for recognition, human desire is the desire of desire. There is here therefore an absolutely primitive structure, one that makes possible psychoanalysis. We could even say that, at bottom, the analytic cure consists in bringing to language exactly what has been excluded from language. I believe it is to a German psychoanalyst, Alexander Mitscherlich, that we owe the introduction of the idea of "desymbolization" as a way of accounting for the neurotic and eventually the psychotic fact.[1] Illness, at least as regards its

[1] Alexander Mitscherlich (1908–1982) wrote a precursor book in 1963, *Toward a Society without a Father: A Contribution to Social Psychology*,

linguistic aspect, consists in a decomposition of the symbolic function and the analyst's task is to resymbolize, that is, to reintroduce the patient to the linguistic community.

We can speak not only of desymbolization, but even of excommunication to express this breakdown in the linguistic expression of desire. What Freud called "censorship," at bottom, is a linguistic phenomenon. Let me recall the origin of this word in Freud: it is a transposition into the psychic structure of a social phenomenon of language. We know that censorship takes place on the border between two countries, two political regimes. One blacks out a letter, correspondence . . . words, elements of communication. There is a kind of linguistic exclusion. We might argue about everything Freud said about repression, but this does not set aside the fact that psychoanalysis is only possible as *praxis* because in fact one can break through this prohibition and, in a way, reintroduce into the linguistic community those who have been excommunicated from it, and thereby resymbolize what had been desymbolized.

The second hypothesis is that human desire has a dialogical structure. The psychoanalytic model has always struck me as being a monological one. Freud always presents his model as a sort of egg closed in on itself. He represents it through a schema: preconscious, conscious, unconscious, or, in the second topology: superego, ego, id, but there never is the other. The other is never thematized as an element of the structure even though the analytic experience is the relationship of desire to another. Analytic experience consists in bringing back old relations to others – father, mother, all those who stand in some relation to a child's desires – but this is an experience that passes through language.

Bearing witness to this are all the fundamental dramas that psychoanalysis, at least Freudian psychoanalysis, revolves around. (Jungians would put it in other terms.) But as it turns out, relations with the father and the mother are linguistic ones, since any child is born into a setting where people have talked about him or her before the child comes along, and where the father and

trans. Eric Mosbacher (New York: Harcourt Brace and World, 1969). With his wife, Margarete, he is the author of *The Inability to Mourn: Principles of Collective Behavior*, trans. Beverley Placzek (New York: Grove Press, 1975).

mother are not simply sources of food or progenitors, but people who introduce the child into a language community. The well-known triangular relation, the oedipal relation (which Freud sometimes presented in biological terms by saying there are three persons for two sexes), is a dialogical structure of desire. This is why the purely biological representation that is drawn from it completely leaves out the language side of this relationship. Human desire is a desire addressed to . . . and therefore passes through this mediation of language.

A third element prepares for the entry of the narrative element: We are in relation to reality and to others by way of the imaginary, but an imaginary that can be deceptive, a place of illusion. In this regard, Lacan is correct: We think we are intending the Other, but we reach another other than the Other (what he calls the object *a*). Psychoanalysis begins as a result with a kind of fundamental misunderstanding, an error, an illusion. Intending the Other takes place through the fantasy. At bottom, this is the problem for psychoanalysis: What does each of us make of our fantasies? A good, a bad usage of fantasies . . . for a part of our life is fantasy in the sense of a make-believe that conceals reality.[2]

What relation do human beings enter into not just with other men and women, but with those fantasies through which they do or do not encounter these others? Can a person live with his fantasies, support them, transform them into something creative, or on the contrary do these fantasies cut off his access to reality, in this way becoming sources of suffering? I ran into the same problem in literature: Does literature – another kind of make-believe – give us access to a deeper acquaintance with things or is it an obstacle? Both things are possible. I think of the figure of Don Quixote, who lives in an imaginary, fantastized relation to others. We know the childish elements of this relationship: He fights windmills which are deceptive elements, but the whole story of Don Quixote is, at bottom, about the progressive reduction of this fantasized element leading to a conquest of an imagined truth,

[2] Jürgen Habermas, in his general theory, tries to show that this is parallel to the concealing function uncovered by the critique of ideologies; cf. his *Knowledge and Human Interests*, trans. Jeremy J. Shapiro (Boston: Beacon Press, 1971).

one that is creative and not based on illusion. The opposition that Lacan sets up between the imaginary and the symbolic seems to me quite useful. In this context, the imaginary is considered as misleading and the symbolic leads us to an order that really is constitutive of human reality – the fundamental order of language.

I think that this third element, I mean the relation to fantasy, to a falsifying imaginary, is very important because we have here a virtually pathological aspect of the symbolic function. Here the symbol, rather than "giving rise to thought" and to knowing, is a source of illusion and mystification. Freud brought to all this something absolutely fundamental, the illusory character of the imaginary. We rediscover here the old tradition of French moralists, of Montaigne and Pascal, but also of the Platonists and I find the same thing in Spinoza, I mean that the imagination is a deceptive function. The misleading imagination, there lies the central problem. Maybe Lacan exaggerated the scope of fantasy in the imaginary. But in so doing, he rejoined, at bottom, a long tradition of critics of the imagination, beginning with Montaigne and Pascal, and continued by the great French moralists of the eighteenth (such as La Rochefoucauld) and the nineteenth centuries. There is a trial of the imaginary in philosophy, as, for example, when Spinoza calls *imaginatio* precisely the deceptive level of knowledge. The deceptive, falsifying imagination is the central problem. What, in my opinion, attaches psychoanalysis to what is most profound in the moral and psychological culture of the West, is its having seen in the imagination a kind of Janus Bifrons, with one side that is "illusion" and another that is "creation."

Next, I believe, comes the fourth dimension: the narrative one. The relation of desire with the other or with the fantasy was in a way a kind of instantaneous insight. But it is necessary to bring in time, the time of a lifetime. A life unfolds from birth to death and is necessarily a central problem for analytic experience inasmuch as each age is bound up with the other ages of life. Freud himself takes account of this temporal aspect with the fundamental role of infancy and turns psychoanalysis into a kind of archeology. Psychoanalysis, as an archeology of desire, has to deal with beginnings, with developments, and hence with a temporal dimension.[3] I will say that this temporal dimension becomes a narrative element and seems to me to play two roles in analysis: on the one hand, in the constituting of the illness and, on the other, in the carrying out of the cure.

In the constituting of the illness, because what we have called "desymbolization" is also a "denarrativization," that is, the patient is not capable of constituting an intelligible, acceptable story of his life. The symptoms appear as fragments, bits and pieces of narratives that cannot be put together into a coherent narrative. In this case can we not consider the analytic cure as a return at the same time to language, to communication, to truth, to language in opposition to excluding things from language, to communication beyond the oedipal conflict, to truth beyond fantasy, all of this by a kind of narrative restructuration of one's personality?

On this point, I would very much like to have a discussion with analysts to learn how they behave in relation to the narratives they hear from their patients. It seems to me, as regards the cure, that each session of analysis will include some narrative element, as when one recounts a dream.

But we need to emphasize that what one calls a dream is not a dream as dreamed but the narrative of a dream. It is a mistake to assume that there is a direct equivalence between the dream and the dream as recounted. Freud himself never thought to theorize about this quite basic fact, and he nullifies this equivalence when, in his theory of rationalization, he shows that one of the effects of this rationalization is to put things in order, and a narrative order is one of the possible superimposed orders. So the narrative element is taken for granted in the analytic experience.

For another thing, in narrative, and precisely in narratives based on fantasies, there are all kinds of conflictual episodes. The patient believes that his father, when he was a child, was this or that. I

[3] Here I note in passing the role, which is so important for a number of French analysts, of the notion of what Freud calls "after the factness" (*Nachträglichkeit*), indicating by this that a traumatism is only operative when it has been repeated by another traumatism that reactualizes it and thereby retrospectively recreates the destructive, dangerous character of this first occurrence.

allude here to the well-known episode that the young Freud discussed at such length about the theory of the seduction of the child by the father. Is this a pseudo-memory that gives a pseudo-narrative or is it a true memory? Can we not say that the whole purpose of the cure is to aid the patient to construct the narrative, the story of his life, with the character of intelligibility, of acceptability missing from those bits and pieces of inconsistent and unsupportable narrative that the patient brings with him? If such be the case, then the narrative dimension needs to be incorporated into the theory itself, not just at the level of therapeutic practices but at the very level of the theory itself; that is, that the equivalence between what I am and what I say that I am has to be taken totally seriously. In other words, the identity between self-understanding and any narrative about oneself has to be integrated into psychoanalytic theory. But, then, with this narrative dimension it is no longer possible to preserve the economic, I would even say quasi-energetic model of Freudianism. It is necessary to reincorporate the linguistic element, the dialogical element, the element having to do with the relation between appearance and truth in the imaginary (an element one can call Platonic), and the narrative element, and to coordinate these four elements to make up the basis of a theory appropriate to the analytic experience, a hermeneutics.

I will say that psychoanalysis is a hermeneutics in the sense that human beings are beings who understand themselves by interpreting themselves, and the way in which they interpret themselves is a narrative one. Narrative is the mode of self-understanding for a being when he considers himself from the point of view of temporality, of time as lived in daily life, but also that of the long time span which is the history of a life from birth to death. What I now need to say is that we cannot purely and simply transpose a narrative model taken from literature to psychoanalysis, nor to philosophy, when we are speaking about ourselves, for one fundamental reason: Literary narratives have an ending; we know the beginning and the ending, whereas the story of our life is an open-ended story. It is open-ended about the beginning. Our oldest memories never link up with the first act, our birth, our conception. My beginning will never be part of my memory. To be sure, one of the problems for analysis is to return further back in memory, but one element will never be remembered: my absolute beginning in my conception. Even if we follow Otto Rank regarding the birth trauma that leaves its traces, the conception that leads to my existence will never be a memory. But above all, and as another point, my death is still before me and will never be told by me, whereas a narrative can include death. Every narrative bears within itself, if not the hero's death, at least that of other "heroes."

In this sense, the narrative structure of existence is not literary because it is open-ended. This is why there is a great fragility to the narrative function when it comes to life. We can tell several stories about ourselves because the criterion for an ending escapes us. Here I come back to a Greek proverb that Plato and Aristotle cite, namely, that one cannot say of a person that he or she was happy until they are dead. In a certain way, the meaning of a life is also in its conclusion, and its conclusion reacts retrospectively on its earlier phases, on its beginnings.

To conclude, since I find myself here speaking to Jungians and not Freudians, I would like to mention briefly two points that struck me and that I think ought to be brought up. First, the most dramatic problems of life are not those of infancy (something not found in Freud). Jung's patients were not at all the same ones as Freud's. Freud's were young repressed women in the Vienna of Franz-Joseph, whereas those of Jung, it seemed to me, were older men and women confronted with a challenging truth, at a moment when one added up the balance of one's life, where one sought its meaning the closer one got to its end. And here is where what I would like to call the projective element of narrative comes into play.

Since our lives are not over, we do not know the end of our story, and the narrative we tell of ourselves stands in relation to what we still expect from life. The only narrative that is accessible to us is based on what Gadamer, like Koselleck, has called a "horizon of expectation." This idea that time is both the retention of a past and the pro-tention of a future, memory and expectation, comes from Saint Augustine. It was taken up by Husserl, then by Heidegger, with the idea that a human being is fundamentally and in the first place a being ahead of itself, *vorweg*, on the way, hence that the most important structure of time has more to do with the future along with its horizon of death.

As I was saying, in literary narrative, the story ends and one knows how it ends, even if the end is open-ended. There is an end to the book – the last page. We do not know, on the contrary, the last page of the text that is our life, and it is the orientation toward the future, the dialectic between expectation and memory that means that we have to project our futures. Here it would be necessary to consider how analysis, how the psychoanalytic instant, ties together these two elements: What does a person expect of his life, what does he project as his future and what does he understand to be his past? There is, of course, an exchange between these two. There is a retroactive effect of our vision of the future on the way we reread our past. What completely distinguishes the narrative of a life from a literary narrative, in a kind of Heideggerian way, I would say, is that one can project one's future only starting from the deepest-lying resources. And this restructuring of these deep-lying resources is governed by the narrative restructuration they give rise to. And here is where I see the place for psychoanalysis. At the same time, this narrative structuring always remains in relation to a capacity to project one's future. Sartre put this well with his idea of an existential project. The existential project overflows memory and narrative. I think that our narrative identity has to be taken up entirely starting from this relationship between expectation and narrative.

Postscript: Listening to Freud
One Last Time

At the end of this conference, which has brought together analysts and non-analysts, artists, writers, and philosophers, I do not want to give another paper, or to try to sum up the result of our discussions by borrowing a line from each speaker. I will limit myself to leaving the last word to the teacher without whom the question that has brought us together at Cerisy-la-Salle would never have been posed.

I have spoken about the relations between art and Freudian systematic theory. In doing this, I meant to refer to the analogical transposition to works of art of the procedures of interpretation that apply to dreams and neuroses. In this regard, *The Moses of Michelangelo*, the *Leonardo da Vinci* seemed to me exemplary of what we can call the psychoanalytic point of view on the work of art. There is something else in Freud, which did not come up in our discussions, that will allow me at least to point to the problem at the moment the conference is coming to a close. This something else is the vision of culture that appears in Freud's last writings: *Civilization and Its Discontents* and *The Future of an Illusion*. I want to propose this last reading of Freud to you for two reasons: First, it is the most encompassing one; I mean that it encompasses all of us, since it takes as one all of art, ethics, religion, and science and in this way gives an aim, a horizon to all our discussions. Next, these are the most problematic, the most contestable of Freud's views – even if the tone becomes more and more dogmatic – because they are most profound ones. They plunge down to the roots of human signs with an eagle's eye which was also that of Marx and Nietzsche.

The meaning of culture – that great envelope within which we come here to inscribe ourselves – is circumscribed by Freud by means of three questions: To what point can we lower the cost of the instinctual sacrifices imposed on human beings? How to reconcile them with what among such renouncements are inevitable? Finally, how to offer individuals satisfying compensations for these sacrifices? These three questions are not, as one might at first think, questions that Freud came up with in regard to culture. These questions constitute culture as culture. What, in fact, is in question in all the discussions about prohibition and drives is just this triple problematic: the lowering of the instinctual cost, reconciliation with the inevitable, and compensation for the sacrifice.

The elaborating of these three questions, which give us access to culture taken as a whole, is noteworthy in that it is strictly contemporary with Freud's work on the handling of the theory of drives, founded up to then on the opposition between object-libido and ego-libido or narcissism. It was now necessary to work with a new pair of drives and to introduce the death drive, over against Eros, which from here on will encompass both object- and ego-libido. I do not want to examine here the many reasons for this considerable reworking, but just to consider its impact on the definition of what we have just spoken of as the "task of culture." The connection between the introduction of the death drive and the triple question by which we defined this task seems quite hidden at first. It is in fact well hidden; it is the very destiny of pleasure. The problem of pleasure would be a simple problem, as would the task of culture, if human beings were only looking for pleasure and fleeing pain. Given this hypothesis, the task of culture would be just one slightly peculiar province of what we could call a general erotics, and we would never encounter anything irreducible or inevitable capable of accounting for what Freud calls, using a strange but powerful term, "discontent" (*Unbehagen*). This discontent, this unease, seems in fact inherent to culture as such. Human beings are unsatisfied as cultural beings, because they also pursue death, their own death and that of others. *Civilization and Its Discontents* lays out the implication of this strange and scandalous drive, which *Beyond the Pleasure Principle* had described in terms of its quasi-biological aspects. The death drive in these last writings is unmasked and revealed to be anti-culture. On the biological or psychobiological plane, we never grasp this except as somehow implicit in Eros. It is Eros that makes use of this drive by turning itself into something other than a desire for life, in the form of aggression. For example, this new drive can be intermixed with Eros in the form of sadism. This is why it is through masochistic satisfaction that we catch sight of it at work as directed against life itself. There follows a progressive revelation of the death drive across the three biological, psychological, and cultural levels. At the first of these levels, in *Beyond the Pleasure Principle*, Freud calls it a silent drive. But in repeating itself from level to level, the struggle between Eros and death becomes ever more manifest. It attains its complete meaning only at the level of culture. We can then speak of the clamor of war: "And now, I think, the meaning of the evolution of civilization is no longer obscure to us. It must present the struggle between Eros and Death, between the instinct of life and the instinct of destruction, as it works itself out in the human species. This struggle is what all life essentially consists of, and the evolution of civilization may therefore be simply described as the struggle for life of the human species. And it is this battle of the giants that our nurse-maids try to appease with their lullaby about Heaven."[1] In truth this is a strange sort of battle, since on one side culture slays us so that we may live, by using guilt feelings to its profit and against us, and on the other side we have to loosen its grip in order to live and get on with life.

Someone will say: we have completely lost sight of aesthetics! And someone else will add that it is not really a question of art in these writings on culture but of ethics and religion. I would like to show, nevertheless, at the close of this conference, that it is by starting from this bird's-eye view that we can, on the contrary, plunge into the problem we have all touched on in a more or less lateral way: the problem of the relations among art, satisfaction, and death.

The problem of pleasure suddenly takes on an immense and tragic meaning. In the general perspective opened by the death

[1] S.E. 21:122.

drive, human beings can find pleasure only in a symbolic way. The definition of pleasure as a simple reduction of tension now appears to be laughable. Human beings are also beings who invent and renew their tensions through impossible tasks. Pleasure per se, without remainder, is inaccessible to them. But above all else, human beings are confronted with a difficulty in living that Freud more than once speaks of as the harshness of life. Human life is hard, whence the great problem: how to endure it? In particular, how to accept death? For humans are at the same time the beings the least well prepared to resolve this problem – they alone have a long childhood. And, for Freud, childhood is not principally the happiness of the first weeks and months of life, it is dependence on authority, submission, the need to be reassured and consoled, it is the Oedipus complex and the threat of castration. This is why we are never done with our childish consolations. In the *Phaedo*, Plato had already referred to this child who, in each of us, aspires to listen again to its nursery lullabies. Freud echoes this at the end of *Civilization and Its Discontents*: it is the battle between giants heard of earlier that our nursemaids want to calm by saying "*Eiapopeia vom Himmel!*" [lullaby from heaven]. In this verse from Heine, the sublimity of religion, philosophy, and art becomes the ironic echo of our nursery rhymes. And, at the same time, this irony dumps us back into the heart of our ultimate problem: How does art insert itself into this battle between two giants and where does it situate itself in relation to our nursemaid's lullabies?

The economic problem of art, which I earlier referred to in an abstract way and in a purely analogical fashion, now takes on another dimension. It is a question of situating art, of gaining a perspective on it, in relation to other cultural expressions, and as a function of the economic task of culture considered overall under the sign of Eros, Thanatos, and Ananke.

Illusion is the regressive answer. Religion defends people against the overwhelming, crushing superiority of nature by restoring the image of a father who is both a protector and demanding at the same time. It satisfies the three functions of culture listed earlier – to lower the cost of instinctual sacrifices, to reconcile us to unavoidable renouncements, and to compensate us for the sacrifice through some form of vicarious satisfaction – but at the price of a "collective neurosis," which Freud places under the heading of a "return of the repressed." It is in contrast to this return of the repressed that aesthetic satisfaction finds favor in Freud's eyes. Art is the non-obsessional, non-neurotic form of a substitute satisfaction. The "charm" of aesthetic creation does not come from a memory of a parricide. Let us recall our earlier analysis of preliminary pleasure, with its seductive bonus: technique creates a formal pleasure, thanks to which our fantasies can be exhibited without any shame, at the same time that it lowers all the thresholds of inhibition. No fictional restoration of the father comes along here to make us regress toward infantile submission. Instead we play with our resistances and drives and obtain in this way a general lessening of every conflict. Here Freud is very close to the tradition of catharsis in Plato and Aristotle. It still needs to be discovered, of course, whether religion is really only a return of the repressed and art only a general lowering of tensions through a kind of seduction. I shall not discuss all this. I am seeking simply to understand what is at issue, so as better to understand myself.

So should we say that in the end Freud was simply satisfied with this assertion regarding the cathartic function of art? Here is where I see a second front, that of the reality principle. This is one aspect of Freud that has been little explored. And I am quite aware of the uncertain character of my reading in regard to this point, which, however, touches bottom concerning the Freudian enterprise and its ambitions. In fact, I am more and more persuaded that Freud's philosophical ambitions were quite large and that they hang on the radical meaning of the relation between the pleasure principle and the reality principle. On the one side, Freud is a pessimist about pleasure like Epicurus. Pleasure is merely a kind of relaxation, a wiping away. In the end, it is Nirvana, the zero degree of pain and tension. At the limit, the pleasure principle and the death drive are indistinguishable. The supreme illusion has to do with the meaning of pleasure; and this supreme illusion takes refuge in narcissism. In this regard, the well-known essay "On Narcissism: An Introduction" is very important.[2] The great storehouse of libido is narcissism. We first love ourselves. From this love we find a way to love mother, father, and so forth, but the dissolution of object-libido leads back to the narcissism underlying all these attachments. And, in the end, it is against this

[2] S.E. 14:73–102.

narcissism that the reality principle has to be opposed. Already in 1917, in an essay that first appeared in Hungarian, titled "A Difficulty in the Path of Psychoanalysis," Freud denounced narcissism's resistance to truth: first as the resistance to Copernican astronomy, which teaches us that our earth is not the center of the universe, then to Darwinian biology, which teaches that our species is not the apex of life, and finally to Freudian psychoanalysis, which reveals to us that the ego is not the master in its own house.[3] These three great discoveries are at the same time the three great humiliations that narcissism must undergo.

This short text is a good introduction to the reality principle. Multiple senses are conveyed by this simple word "reality" in terms of ever deeper layers. Reality is first of all what stands opposed to fantasy, it is the fact that every human being fights against, the opposite of the dream, of hallucination. Then in a more analytic sense, it is adaptation to time and to the necessities of life in society. In this sense, in the essays on metapsychology, reality is the correlate of the ego and consciousness. Whereas the id is unaware of time, of contradiction, and only obeys the pleasure principle, the ego has a temporal organization and takes account of what is possible and what is reasonable. The reality principle is basically what the Greeks would have called the "fitting," the *officium*. Yet I think it is necessary to go even further. It is not an accident that Freud so often mythologizes the reality principle, calling it necessity (*Ananke*), just as he mythologizes love and death. We have to continue right up to the great tragic trio of Eros, Thanatos, and Ananke. But why this fabrication that suddenly brings Freud close to the German Romantic tradition, to Goethe and Schopenhauer? Is it not that Ananke is a worldview? A worldview that serves as the ultimate riposte to what we have already spoken of as the harshness of life? I am convinced that in the end in Freud there is a Spinoza-like sense of reality or, if you prefer, something like the love of fate, the *amor fati* in Nietzsche. The touchstone of the reality principle is the victory of our love of the whole over our narcissism, our fear of death, over every resurgence of some form of childish consolation. Allow me to recall the closing words of the essay on Leonardo: "We all still show too little respect for Nature which (in the

[3] S.E. 17:137–44.

obscure words of Leonardo which recall Hamlet's lines) 'is full of countless causes [*ragioni*] that never enter experience.' Every one of us human beings corresponds to one of the countless experiments in which these 'ragioni' of nature force their way into experience."[4] I am convinced that it is in this sense of Ananke, as rational and rationalizing resignation, that we have to evaluate the function of art for Freud. If so, here is where we would have to look next.

I think that we can say that, despite his great sympathy for the arts, there is in Freud no complacency regarding what we might call an aesthetic vision of the world. Just as he distinguishes the aesthetic seduction of the religious illusion, he also suggests that aesthetics – or, to put it more correctly, the aesthetic vision of the world – stands halfway along the difficult education into the necessity required by the harshness of life, which makes the knowledge of our death so moving to us, and which counteracts our incorrigible narcissism and blocks our thirst for childish consolations.

I will cite just one or two indications of this. In his interpretation of humor, in 1905, at the end of "Jokes and Their Relation to the Unconscious," Freud seems to make a great deal of this gift of being able to create pleasure from painful feelings. Humor that laughs through its tears, and even the atrocious kind of gallows humor (which makes the condemned person led to the scaffold on a Monday morning say, "here's a week that begins badly") seems to have some value to his eyes. Interpreted in economic terms, this consists in a bonus payment of pleasure derived from the store of painful feelings. And yet, already in this text from 1905, one small point stands as a warning: "We can only say that if someone succeeds, for instance, in disregarding a painful affect by reflecting on the greatness of the interests of the world as compared with his own smallness, we do not regard this as an achievement of humor but of philosophical thought, and if we put ourselves into his train of thought, we obtain no yield of pleasure. Humorous displacement is thus just as impossible under the glare of conscious attention as is comic comparison; like the latter, it is tied to the condition of remaining preconscious or automatic."[5]

---

[4] S.E. 11:137.
[5] S.E. 8:233.

Next, in 1927, Freud wrote an additional note on "Humor," which is harsher and in which he extends his conclusion to every feeling of the sublime. Humor takes us beyond our unhappiness only by rescuing narcissism itself from disaster: "The grandeur in it clearly lies in the triumph of narcissism, the victorious assertion of the ego's invulnerability. The ego refuses to be distressed by the provocations of reality, to let itself be compelled to suffer. It insists that it cannot be affected by the traumas of the external world; it shows, in fact, that such traumas are no more than occasions for it to gain pleasure. . . . Humor is not resigned; it is rebellious. It signifies not only the triumph of the ego but also of the pleasure principle, which is able here to assert itself against the unkindness of the real circumstances."[6] And from where does humor draw this power of withdrawal and denial? From the superego that condescends to allow the ego this small payment of pleasure. Freud concludes, "It is also true that, in bringing about the humorous attitude, the super-ego is actually repudiating reality and serving an illusion. . . . And finally, if the super-ego tries, by means of humor, to console the ego and protect it from suffering, this does not contradict its origin in the parental agency."[7]

I acknowledge that we cannot judge art or anything about art on the basis of so circumscribed an emotion as humor. Still, with humor, we have reached a point where the pleasure of seduction seems to come down to philosophical resignation. It is at this point precisely that Freud opposes a haughty denial. It is as though he were saying to us: "Accept life and death? Yes, but not at such a low price!" Everything, for Freud, lets us understand that true, active, personal resignation to necessity is life's great masterpiece and this no longer has to do with something aesthetic.

Someone will say: Freud's ultimate worldview is the scientism of the end of the nineteenth century, which is not all that original a thing to say. I do not deny it, but if Freud is a scientist, his scientism does more than characterize the spirit of the age which he shares. The note he gives to his scientism, in that it is neither Copernican nor Darwinian (the scientism that inspired his early system, that of the *Project of a Scientific Psychology*), interests me more than the framework in which he expresses it. I hear this note

[6] S.E. 21:162–3.
[7] Ibid., 166.

as a surpassing of scientism in a Spinoza-like direction. Once we have encountered the two enigmas of "pleasure" and "death," scientism has to overcome itself. The reality about which every scientist speaks then becomes Ananke and the reality principle one of resignation, but a resignation of a rare quality. In considering the conversion of creative energy under investigation in his study of Leonardo, Freud writes, "Lost in admiration and filled with true humility, he all too easily forgets that he himself is a part of those active forces and that in accordance with the scale of his personal strength the way is open for him to try to alter a small portion of the destined course of the world – a world in which the small is still no less wonderful and significant than the great."[8]

Perhaps on this basis we can outline an ultimate reconciliation of art and this quality of resignation. If art does not reach philosophical wisdom, it is nevertheless irreplaceable. In a word, the real resolution of conflicts is impossible; all that is achievable is their symbolic resolution. Dreams, games, daydreams, poetry all play dice with death. They play, but in the end they lose. Still, faced with this final defeat, they point us to wisdom and, who knows, to a reinterpretation of old-time religion. But, at least, before we reach such wisdom, and in waiting for it, dreams, games, and poetry give us ways to endure the harshness of life and – floating between illusion and reality – lead us to cry out with Leonardo: "*O mirabile necessità!*" Yes, admirable necessity! For can we love necessity without loving those "countless causes . . . that never enter experience"?[9] Can we love necessity without loving possibility? If so, is it not art alone then that gives us the vision of the possibilities that haunt it, that give signs of themselves in it, not just to our resignation, but to our courage and our joys?

I hope that these questions can end our conference and start our thinking.

[8] S.E. 11:76
[9] Ibid., 11:137 (drawing on a verse from *Hamlet*).

Postface
Desire, Identity, the Other

Psychoanalysis for Paul Ricoeur after *Freud and Philosophy*
Vinicio Busacchi[1]

Man is a being who understands himself in interpreting himself
and the way he interprets himself is through narrative.
Paul Ricoeur, "Narrative: Its Place in Psychoanalysis"

The Long Route of Ricoeur's Dialogue
with Psychoanalysis

Paul Ricoeur's confrontation with the work of Sigmund Freud is
a complex dialogue between a philosophical and a scientific tradition, one the richest and densest he has undertaken. The importance of this confrontation is not just central, it is strategic. It
would be a mistake to think that, having begun with a phenomenological interpretation of the unconscious in the context of a
"phenomenology of the will" (*Freedom and Nature*, whose first
French edition dates from 1950), this confrontation reached its
apogee and fulfillment in the years of his initial hermeneutic turn,
in the 1960s, with his key work, *Freud and Philosophy: An Essay
on Interpretation* (French edition 1965), and again, in part, with
the essays in *The Conflict of Interpretation: Essays in Hermeneutics*

[1] Vinicio Busacchi is a philosophy fellow at the University of Caligari,
who also works with the professor of hermeneutics at the University of
Naples.

(French edition 1969), only to be followed by a few essays on the epistemology of psychoanalysis (from 1977 and 1978) and other articles of secondary importance. If it is true, on the one hand, that psychoanalysis after *Freud and Philosophy* no longer was the object of so focused or intense an attention, it remains that reflection on psychoanalysis marks all the work of Paul Ricoeur, not only because Freud's presence is almost uninterrupted – albeit of varying "intensity" – over a long course of development, but especially because his presence touches every speculative level of Ricoeur's reflections (methodology, epistemology, theory, linguistics and hermeneutics, anthropology and philosophy, ontology, ethics, and theology). In fact, the "Freudian lesson" will always be present as a turning point for his reflections – sometimes accompanying it, sometimes guiding it, up to the last works. In this regard the essays, articles, and lectures devoted to psychoanalysis starting from the early seventies are important, as are also such works as *Le Discours de l'action* (1977), *Time and Narrative*, volume 3: *Narrated Time* (French edition 1985); *Oneself as Another* (French edition 1990), and *Memory, History, Forgetting* (French edition 2000).

These works mark out the itinerary of a long ongoing dialogue, beginning in Ricoeur's last year at the lycée in Rennes with his teacher there, Roland Dalbiez,[2] and pursued through his encounter with Gabriel Marcel and his study of the texts of Karl Jaspers and Edmund Husserl. The phenomenological method of the latter led Ricoeur to undertake an eidetic analysis of the unconscious, which led him – in *Finitude and Guilt*, the second part of his trilogy on the philosophy of the will – to an analysis of the notion of guilt (a discussion wherein psychoanalysis already played a role during the first half of the fifties)[3] and to a "philosophical repetition" of reflection on its confession or avowal, which made use of

---

[2] A lucky chance that, since Dalbiez was, as is well known, the first French philosopher to publish a book on psychoanalysis, a serious and well-informed one: *Psychoanalytic Method and Freudian Doctrine*, 2 vols., trans. T. F. Lindsay (London: Longmans, Green and Co., 1941).

[3] See, for example, Paul Ricoeur, " 'Morality without Sin' or Sin without Moralism?" *Cross Currents* 5 (1955): 339–52. This essay was instigated by the publication of a book by the psychoanalyst Angelo Hesnard,

psychoanalysis to interpret its symbols and myths. Following this philosophy of confession came Ricoeur's hermeneutic turn and the discovery of the conflict of interpretations, in which his study of Freud would play a central part.[4] Next, in the seventies, Ricoeur moved from the topic of "passivity" (numerous important corrections to the concept of the involuntary developed in his first work can be found in his "semantics of action") to an elaboration of the epistemology of the "hermeneutic arc." In the eighties, Ricoeur next took up the theory of narrative and the question of a "narrative identity" leading to the developments having to do with the philosophy of human identity in *Oneself as Another*, his philosophical "summa" from the end of that decade.[5] In the nineties, he moved from reflection on the challenge of translation,[6] which includes an explicit reference to the psychoanalytic concept of the work of translation (a well-known image used by Freud already in his *Interpretations of Dreams*), to other themes still marked by psychoanalysis: the work of memory and that of mourning (in *Memory, History, Forgetting*).

Morale sans péché, in 1954, in which the author proposed to deepen the ethical meaning of mental illness. It should also be noted in passing that in his "Intellectual Autobiography," in Lewis Edwin Hahn, ed., *The Philosophy of Paul Ricoeur* (Chicago: Open Court, 1995), Ricoeur affirms that it was precisely this theme of guilt that pushed him toward Freud and that his passage through psychoanalysis was in that respect, "of critical importance," (21) even though he had been thinking of giving less place to that topic.

[4] Paul Ricoeur, *Freud and Philosophy: An Essay on Interpretation*, trans. Denis Savage (New Haven: Yale University Press, 1970); *The Conflict of Interpretations: Essays on Hermeneutics* (Evanston: Northwestern University Press, 1974).

[5] Among other things, his reflection on Freud had contributed to pointing out the centrality of desire in the elaboration of ethics. In *Oneself as Another*, trans. Kathleen Blamey (Chicago: University of Chicago Press, 1992), we see it in the broadest sense of the term, which includes Spinoza's *conatus*, Leibniz's "appetition," Freud's libido, and Jean Nabert's desire for being and effort to exist. We can also cite his interpretation of "conscience" – in its (hidden) dimension, the superego – as the third form of alterity (ibid., 353).

[6] Paul Ricoeur, *On Translation*, trans. Eileen Brennan (New York: Routledge, 2006).

Recognition was the last big philosophical topic for Paul Ricoeur, in *The Course of Recognition*,[7] but we can also cite posthumously available writings, especially one small "fragment," his last one, on the "levels of meaning between the event and the structure of being in the world." This short text is no more than a sketch that is of symbolic rather than philosophical value, but it shows how Ricoeur's dialogue with Freud continued right up to the end. Only one proper name appears in it, that of the "great Viennese."[8]

It was a long road, then. A continuous but winding, even torturous one marked by corrections, abandonments, surpassing. The most evident contrast between *Freud and Philosophy* and the later texts lies in the shift in the point of interest. We move from psychoanalytic theory to psychoanalytic practice – more generally speaking, to analytic "experience" (as can be seen in the essay titled "Image and Language in Psychoanalysis")[9] – and to a progressive abandonment of certain Freudian concepts.[10]

[7] Paul Ricoeur, *The Course of Recognition*, trans. David Pellauer (Cambridge, MA: Harvard University Press, 2005).

[8] See, for example, the reference to the "anthropological level" in Ricoeur's final fragment in *Living Up To Death*, trans. David Pellauer (Chicago: University of Chicago Press, 2009), 90. On the right of this sketch we find the "mythological" pair Eros/Thanatos along with the heading "vital impulse ≠ death drive." Below this is a question: "[what is the] structure of being in the world?" with the response "*Desire*" and, beneath this, "Being in Life." It is not difficult to make sense of the meaning of these notations. They are a clear expression of a resistance to any Freudian (and Heideggerian) pessimism about life "being-unto-death," to which Ricoeur opposes the vision of life as a "resistance" to death and a "victory" over death.

[9] This had already been noticed by John B. Thompson in his edited collection of Ricoeur's essays published as *Paul Ricoeur: Hermeneutics and the Human Sciences* (Cambridge: Cambridge University Press, 1981), 24.

[10] One can see this in "The Self According to Psychoanalysis and Phenomenological Philosophy." It is explicit in "Narrative: Its Place in Psychoanalysis," where Ricoeur speaks of an "increasing dissatisfaction as regards Freudianism." In this respect, this essay is more representative than others, for here – a study of Heinz Kohut's selfpsychology – Ricoeur will follow a partly analytic (that is, one at a level of discourse where the philosopher "lets [himself] be instructed" by analytic experi-

The change in perspective already perceived in the 1965 essay is due to a dissonance between Freudian theory and the very nature of its discovery,[11] but also to a profound change in paradigm in Ricoeur's philosophy. In the seventies and eighties, he moves from the hermeneutics of the symbol to that of the text and of narration, developing an increasing clear concern for narrative themes – even as regards his philosophical anthropology – to the detriment of other themes (that of the body, for example); that is, to the detriment of the properly physical or "energetic" horizon. We recall how it was a "double epistemology," one divided between an "energetics" and a "hermeneutics," that had characterized Freud's psychoanalysis in *Freud and Philosophy*, and how this reading was opposed to the linguistic reduction carried out by Jacques Lacan. This double epistemology could be interpreted, according to Ricoeur, either as an indication of the epistemic fragility of Freudianism, or as its characteristic, insurmountable feature. With the later narrative orientation of Ricoeur's philosophy, it became difficult for him to maintain this position. He himself admits having experienced difficulties in holding onto the energetic element within the framework of this later perspective.[12]

ence), partly dialectic way of putting things (where analytic experience enters the sphere of philosophical reflection), one already present in *Freud and Philosophy*. This is the first time Ricoeur carries out this kind of approach in regard to a psychoanalytic school other than the Freudian one.

[11] In analytic experience, in effect, there is more than appears in the discourse of Freud's metapsychology.

[12] "It is no longer possible to preserve the economic, I would even say quasi energetic model of Freudianism. It is necessary to reincorporate the linguistic element, the dialogical element, the element having to do with the relation between appearance and truth in the imaginary (an element one can call Platonic), and the narrative element, and to coordinate these four elements to make up the basis of a theory appropriate to the analytic experience, a hermeneutics" ("Narrative: Its Place in Psychoanalysis," 208).

The Epistemology of Human Desire and the Dialectic of Recognition

Ricoeur's reflection on psychoanalysis after *Freud and Philosophy* unfolds along two principal lines of interpretation: one that is epistemological *stricto sensu* (along which can be arranged the texts in this volume already mentioned: "Image and Language in Psychoanalysis," "The Question of Proof in Psychoanalysis," and "Psychoanalysis and Hermeneutics") and one that we can call hermeneutic-narrative (along which would be found the essays "The Self . . . ," "Narrative . . . ," and even "Life: A Narrative in Search of a Narrator").[13]

As regards the first line, the principal text is *Le Discours de l'Action*, an important work based on courses taught at the Catholic University of Louvain starting in 1970 devoted to the contribution of language to a philosophy of action. Psychoanalysis comes in at the moment of a search for a possible mediation "between the philosophy of action, with its twofold phenomenological and linguistic constitution, and the sciences of behavior," and more precisely within the framework of an epistemological inquiry into the duality between the universes of action and of movement, to which gets attached the duality between "motives" and "causes." Against the idea of an opposition between them, Ricoeur raises objections and shows that it is only partly correct: motives and causes can also coincide.[14] If, on the side of a philosophy of action, this mediating function is exercised by linguistic analysis, on the side of the human sciences it is exercised precisely by psychoanalysis.[15] To put it in a few words, Freud's psychoanalysis showed the possibility of a double epistemology compatible with the element of human desire because it itself carried a double epistemic value, at the crossroad between nature and culture,

---

[13] A third group of texts – made up of "Psychoanalysis and Moral Values," "The Atheism of Freudian Psychoanalysis," and "Psychoanalysis and Art" can be placed on a more minor line of inquiry, one devoted to "psychoanalysis and culture."

[14] See Paul Ricoeur, "Le Discours de l'action," in Dorian Tiffenau, ed., *La Sémantique de l'action* (Paris: C.N.R.F., 1977), 16.

[15] Ibid., 19.

between force and meaning.[16] Here a new shift is produced in relation to the position upheld in *Freud and Philosophy*: The double aspect of psychoanalytic epistemology, previously interpreted as a problematic feature of Freudianism and a sign of its fragility, is now raised to the level of an exemplary attempt to elaborate a new epistemological concept, an effort that will shortly thereafter be named the theory of the hermeneutical arc, which Ricoeur will attempt to demonstrate at work in several different domains (texts, action, history) by synthesizing the basic idea conveyed in his well-known formula: "to explain more in order to understand better."[17]

Ricoeur returns to the character of human desire in the essay "Image and Language in Psychoanalysis," in a key, dense passage that I will cite *in extenso*:

> The analytic situation offers desire what Freud, in one of his technical texts, calls "a playground in which it [the patient's compulsion to repeat] is allowed to expand in almost complete freedom." Now why does the analytic situation have this virtue of reorienting repetition toward remembrance? Because it offers desire an imaginary face-to-face relation in the process of transference. Not only does desire speak, it speaks to someone else, to the other person. This second starting point in analytic practice, too, does not lack theoretical implications. It reveals that from its beginning human desire is, to use Hegel's expression, the desire of another's desire and finally for recognition.[18]

The principle themes of Ricoeur's reflection on psychoanalysis after *Freud and Philosophy* are brought together here in a syn-

---

[16] Ibid., 45.

[17] In "Explanation and Understanding," Ricoeur writes that "rather than constituting mutually exclusive poles, explanation and understanding would be considered as relative moments in a complex process that could be termed interpretation." In *From Text to Action: Essays in Hermeneutics II*, trans. Kathleen Blamey and John B. Thompson (Evanston: Northwestern University Press, 1991), 126. On this topic, see also Jean Ladrière, "Expliquer et comprendre," in Myriam Revault d'Allonnes and François Azouvi, eds. *Ricoeur* (Paris: Éditions de l'Herne, 2004), 68–77.

[18] Above, 96.

thetic manner. Beyond the implicit question of the epistemology of desire and the evident concentration on the analytic experience, we find the theme of the linguistic vocation of human desire – a theme that, for one thing, points back to the confrontation with Lacanian theory (and more generally with linguistics) and, for another, points ahead to the discourse of narrative hermeneutics and through it, the question of the "other" (and beyond it to the question of recognition). With regard to this latter point, Freudian doctrine had appeared to Ricoeur, at the time of *Freud and Philosophy*, insufficient and substantially in conflict in relation to Freudian *praxis*. In this theoretical elaboration, Freud presents human beings as a system closed in on themselves, like an egg. As Ricoeur writes in his essay on narrative and psychoanalysis: "He represents it through a schema: preconscious, conscious, unconscious, or, in the second topology: superego, ego, id, but there never is the other. The other is never thematized as an element of the structure even though the analytic experience is the relationship of desire to another."[19] It was principally due to such inadequacy that Ricoeur turned to Heinz Kohut to articulate a confrontation between three philosophical and paradigmatic models of the relation between subjectivity and intersubjectivity – those of Hegel, Husserl, and Levinas. This question of the other is taken up again and developed in magisterial fashion, as is well known, in *Oneself as Another* – which includes a direct confrontation with Levinas – and subsequently in *The Course of Recognition*, precisely by means of this latter theme. Yet ought we not also to recall that one of the first instances of this discussion can be found in the Hegelian dialectic of the master and the slave, which Ricoeur links to Freud's psychoanalysis, as we saw in the passage just quoted from "Image and Language"?

Narrative Identity and Analytic Experience

Our second thematic line (which is closely connected to the first one) points directly to *Oneself as Another* and the concept of narrative identity, the heart of that work and of Ricoeur's "hermeneutic phenomenology of selfhood." Made central in the sixth

[19] Above, 204.

study of that work, it takes its origin from a confrontation with the problematic of personal identity (in the fifth study).[20] Yet the question goes back even further, as we know from the general conclusions at the end of the third volume of *Time and Narrative* in the context of the discussion of the first aporia of temporality. Narration is the key, Ricoeur maintains, to bring together a duality in identity – which otherwise would be impossible – as transmitted to us by the philosophical tradition. This comes down to the alternative between a substantial subjectivity (Descartes) and an illusory one (Hume, Nietzsche). The dilemma disappears if for identity thought of in the sense of an *idem*, we substitute identity understood in the sense of an *ipse*. The difference between *idem* and *ipse* is nothing more than the difference between substantial or formal identity and narrative identity.[21] It will be helpful at this point to recall another passage from "Image and Language in Psychoanalysis":

> Therefore to speak of oneself in psychoanalysis is to move from an unintelligible to an intelligible narrative. The analysand, after all, enters analysis not simply because he is suffering, but because he is troubled by symptoms, behaviors, and thoughts that do not make sense to him, which he cannot coordinate within a continuous and acceptable narrative. The whole of analysis will be only a reconstruction of contexts within which these symptoms take on meaning. By giving them, by means of the labor of talking about them, a reference framework wherein they can be appropriated, they are integrated into a history that can be recounted.[22]

Narrative, for Ricoeur, in the eighties and nineties, is the royal road for speaking of a life history, since only narrative allows us to make explicit the temporal interconnections of action and thereby to really account for the historical dimension of subjectiv-

---

[20] On the relation between this concept in Ricoeur and Freud's psychoanalysis, see Muriel Gilbert, *L'Identité narrative: Une reprise à partir de Freud dans la pensée de Paul Ricoeur* (Geneva: Labor et Fides, 2001).

[21] See Paul Ricoeur, *Time and Narrative*, vol. 3, trans. Kathleen Blamey and David Pellauer (Chicago: University of Chicago Press, 1988), 246–8.

[22] Above, p. 97.

ity. This is all the more so in that the subjects of a narrative can be not just fictive characters but also real individuals.[23] There is an important development here in regard to psychoanalysis. It allows Ricoeur to establish a parallel with the "narrative situation" that is established in therapy,[24] where the patients become subjects, characters in a narrative, an "emplotment," and at the same time make themselves the narrator of their own story, or life.

[23] However, Ricoeur does indicate a basic distance between the narrative model drawn from literature, even when it is psychoanalytic or philosophical ("when one talks about the self"), and the narrative of one's own life, which remains open-ended since we do not really know either the beginning or the ending. Here we come up against a particularly delicate question, for the lack of a "narrative unity of a life" – which gets constituted through narration – poses serious problems for the constitution of an identity. (Regarding this question, Ricoeur writes in *Oneself as Another*: "How, indeed, could a subject of action give an ethical character to his or her own life taken as a whole, if this life were not gathered together in some way, and how could this occur if not, precisely, in the form of a narrative?" [158] "Life must be gathered together if it is to be placed within the intention of genuine life. If my life cannot be grasped as a singular totality, I could never hope it to be successful, complete" [160].) To address this problem, he turns not to Freud but to Jung (as well as such philosophers as Husserl, Heidegger, and Gadamer – see above p. 209). Jung as a source for Ricoeur, however marginal, goes back to the time of the *Symbolism of Evil* (French edition 1960). Jung considered the Freudian model to be inadequate because it emphasized the centrality of the oedipal relation as in the establishing of neuroses and the therapeutic process, whereas for him, Jung, the most dramatic problems in life had to do with the meaning of life in its progression toward an end. Here is where the idea of a "horizon of expectation" comes into play. If the narrative moment functions to connect the projective element – thanks to which I can, in relation to my death, enter into a horizon of expectation, or in other terms, prefigure myself without having to narrate this (just as I can represent my birth to myself) – it becomes possible to reconstitute one's life in terms of a kind of unity. "To prefigure my own life" surely does not mean to reconstitute it in some narrative unity: I can prefigure my death but this does not mean that I can narrate it.

[24] See here, "The Question of Proof in Psychoanalytic Writings."

The Ethical Challenges of the Work of Translation

Following *Oneself as Another*, Ricoeur's relations with psycho-analysis – indicated in the nineties and beyond by a return to Freud – will be concentrated on a few short texts from Freud's metapsychology (*Remembering, Repeating, and Working Through* [1914] and *Mourning and Melancholy* [1915]) as well as on such key concepts as the "work of memory" and the "work of mourning," already referred to above. One might see this as a lessening of interest in psychoanalysis or even as marginalizing it, whereas to the contrary it persists in the circle of Ricoeur's reflection in relation to themes of the highest importance: translation, memory, forgetting, and – as we have already seen – recognition.[25] The idea of a "work of translation," around which circle the other terms, is central here. We have already mentioned how Freud makes use of the idea of translation to describe the process of interpreting dreams and, more generally, for the transposition of unconscious contents into conscious thoughts. This process had been interpreted by Ricoeur since the sixties as a kind of process of recognition, comparable to the Hegelian schema at work in the master-slave dialectic. "It is of this quasi-Hegelian operation that Freud speaks in the celebrated saying: *Wo es war, soll ich werden* – 'Where id was, there must ego be.' "[26] But the concept of "work" also takes on a special importance. From *Freud and Philosophy* on, Ricoeur has argued that the analytic "treatment" is a kind of work, for "psychoanalysis is also a struggle against resistances." In other words, it is not a question of a simple process of transposition, but of a real challenge of translating the unrepresentable

---

[25] One should add, in light of what has been said, the importance of psychoanalysis in the specific context of *The Course of Recognition*. It is crucial (albeit not in an exclusive manner) to the central concept of human being that lies behind this work. The focal point of this relation undoubtedly comes in the chapter on the "phenomenology of the capable human being" in the recognition of oneself by oneself – more precisely, at the moment of "being able to narrate and to narrate oneself," which follows the moment of "being able to speak, to act," before that of "imputability."

[26] Paul Ricoeur, "The Question of the Subject," *The Conflict of Interpretations*, 241.

(that is, what is held down by the tyranny of its force) into something representable (i.e., what can be brought into the circle of meaning).[27] And furthermore it is a question of an ethical challenge, because what is at stake is the patient's mental health.

This theme of translation drew Ricoeur's philosophical interest principally during the nineties, to such a degree that we can see in it another variant of his hermeneutics, even a new paradigm.[28] Two important texts here are "Translation as Challenge and Source of Happiness" (1997) and "The Paradigm of Translation" (1999).[29] In the first one, Ricoeur suggests "comparing the 'translator's task' . . . with 'work' in the double sense Freud gives to the word when, in one essay, he speaks of the 'work of remembering' and, in another essay, he speaks of the 'work of mourning.' "[30] To translate, to use an expression from Franz Rosenzweig "is to serve two masters: the foreigner with his work, the reader with his desire for appropriation."[31] "Author, foreigner, reader all inhabit the same language as does the translator. This paradox comes from an unparalleled paradox, doubly sanctioned by a vow of faithfulness and a suspicion of betrayal."[32] This is precisely where we find the reason for the *ethical* challenge of translation in hermeneutics.

To conclude, the theme of work also appears in *Memory, History, Forgetting.* Here the concepts of a "work of memory" and a "work of mourning" are recalled in order to articulate an important analogy between the paradoxical situation of an "excess of memory" and an "excess of forgetting," which, according to Ricoeur, characterizes our current relation to history – and this double phenomenon is described using psychoanalysis as a "compulsion to repeat" and "repression."[33]

[27] See above, pp. 27–8.

[28] See here Dominico Jervolino, *Ricoeur: Herméneutique et traduction* (Paris: Ellipses, 2007).

[29] Both texts are now available in Paul Ricoeur, *On Translation*, trans. Eileen Brennan (New York: Routledge, 2006). A different translation of "The Paradigm of Translation" appears in Paul Ricoeur, *Reflections on the Just*, trans. David Pellauer (Chicago: University of Chicago Press, 2007), 106–20. – Trans.

[30] Ricoeur, *On Translation*, 3.

[31] Ibid., 4.

[32] Ibid.

[33] See *Memory, History, Forgetting*, 801–32.

Origin of Texts

"The Question of Proof in Psychoanalysis" was first published in the *Journal of the American Psychoanalytic Association* 25 (1977): 835–71. The original French manuscript, along with many notes, is now in the Ricoeur archive of the Ricoeur Foundation, under the same title. Ricoeur published a shorter version of this text, without the notes, as "La question de la prevue dans les écrits psychanalytiques de Freud," in *Qu'est-ce que l'homme? Philosophie/Psychoanalyse. Hommage à Alphonse de Waelhens* (Brussels: Éditions de la Faculté universitaire Saint-Louis, 1982), 519–619. The version presented here is the original long version with the notes Ricoeur had prepared for the American version.

"Psychoanalysis and Hermeneutics" was first published in Japanese as "Seishinbunseki to Kaishakugaku," *Shiso* (1978), and in French in *Nichifutsu Bunka* ("La culture nippo-française"), no. 26 (February 1979), following a lecture Ricoeur gave during a trip to Japan. The French manuscript is now in the Ricoeur archive.

"Image and Language in Psychoanalysis" was first published in Joseph H. Smith, ed., *Psychoanalysis and Language, Psychiatry and the Humanities*, vol. 3 (New Haven: Yale University Press, 1978), 293–324. The original French manuscript is now in the Ricoeur archive under the same title. It had not previously appeared in French.

"The Self in Psychoanalysis and in Phenomenological Philosophy," was first published in *Psychoanalytic Inquiry,* 6

(1986): 437–58. An Italian translation was published in 1986. It had not previously been published in French. The original French manuscript is now in the Ricoeur archive.

"Psychiatry and Moral Values," was first published in the *American Handbook of Psychiatry, vol. 1: The Foundations of Psychiatry,* ed. S. Arieti (New York: Basic Books, 1974), 976–90. The original French manuscript is now in the Ricoeur archive under the English title. It includes notations about passages to be included drawn from Ricoeur's *Freud and Philosophy.*

"The Atheism of Freudian Psychoanalysis" was published in French in *Concilium* ("Problèmes frontiers") 16 (1966): 59–71. An earlier English translation by Ruth Dowd, R.S.C.J. appeared in the English version of this issue: *Concilium* ("Fundamental Theology: Is God Dead?") 16 (1966): 59–72.

"Psychoanalysis and Art" is the text of a lecture given to the Washington School of Psychiatry as the Edith Weigert Lecture, in 1974. It was published as "Psychoanalysis and the Work of Art" in Joseph H. Smith, ed., *Psychoanalysis and Language, Psychiatry and the Humanities,* vol. 1 (New Haven: Yale University Press, 1976): 3–33. The original French manuscript is now in the Ricoeur archive. It had not previously been published in French.

"Life: A Story in Search of a Narrator," was first published in an earlier English translation in M. C. Doeser and J. N. Kraay, eds., *Facts and Values: Philosophical Reflections from Western and Non-Western Perspectives* (The Hague: Martinus Nijhoff, 1986), 121–32. An Italian translation was published in 1994. The original French manuscript is now in the Ricoeur archive.

"Narrative: Its Place in Psychoanalysis" first appeared with the title "La component narrative della psicoanalisi" in the Italian journal *Metaxu* in 1988. The Italian version was based on the translation of an edited transcription of a talk that Ricoeur gave in Rome that year to a group of Jungian psychoanalysts. Ricoeur retained the original version of the transcription in his files. The version published here is longer than the text that appeared in Italian in 1988.

"Postscript: Listening to Freud One Last Time" comes from Ricoeur's closing remarks to a conference on Art and Psychoanalysis at Cerisy-la-Salle in 1962. The French version was first published in A. Berge et al., *Entretiens sur l'art et la psychanalyse* (Paris/ The Hague: Mouton, 1968): 361–8.

Index

Socrates, 187, 198
Sophocles, 113n44, 160, 164,
    165
Spinoza, Baruch, 137, 206, 216,
    222n5
sublimation, 118, 125, 139–42,
    159, 180–1, 183, 184, 185
symbol, 23n23, 31, 99, 112, 113,
    155, 196
  function, 206
  hermeneutics of, 224
  religious, 156

text, idea of, 23–4, 25, 28, 30,
    50, 53, 62, 69, 100, 170,
    172, 175, 224
  quasi-text, 196
  world of, 193
time, 206, 216
tradition, 191
tragedy, 37, 123, 124, 125, 143,
    145, 153, 165, 199, 213
transference, 14, 15, 16, 27, 28,
    37, 54–5, 67, 74, 75, 76, 78,

79, 80, 81, 83, 88, 91, 95,
    143, 202
translation, 23, 26, 27, 47, 54,
    67, 68, 96, 113n42, 172,
    173, 174, 175, 184, 222,
    230–1

uncanny, 176
understanding, 14n3, 35, 81
utopia, 196

values, 141–2
Verdun, Nicolas de, 177
verification, 43, 46, 51
violence, 136–7

Weber, Max, 144
wisdom, 219
wish fulfillment, 150, 155, 161,
    167
Wittgenstein, Ludwig, 33, 63
Wolf Man, 21, 60
working through, 21, 48, 59, 75,
    79, 81–2, 142–3